PUBLIC OPINION AND FOREIGN POLICY

PUBLIC OPINION AND FOREIGN POLICY

AMERICA'S CHINA POLICY, 1949–1979

Leonard A. Kusnitz

Contributions in Political Science, Number 114

Greenwood Press
Westport, Connecticut • London, England

Library of Congress Cataloging in Publication Data

Kusnitz, Leonard A.
   Public opinion and foreign policy.

   (Contributions in political science, ISSN 0147-1066   ;
no. 114)
   Bibliography: p.
   Includes index.
   1. United States—Foreign relations—China. 2. China—
Foreign relations—United States. 3. China—Foreign
opinion, American. 4. Public opinion—United States—
History—20th century. I. Title. II. Series.
E183.8.C5K87   1984   327.73051   83-26508
ISBN 0-313-24264-X (lib. bdg.)

Library of Congress Catalog Card Number: 83-26508
ISBN: 0-313-24264-X
ISSN: 0147-1066

First published in 1984

Greenwood Press
A division of Congressional Information Service, Inc.
88 Post Road West
Westport, Connecticut 06881

Printed in the United States of America

10 9 8 7 6 5 4 3 2 1

Copyright Acknowledgments

Grateful acknowledgment is given for permission to use the John Foster Dulles Papers, Princeton
University; the Adlai E. Stevenson Papers, Princeton University; and the V.K. Wellington Koo
Papers, Rare Book and Manuscript Library, Columbia University.

Contents

Figures

Acknowledgments _____

Writing these acknowledgments is a pleasure in that I can thank those persons who made completion of this work possible. This group is numerous and diverse, sharing, perhaps, only the trait of generosity. Without these individuals, none of what I have accomplished would have been possible.

Those I worked with at the University of Chicago deserve a special vote of thanks. Dr. Benjamin I. Page first interested me in the subject that grew into this book. His enthusiastic encouragement of this project, as well as his keen insights into its problems and prospects, was invaluable to this manuscript's completion. Dr. Tang Tsou, for his part, was instrumental in aiding me in interpreting the past thirty years of Sino-American relations. Dr. Lloyd I. Rudolph was also tremendously helpful through his many insightful criticisms of this book's earlier drafts. Any errors and omissions contained within this work are, of course, solely my responsibility. It should be noted that all views expressed in this work are solely those of the author and not the U. S. government.

Several others who have read portions of this book and provided me with useful comments also deserve mention. Among those who helped me in this manner were Eshan Feroz, Charles Lipson, and Ronald Toles. Those kind enough to help me with various logistical and empirical problems include Il Byun, Wilhelmina Crawford, Andrew Filardo, Jeffrey Friedman, Thomas Jilly, Leo Kocher, Thomas Levergood, Richard Lipinski, Richard Perlstrom, E. Bradley Pewitt, John Radke, Richard Rosengarten, Mark Solinski, Mitchell Stein, and George Tzanetopoulos. Special thanks must also be given to Tom Smith who aided me in procuring certain otherwise unavailable data. Robert Y. Shapiro was also quite generous with his time and polling data. Special thanks are also due John W. F. Dulles, Adlai Stevenson, and Patricia Koo Tsien for allowing me to use private collections of papers under their control.

My warm thanks also extend to those who provided me with housing and encouragement while I did field research. In the Washington, D.C., area, I am eternally grateful for the sufferance of Stuart and Sally Horn and their children, Gayle and Stephanie. In the New York area, I wish to thank Harvey and Judy Goldman and their children, Cari and Mark. Both of these families did the impossible—put up with me for weeks on end without complaint.

Finally, I would like to thank the two persons who *really* made this book possible. I would like to extend both my love and thanks to my parents, Norman and Esther, who warmly encouraged this project.

PUBLIC OPINION
AND
FOREIGN POLICY

1

Introduction

Public opinion in a democracy wields the scepter.

—Charles Evans Hughes

The notion of a constrained or a democratic foreign policy may be simply a pleasing myth, one which gives solace and recommends silence to the general public . . .

—Bruce Andrews

To what extent are the policies of governments responsive to the preferences of their citizens? This question is central to a variety of normative and empirical theories of democratic politics, yet evidence bearing on an answer is surprisingly inconclusive. Despite a good deal of research, the extent to which democratic states respond to public opinion remains unclear. This relationship remains even more clouded for foreign than for domestic issues. As Bernard Cohen has put it, "We know strikingly little, in an assured way, about the impact that the body of non-governmental opinion has upon the men who formulate and execute American foreign policy."[1] In order to shed some light on this "external" question, the degree to which federal government policies in the United States have responded, or failed to respond, to the Far Eastern preferences of the public since the late 1940s will be systematically assessed. Specifically, the role that the American people have played in the formation of this nation's policies toward China will be closely examined.

Research, though not speculation, into the effect of public opinion on foreign policy is a relatively recent phenomenon. Classical notions of statecraft, which trace their genesis as far back as the Peace of Westphalia, have long discouraged such analyses.[2] In an international environment perceived to be anarchic, the survival of the state was seen as the prime goal of a nation's foreign policy. Individual interests and opinions had to be subordinated to the state's survival, since this was—by definition—a precondition for societal prosperity. Edward L. Morse has made just this point in concluding that the "principle of *primacy of foreign policy* over domestic affairs was a norm of statecraft that served to free the sovereign rulers of Europe to act in foreign policy autonomously of domestic interests."[3] The notion of politics stopping at the water's edge is by no means a new one.

The first systematic breach of this Westphalian theoretical wall did not occur until the late nineteenth and early twentieth centuries. Perhaps the initial individual to address the impact of non-governmental opinion on foreign policy in more than a tangential manner was the reform-minded English journalist and scholar J. A. Hobson.[4] The influential public Hobson identified was an exceedingly narrow group; nonetheless, his work is among the first systematic concessions that a government's foreign policy may be, at least in part, shaped by forces outside the state apparatus. Hobson, in seeking to explain the nascent colonial empires of his time, argued that the wealthy were influencing states in order to "find profitable employment for [their] capital which would otherwise be superfluous."[5] In other words, "it was Messrs. Rockefeller, Pierpont Morgan, and their associates who needed Imperialism and fastened it upon the shoulders of the great Republic[s] of the West."[6]

From Hobson's time on, the analytical pendulum has swung back and forth between those who felt that the views of the public had too much weight in the formation of policy and those who felt that such attitudes had too little impact. Interest in the subject of public opinion and foreign policy formation has, further, undergone somewhat of a renaissance since the Second World War. Four reasons largely account for this surge of interest. First of all, technical developments in polling and data handling have allowed for a clearer consideration of this still murky field. Secondly, the experiences of the 1940s had an important effect on many analysts. Having fought authoritarian dictators in World War II, and the prospect of facing a new totalitarian enemy across an "iron curtain" sensitized a number of Americans to the question of democratic policy making.[7] America's involvement in Vietnam was a third factor in stimulating interest in this field. Analysts took this involvement to show both the strengths and weaknesses of the public in dealing with their leaders. Finally, the surge in attention paid to public opinion and foreign policy making reflects, in part, growing perceptions of economic interdependence—a process that, if occurring, will serve to increase the domestic repercussions of acts in the international arena.[8]

PUBLIC OPINION AND FOREIGN POLICY: A RETROSPECTIVE VIEW

Much of the previous research into the impact of the public on foreign policy has been characterized by one thing—disagreement. These contrary conclusions often stem from the impressionistic nature of much of the evidence in this field. Anecdotal discussions of opinion and policy changes continue to be numerically dominant if for no other reason than the seeming accessibility of this subject to journalists and past public officials. It is difficult to pick up a newspaper or read a memoir without encountering the posited power of the public. While these accounts are valuable in adding to our understanding of the dynamics of individual situations, they must be recognized for what they are—assertions, not proven facts.[9]

An especially fertile ground for uncovering statements in this assertive mode can be found in works that deal with the Vietnam War. Opinion has been both praised and condemned as regards its influence on America's Indochina involvement. Thomas Powers has, in a positive sense, traced the war's end to "ordinary citizens . . . [who] simply refused to tolerate the war or the official assumption that there was no alternative war."[10] Richard Nixon has also hinted at some public input into America's Asian disengagement decision. The ex-president pointed in this direction when he recalled in 1977 that "nobody can know what it means for a President to be sitting in the White House working late at night and to have hundreds of thousands of demonstrators charging through the streets. Not even earplugs could block the noise."[11]

The conclusion that the public hastened America's withdrawal from Vietnam has, however, also been stood on its head. Many recent accounts have argued that the fear of a domestic political backlash resulting from an Indochina withdrawal led to the prolongation of the United States' stay in Southeast Asia. This occurred despite Washington's knowledge that the hope of eventual victory was an illusion. Typical of these works is Daniel Ellsberg's 1971 article on the war which "reluctantly concluded" that

we have elected and been led by presidents who were . . . willing to kill large numbers of Asians, destroy Asian society, and sacrifice large numbers of Americans from time to time, mainly for the reason that their party and they themselves would be in political trouble if they did not.[12]

Arguments like Ellsberg's, focusing on the fear of a domestic political reaction as a constraint on policy, often have been made with regard to America's China policy. Hans Morgenthau, one of the most important of post-war political scientists, for example, described the Eisenhower Administration's policy toward the mainland as "irrational." It was not rational since Washington recognized what should be done but was prevented from adopting these moderate policies due to the fear of a public outcry. The Republican Administration of the 1950s was "too responsible to do what the opposition wanted it to do but prevented by its fears of public opinion from devising and executing a positive policy of its own. . . . "[13] Similar impressionistic accounts focusing on China policy and opinion for those who went before, and those who followed, Eisenhower in office are not hard to find.[14]

Accounts such as Morgenthau's and Ellsberg's have been buttressed by writers with a larger focus. Perhaps the classic disparaging remark concerning public opinion's role in the policy process rose from the pen of the philosopher-journalist Walter Lippmann. Writing in his *Essays in the Public Philosophy*, Lippmann suggested that

the unhappy truth is that, the prevailing public opinion has been destructively wrong at critical junctures. The people have imposed a veto upon the judgments of informed and responsible officials. They have compelled the governments ... to be too late with too little, or too long with too much, too pacifist in peace and too bellicose in war, too neutralist or appeasing in negotiation or too intransigent. Mass opinion has acquired mounting power in this century. It has shown itself to be a dangerous master of decision when the stakes are life and death.[15]

Acceptance of arguments in this vein has led a number of individuals to suggest that the "yielding of some of our democratic control of foreign affairs is the price that we may have to pay for greater physical security" in a nuclear age.[16]

Despite these expressed fears concerning opinion's power over foreign policy, it nevertheless remains true that the United States leads "the world in ritualistic deference to [the worth of] public opinion."[17] Government officials rarely tire of noting that "the long range foreign policy of the United States is determined by the American people."[18] Whether believed or not, a current incantation among Washington decision-makers, for example, is that "we can't engage in a war that is not supported by American public opinion."[19] Such sentiments are, in part, normatively based, and it remains unclear whether they represent the true reality of everyday events. As V. O. Key, Jr., has written, "The interaction between government and public opinion in the day-to-day work of government presents, it must be conceded, a phenomenon about which systematic data are limited."[20]

Attempts to gather this systematic data have continued to remain rather "limited." Among the first to deal in a more rigorous fashion with the question of public input into foreign policy, though, was Gabriel Almond.[21] The focal characteristic of Almond's pioneering work involved the splitting of the public into segments attentive and non-attentive to external policy concerns. Almond, and those who built upon his work, concluded that only a fraction of the public could be considered interested in issues of foreign policy. The vast majority of persons—70 to 90 percent—were seen to be relatively untroubled by foreign concerns and were thought to only "participate in policy making in indirect and primarily passive ways."[22] The attentive public, however, also had a somewhat constrained role in the policy process. It entered into this process only at two- and four-year intervals, when it bought "or refused to buy the 'policy products' offered by the competing elites."[23]

Those working within this "attentive paradigm" do not completely ignore the rest of the public when describing the process of foreign policy formation. The mass public is argued to enter into the policy process by having its "moods, interests, and expectations set limits on the discretion of [its] representatives."[24] These limits, though, are conceded to be quite broad: "As a passive mass . . . the mass public lies virtually outside the opinion policy relationship. Its only function is that of setting the outer limits within which decision-makers and opinion-makers feel constrained to operate and interact."[25] This rather vague formulation of the inattentive public's role becomes clearer once this literature is located within its pluralist context. James Rosenau has helped accomplish this task through his explicit formulation of the "attention group" notion implicit in Almond's work.[26] Arising out of the mass public, these attention groups are akin to David Truman's potential (latent) interest groups.[27] Such groups are not formal organizations; they are, rather, persons who on the basis of "shared attitudes" are mobilizable to protect the constitutional outlines of the political system. These outlines are very broad, perhaps so broad as to be operationally useless when dealing with most policy concerns.

These pluralist proposals have been closely examined by a number of researchers. Perhaps the most important of these empirical examinations has been conducted by Donald Devine.[28] After reviewing policy and opinion in seven areas, Devine concluded that the attentive public does have a greater impact on policy than does the public at large. The data used to support this conclusion, though, are inexplicit and open to alternative interpretation.[29] The generally ambiguous and inconclusive findings within the attentive public paradigm of opinion research have led to many recent analysts' reconsideration of the general public's role in the policy process.[30] This work has been further encouraged by a concern over the possible implications of the attentive view for democratic theory.[31]

A LOOK AHEAD

This study operates at the aggregate (national) level of opinion. A study of responsiveness at this level is, presumably, of great importance to democratic theorizing. New work has begun along these lines, though rarely has it concentrated solely on an issue of foreign affairs. These recent studies, furthermore, have been reluctant to draw causative conclusions due to methodological concerns. It is to alleviate this dual problem—as well as to highlight the past thirty years of American opinion and policy regarding China—that this project was undertaken.

In the course of this discussion some light hopefully will be shed on the reasons why past opinion-policy studies have reached disparate conclusions. It will be suggested that an over-mechanistic outlook on opinion and policy, as well as an implicit search for a constant public preference-government action relationship operative at all times, has led to an abundance of confusion in this field. If historical conditions were more religiously taken account of, the mystery behind many different events might quickly disappear. This, of course, does not mean that no general conclusions can flow out of opinion and policy research. Indeed, it is posited here that public preferences, whether led or followed by officials, are important determinants of America's foreign policy. This is due, we suggest, to the very real fear of office-holders that their actions *may* later bring down upon them the electorate's wrath.[32]

Before directly examining this thesis in light of our case study, it is valuable to make explicit the problems that plague all preference and policy studies. An understanding of these difficulties, as well as an explanation of the method to be used in order to gain causative insights, is important for later evaluation of our findings. It is to this task that we now turn.

NOTES

1. Bernard C. Cohen, "The Relationship between Public Opinion and Foreign Policy Maker," in *Public Opinion and Historians: Interdisciplinary Perspectives*, ed. Melvin Small (Detroit: Wayne State University Press, 1970), p. 66.

2. David S. Yost, "New Perspectives on Historical States-Systems," *World Politics* 32 (October 1979): 151-168, has traced these notions of statecraft even further back into history to the fifteenth century.

3. Edward L. Morse, *Modernization and Transformation of International Relations* (New York: The Free Press, 1976), p. 28. The American founding fathers were, in some ways, influenced by this notion. In their hands it took on a Lockean hue. See Arthur M. Schlesinger, Jr., *The Imperial Presidency* (New York: Popular Library, 1974), pp. 19-21, and John Locke, *Treatise of Civil Government and a Letter Concerning Toleration* (New York: D. Appleton-Century Co., 1937), pp. 97-99, 108-114.

4. John A. Hobson, *Imperialism: A Study* (London: George Allen and Unwin, 1902). See also his *The Evolution of Modern Capitalism: A Study of Machine Production* (New York: Charles Scribner's Sons, 1898).

5. Hobson, *Imperialism*, pp. 77-78.

6. *Ibid.*, p. 77. This external expression of the "influential public" has been argued to have had a domestic analog in the policies of the turn-of-the-century Republican party in the United States. On this point, see Walter Dean Burnham, *Critical Elections and the Mainsprings of American Politics* (New York: W. W. Norton and Co., 1970).

7. Not all analysts drew the same conclusions from these events. Some, like Lester Markel, "Opinion—A Neglected Instrument," in *Public Opinion and Foreign Policy*, ed. Markel (New York: Council on Foreign Relations, 1949), pp. 3-46, argued for an end to "white-shuttered diplomacy" and for more public input into foreign policy formation. Others, exemplified by Thomas A. Bailey, *The Man in the Street: The Impact of American Public Opinion on Foreign Policy* (New York: Macmillan Co., 1948), esp. pp. 13, 318, drew the opposite conclusion, that the degree of popular control of foreign policy would have to be lessened in the post-war world.

8. On economic interdependence see Robert O. Keohane and Joseph S. Nye, *Power and Interdependence* (Boston: Little, Brown and Co., 1977). For an opposing view which sees economic and political interdependence as more an academic illusion than a reality see Kenneth N. Waltz, "The Myth of National Interdependence," in *The International*

Corporation, ed. Charles P. Kindleberger (Cambridge, Mass.: M.I.T. Press, 1970), pp. 205-223.

9. A similar point is made by Bernard C. Cohen, *The Public's Impact on Foreign Policy* (Boston: Little, Brown and Co., 1973), pp. 8-20.

10. Thomas Powers, *The War at Home: Vietnam and the American People, 1964-1968* (New York: Grossman Publishers, 1973), p. xii. Also in this vein is the documentary film on public opinion and the Vietnam War which shares its title with Powers's book.

11. Quoted in Charles W. Kegley, Jr., and Eugene R. Wittkopf, *American Foreign Policy: Pattern and Process* (New York: St. Martin's Press, 1978), p. 202. See also Seymour M. Hersch, "Kissinger and Nixon in the White House," *Atlantic Monthly*, May 1982, p. 48.

12. Daniel Ellsberg, "Politics, Intervention and Escalation," *Peace with China? U.S. Decisions for Asia*, ed. Earl C. Ravenal (New York: Liveright, 1971), p. 136. See also Leslie H. Gelb, "Vietnam: The System Worked," *Foreign Policy* 3 (Summer 1971):140-167; Bruce Andrews, *Public Constraint and American Policy in Vietnam* (Beverly Hills: Sage Publications, 1976), esp. pp. 7-12; and Daniel Ellsberg, "The Quagmire Myth and the Stalemate Machine," *Public Policy* 2 (Spring 1971):217-274. For a contrary view see Aaron Wildavsky, "The Two Presidencies," *Trans-Action* 4 (December 1966):10.

13. Hans J. Morgenthau, "John Foster Dulles," *An Uncertain Tradition: American Secretaries of State in the Twentieth Century*, ed. Norman A. Graebner (New York: McGraw Hill, 1961), p. 302.

14. Ross Y. Koen, *The China Lobby in American Politics* (New York: Macmillan Co., 1960); Chester A. Bowles, *Promises to Keep: My Years in Public Life, 1941-1969* (New York: Harper and Row, 1971); Theodore H. White, *In Search of History: A Personal Adventure* (New York: Warner Books, 1978); A. T. Steele, *The American People and China* (New York: McGraw Hill, 1966); and James C. Thomson, Jr., "Dragon under Glass," *Atlantic Monthly*, October 1967, pp. 55-61.

15. Walter Lippmann, *Essays in the Public Philosophy* (Boston: Little, Brown and Co., 1955), p. 20.

16. Bailey, p. 13. Analysts focusing on non-nuclear eras have also, at times, reached equivalent conclusions. See, for example, Lynn M. Case, *French Opinion on War and Diplomacy during the Second Empire* (Philadelphia: University of Pennsylvania Press, 1954). Robert A. Dahl, *Congress and Foreign Policy* (New York: Harcourt, Brace, 1950), p. 5., notes, in a similar fashion, that a foreign policy that is completely democratic can also be totally suicidal.

17. Robert Weissberg, *Public Opinion and Popular Government* (Englewood Cliffs, N.J.: Prentice-Hall, 1976), p. 3.

18. Dean Rusk, "The Anatomy of Foreign Policy Decisions," *Department of State Bulletin* (hereafter *DSB*) 53 (27 December 1965):506-507. This comment can be compared to one made by Rusk at a 20 February 1961 "informal talk" to State policy officers (*American Foreign Policy: Basic Documents, 1961* [Washington: State Department, 1965], pp. 26-27). The new secretary of state suggested

If we sit here [in the State Department] reading editorials and looking at public-opinion polls and other reports that cross our desks, we should realize that this is raw, undigested opinion expressed in the absence of leadership. We cannot test public opinion until the President and the leaders of the country have gone to the public to explain what is required and have asked them for support for the necessary action. I doubt, for example, that three months before the leadership began to talk about what came to be the Marshall plan, any public-opinion expert would have said that the country would have accepted such proposals.

19. A "high Pentagon official" quoted in the 4 February 1982 *New York Times* (hereafter *NYT*) in regard to the possibility of sending American ground troops to El Salvador.

20. V. O. Key, Jr., *Public Opinion and American Democracy* (New York: Alfred A. Knopf, 1961), p. 431.

21. Gabriel A. Almond, *The American People and Foreign Policy*, rev. ed. (New York: Frederick A. Praeger, 1960). Almond's ideas were, in many ways, anticipated by Martin Kriesberg, "Dark Areas of Ignorance," in Markel, ed., pp.49-64.

22. Almond, p. 139. James N. Rosenau conceives of the attentive public, at the low end of his estimate, as comprising 10 percent of a nation's adult population (*Public Opinion and Foreign Policy* [New York: Random House, 1961], p. 40). While Almond is slightly more generous in his estimate, it is also possible to find estimates even lower than Rosenau's. Alternatively, Barry Hughes, *The Domestic Context of American Foreign Policy* (San Francisco: W. H. Freeman, 1978), pp. 23-24, sees the "mass public" as comprising only 30 percent of the total population, the "attentive public" 45 percent. The "opinion leaders," who hold stable preferences that they communicate to others, comprise the remaining 25 percent of the population in Hughes's model.

23. Almond, p. 5 (quote slightly altered). The attentive public is generally believed to be disproportionately composed of affluent and well-educated citizens.

24. Ibid., p. 139.

25. Rosenau, p. 37.

26. Ibid., pp. 37-39.

27. David B. Truman, *The Governmental Process*, 2d ed. (New York: Alfred A. Knopf, 1971).

28. Donald J. Devine, *The Attentive Public: Polyarchical Democracy* (Chicago: Rand McNally and Co., 1970).

29. Weissberg, p. 246.

30. Some of the more recent studies along aggregate lines include Benjamin I. Page and Robert Y. Shapiro, "Effects of Public Opinion on Policy," paper delivered at the 3-6 September, 1981 American Political Science Convention, New York; Robert Y. Shapiro, "The Dynamics of Public Opinion and Public Policy" (Ph.D. dissertation, University of Chicago, 1982); Alan D. Monroe, "Public Opinion and Public Policy, 1960-1974," paper prepared for delivery at the 31 August–3 September, 1978 American Political Science Convention, New York; Monroe, "Consistency between Public Preferences and National Policy Decisions," *American Politics Quarterly* 7 (January 1979):3-19; and Paul Whiteley, "Public Opinion and the Demand for Social Welfare in Britain," *Journal of Social Policy* 10 (October 1981):455-476.

31. Devine (pp. 119-122), however, does not see this as a great concern since he believes that attentive "status" is available to all that make the effort.

32. This notion is similar, though not identical, to the idea of "anticipated reactions." On this see Carl J. Friedrich, *Man and His Government: An Empirical Theory of Politics* (New York: McGraw-Hill, 1963), pp. 199-215, esp. p. 203; and Robert Y. Shapiro, pp. 95-96 (fn. 1), 105-106. In our view, officials do not anticipate actual reactions, but only the possibility of them.

2

Opinion, Policy, and Problems: Some Methodological Considerations _____

Several theories in political science lead to the prediction of a match between a democratic government's actions and public opinion. Theories of democracy with a normative and "populistic" bent, for instance, generally maintain that national administrators do respond to aggregate citizen preferences.[1] "Running through the history of [such] democratic theories is the identification of 'democracy' with political equality, popular sovereignty, and rule by majorities."[2] Similarly, economic theories of social choice, and positive theories of political behavior based on rationality, have largely led to the same conclusion.[3] Theories involving "groups," on the other hand, suggest that if responsiveness occurs at all, it will be circumscribed by the influence of well-organized and powerful interests in a society.[4] Indeed, some see this exercise of power by private groups to be "the feature of political power most characteristic of American democracy."[5] These groups have been conceived of both in a benign and highly differentiated manner and as sinisterly homogeneous in their concerns, backgrounds, and attitudes.[6]

While it is outside the scope of this book to fully test the propositions inherent in all these notions, a beginning can be made. By first considering whether congruence exists between policy and opinion, and then looking into the causal dynamics of these situations, it should be possible to shed some light on the question of how responsive democracies are when dealing with external issues. This examination will further shed light on whether domestic factors must be taken into account when describing a state's behavior in the international system.[7] Before attempting these tasks, though, it is necessary to make clear the methodology that will stand behind our conclusions. However, even prior to this it is useful to examine some of the problems that plague all studies whose focus is public opinion and policy.

POLLS AND PROBLEMS

The foundation of the empirical research contained within this study, as well as the speculations and conclusions drawn from the data, rests on the soundness of public opinion polls. It is, therefore, appropriate to briefly discuss some of the more important theoretical and methodological problems that accompany the use of these devices. Though we use them in our work, an awareness of the limitations inherent in opinion yardsticks is quite valuable.

The most obvious concern in dealing with public opinion involves the meaning of the term "public." The question of which opinion group is "relevant" to an issue of international importance is critical since the scope of a conflict often determines its outcome.[8] Even the issues selected for attention are, in some ways, dependent on those thought to be relevant. Paul Lazarsfeld noted this when he wrote that "behind the battle over definitions [of who constitutes the 'public'] . . . lie the serious difficulties involved in selecting the problems that are important."[9] In this study we assume that the management of Sino-American relations over the years was an important problem. Policy officials could stress different facets of our relationship with China, but the "problem" was not one that would disappear if unattended.[10] This necessity for action leads to the belief that this issue can be viewed in classical terms—that is, as relevant to the entire population. Given this fact, and our concern with democratic theory, we feel justified in focusing on aggregate national opinion without an overt effort to discern smaller "issue publics."[11]

What a poll response signifies is also a major concern for those dealing with opinion data. It cannot be stated with certainty that a response given is reflective of an interviewee's "true" position. It is plausible that, with a better understanding of a respondent's own interests, altered preferences would be displayed. Such a concern is not merely restricted to the metaphysical planes of "false consciousness," as the problem of a misspecified opinion choice arising out of inadequate information may also arise. For many surveyed, the first information obtained on an issue may be contained within the interviewer's question. In his classic study of three decades past, Almond suggested that this may be the case, as "there are inherent limitations for citizens in modern society to understanding the issues and grasping the significance of the most important problems of public policy."[12] These limitations involve not only an individual's cost of gathering information on the available policy options, but also the course of action the government is following at a particular moment. Indeed, as Christopher Achen argues, "No public opinion surveys are necessary to establish the point. The sheer volume of business in a large nation makes it impossible for even the most studious voter to follow more than a fraction of it."[13]

Partly due to these low information levels, the manner in which survey items are worded also impacts on the responses a poll garners. Uninformed or unconcerned interviewees may listen for cue words for aid in answering a query. Thus polls that mention the president as favoring a policy often display large differences from survey items that do not refer to the chief executive's position.[14] Some analysts, accepting this picture, have even suggested that a comparison of differences in aggregate responses across similar (though not identical) poll items could serve as a rough indicator of the degree of conviction and certainty with which the public holds to their expressed views.[15] This comparison can be attempted even when survey items vary in only the smallest of respects. As Nie, among others, has pointed out,

A question phrased in one way will elicit one response, a seemingly similar question phrased another way may elicit a substantially different response. Often the difference in response is substantial even though the difference in wording of the question is minimal."[16]

While we take note of a wide variety of differently worded polls in this book, the acceptance of this caveat means that, over time, only identical survey items are strictly comparable. This, of course, drastically reduces the number of items from which a researcher may draw solid conclusions. Even here, though, care must be exercised as time may change the meaning of two identically phrased questions.[17]

Since very "few people will admit ignorance even to a reassuring pollster," it is entirely likely that an unsure respondent will also look beyond the question itself for clues about the "right" way to answer a posed query.[18] Harvard psychologist Richard Rosenthal has found, for instance, that unconscious non-verbal cues from an interviewer can significantly shape the answers received.[19] Findings such as these do not mean that all poll responses are tainted; many answers would remain the same no matter who the interviewer was or how the question was framed.[20] Nevertheless, when dealing with opinion polls one must be aware of the fact that "many people simply do not *have* opinions on a number of questions, particularly those that begin to get complicated, remote or vague. When the respondent is pressed by the interviewer for an opinion, therefore, many responses are likely to be capricious."[21] It thus seems as if there is almost a physics of polling; in a manner analogous to the Heisenberg uncertainty principle, when a survey is taken it affects and changes what it purports to measure.

Opinion polls further serve to distort the public's preferences through their forced choice design. Very few polls allow subjects to structure their own responses. Costs, coding problems, and limitations on usefulness all conspire to reduce the number of alternatives presented to a sampling population. Polls that allow a "depends" category, for instance, typically differ in their profile from those that contain only yes/no positions. It is entirely possible that no majority position would appear in most polls were it not for the vastly narrowed universe of options offered to interviewees.

Taken in isolation, a poll response may also confuse the real-world position of individuals on a problem. Presumably persons operate with a hierarchy of priorities. When issues are abstracted from this rank ordering, the individual's actual stance on a concern may become lost. A person, for example, may respond affirmatively to a pollster's proposition that taxes be cut. If given the choice between a tax cut and the local post office's remaining open, however, our citizen may choose to forego salvation from "bracket creep." It is therefore very possible that a discovered lack of congruence may be artificial (and vice versa) when the overall priorities of the public are taken into account. Once it is accepted that persons have rank orderings on and within issues, the problem stressed in Kenneth Arrow's work also arises.[22] Arrow's paradox, simply stated, notes that when all the policy preference functions among a group are collected, no position may command a majority. The important point of Arrow's work, as regards opinion and policy research, is that it shows how "individual opinion need not easily add up to a collective opinion mandate."[23]

A final difficulty in interpreting poll responses also involves the discrepancy between individual and collective desires. The policy individually best for each citizen may lead to collective disaster if it is implemented. It is often unclear when persons answer polling items whether their response has the individual or the society as a reference point.[24] The possibility further exists that differing reference points may vary systematically across a society. If this is the case, it may be true, for instance, that those most integrated into society's mainstream use themselves less often as a reference point than do other citizens.[25] This concern is undoubtedly inappropriate for many polling questions; however, if one tries initially to explain subgroup opinion differences without at least a passing glance at this, errors of interpretation may result.

POLICY AND PROBLEMS

The public's view on policy concerns is of great intrinsic interest. It should be noted, though, that "merely because citizens hold certain opinions on political subjects does not mean that such opinions have inherent political significance."[26] This significance, if it exists, must be demonstrated, not simply assumed. Making this connective link clear is perhaps the main problem in the field of opinion and policy research. As a first step toward accomplishing this task, data descriptive of public policies must be dealt with. This task, though, is not as straightforward as it might initially appear.

A major difficulty in dealing with policy measures arises out of the restricted accessibility of much of the data. Foreign policy, with its often closely held aspects, is especially susceptible to this problem. Through archival research and a close comparative reading of historical accounts, this concern can be somewhat alleviated. Nevertheless, much of the data collected will still remain observer- rather than actor-based. This necessity to infer motivations can lead to problems. Such a difficulty is compounded by the ambiguous nature of many policy moves. Robert Weissberg, in the course of examining opinion and policy on Vietnam, has illustrated this problem:

How do we really know, for instance, whether a President's loudly proclaimed offer to meet with the North Vietnamese to negotiate a peace settlement constitutes a pro-withdrawal policy? Similarly, a threat to step up the bombing if certain actions are not taken might under certain circumstances be interpreted as a "dovish" policy.... Moreover, how do we compare policy pronouncements that have no immediate impact, e.g., "I am willing to make great concessions to the enemy," with actual events.... [27]

This ambiguity is heightened when it is realized that different governmental actors often work at cross purposes in the prosecution of America's external policy. In such cases, an implicit additive model must be brought into play, though the manner of "weighting" each policy output retains a degree of historical arbitrariness.

Ambiguity in policy measures is present even in many seemingly clear cases. Monetary expenditures appear to be a fairly concrete measure of policy, yet this is not always so. The shape of policy, for instance, can look quite different when inflation-adjusted figures are substituted for actual dollar amounts. In foreign matters, these fiscal measures can be further clouded by the transfer of material to the recipient at below-market costs.[28] Problems of unrecorded covert aid, and aid instituted through international organizations upon one government's prompting, must also be faced. Even if all these various figures are available, the discovery of a declining aid curve need not necessarily indicate that a policy change has taken place. Differing world conditions might have led to an upsurge in aid for a number of years followed by a return to relative normalcy. Conditions within the aid recipient (or giver) might also have led to a change in the aid curve without a concomitant shift in overall policy. The cut-off of most economic aid to Taiwan in the mid-1960s occurred not out of American displeasure with Chiang, but was due instead to Taiwan's remarkable economic performance in the previous decade.

Finally, when dealing with policy in the international arena, it must be recognized that not all possible courses of action may be open to a state. This external constraint arises from the nature of international relations. A nation's leadership may be unable to follow the wishes of its people because the behavior of other states makes such overt compliance impossible. Recognition of this possibility once again forces the analyst to focus on the motivations of policymakers and on the less publicized initiatives so common in the field of foreign affairs.

OPINION AND POLICY

Despite all the methodological and conceptual problems associated with opinion polls, they still represent the single best available indicators of citizen preference. Furthermore, though some difficulties certainly do exist, it is, in practice, possible to get a fairly good grasp on the direction of overall policy at any given historical moment. Both these points are crucial, for without polls and policy measures it would be impossible to examine whether instances of democratic responsiveness exist.

For perfect responsiveness to exist, three criteria must be satisfied. These criteria are important not only for how they reflect on democratic theory but also because they are suggestive of a research methodology that can take us beyond the non-causative studies of the past. If a situation of democratic responsiveness exists on an aggregate national level, then (1) the views of the majority must be reflected in the overall policy stance of the government; (2) significant opinion changes must be accompanied by like-directioned policy moves; and (3) the harmony that exists between opinion and policy must result from the government's heeding the public's preferences.

Each of these three facets of responsiveness has been adopted as necessary by this study. The need for policy to fit within a majority framework flows out of the logic inherent in almost all definitions of democracy. Along these lines, Donald J. Devine has written that

since democracy concentrates on a majority, 50 percent plus one [should] be used as the *threshold of policy acceptance*. When a policy has the support of over 50 percent of the public being considered, the policy will be said to have been accepted by that public.[29]

In the course of this study, Devine's criterion is relaxed somewhat to allow the consideration of a wide plurality to also be determining. Within these confines, however, a policy is not considered responsive unless it is in broad harmony with the views of most citizens.

A government, however, could follow many different policy lines within the overall framework set by opinion. It is therefore necessary to go beyond a singular focus on majority opinion to come up with a more sensitive measure of responsiveness.[30] This second, directional method involves looking for statistically significant opinion changes and then examining government policy to see if a similar-directioned move was undertaken.[31] An important advantage of this research design is that the measurement of the degree of fit (or lack thereof) between the public's preferences and the government's policies involves only very simple ordinal measures. Even when the absolute level of policy is difficult to compare with measured opinions, statistically significant changes in a citizenry's preferences are relatively easy to compare with changes in national policy. Though such a method does not allow for a consideration of whether the intensity of policy change is equivalent to the degree of change within the public, it does allow for an examination of the elusive notion of causation within the opinion-policy matrix.

Due to the problems associated with differently phrased survey items, this directional approach can be undertaken only with identically worded items. This approach, however, has an additional advantage:

Assuming no change in sampling procedures, the biases associated with the questions are again held more or less constant and, again without saying what the "real" opinion on an issue is, one can fairly suggest how attitudes on the issue have shifted over time—whether in a favorable or unfavorable direction—if, indeed, they have shifted at all.[32]

These properties of identically worded items allow for an assessment of our third criterion of responsiveness. If opinion and policy are found to be in accord, then close attention to the temporal asymmetries involved in such instances allows the problem of causation to be tackled. This method thus enables us to see when opinion changed before policy and when the opposite temporal sequence occurred. This allows for a closer consideration of the problem of causation than is true in most past studies.

CASE STUDIES AND THEORY

An examination of opinion and policy in the manner outlined here can best be undertaken in the context of an intensive case study. We therefore focus on American opinion and policy toward China since the late-1940s communist takeover. The opinion data selected for this study include all published, and some unpublished, polls relating to Sino-American relations since the mainland's fall. Sources for this material include Gallup and Harris poll releases, the wire service and network polls, and surveys conducted by the National Opinion Research Center (NORC). In addition to these sources, the Roper reports and Archives were consulted, as were the Chicago Council on Foreign Relations opinion studies, the Survey Research Center polls, and private, state, and national polls alluded to in various newspapers, monographs, and articles. The policy measures used in this study also were gathered from a wide variety of sources. Interviews, original documents, private papers, and secondary materials have all been employed in one fashion or another.

Despite the meticulous attention given to American opinion and policy relating to China, the general applicability of our findings must remain somewhat limited. This is due, of course, to this study's sole concentration on the China policy area. As many diverse theorists have pointed out, however, case studies can play an invaluable role in theory construction.[33] Single-issue studies, for instance, can serve either as correctives for past work or as starting points for new theoretical avenues. Case studies also necessarily include the historical dimension often lacking in more mechanistic studies of public opinion and policy change. The avoidance of a "black box" view of the world is a major advantage of such intensive examinations. In areas of research as unresolved as the public's impact on foreign policy, individual-issue research thus can be of great value. Indeed, a case study—as an in-depth examination of an important issue—can often succeed in clarifying a contentious theoretical point where more broadly based research has failed.

NOTES

1. Robert A. Dahl, *A Preface to Democratic Theory* (Chicago: University of Chicago Press, 1956).

2. Ibid., p. 34.

3. Kenneth J. Arrow, *Social Change and Individual Values*, 2d ed. (New York: Wiley, 1963); Amartya K. Sen, *Collective Choice and Social Welfare* (San Francisco: Holden-Day, 1970); and Peter C. Fishburn, *The Theory of Social Choice* (Princeton: Princeton University Press, 1973).

4. The literature on this subject is extensive. For some important representative views see Arthur R. Bentley, *The Process of Government* (Chicago: University of Chicago Press, 1908); David B. Truman, *The Governmental Process*, 2d ed. (New York: Alfred A. Knopf, 1971); E. E. Schattsneider, *The Semi-Sovereign People* (Hinsdale, Ill.: Dryden Press, 1960); Mancur Olson, *The Logic of Collective Action* (Cambridge: Harvard University Press, 1965); Grant McConnell, *Private Power and American Democracy* (New York: Random House, 1966); Theodore J. Lowi, "American Business, Public Policy, Case Studies, and Political Theory," *World Politics* 16 (July 1964):677-715; and Lowi, *The End of Liberalism* (New York: W. W. Norton and Co., 1969).

5. McConnell, p. 3.

6. For a benign and differentiated look at groups involved in the making of foreign policy see Gabriel A. Almond, *The American People and Foreign Policy*, rev. ed. (New York: Frederick A. Praeger, 1960). For a view of these groups as homogeneous in background and make-up see Ralph Miliband, *The State in Capitalist Society* (New York: Basic Books, 1969), and Joyce Kolko and Gabriel Kolko, *The Limits of Power* (New York: Harper and Row, 1972).

7. This controversy is reflective of the level-of-analysis problem in international relations. On this see J. David Singer, "The Level-of-Analysis Problem in International Relations," in *The International System: Theoretical Essays*, ed. Klaus Knorr and Sidney Verba (Princeton: Princeton University Press, 1961), pp. 77-92, and Kenneth N. Waltz, *Man, the State and War: A Theoretical Analysis* (New York: Columbia University Press, 1959). If the international system, taken in isolation, is truly sufficient to explain behavior in the international realm then the study of domestic opinion's influence on foreign policy officials is largely an exercise in recording the tides but ignoring the moon. It should be noted, though, that some systems analysts allow for the possibility that opinion does play a role in policy formation. See, for example, Morton A. Kaplan, *Towards Professionalism in International Theory* (New York: The Free Press, 1979).

8. On this point see Schattsneider.

9. Paul F. Lazarsfeld, "Public Opinion and the Classic Tradition," *Public Opinion Quarterly* 21 (Spring 1957):46.

10. The ability of officials to set the agenda, at least in part, for public discussion has long been commented upon. For a discussion of the manner in which official influence is exerted upon the media to bring about such a result see Gaye Tuchman, *Making News: A Study in the Construction of Reality* (New York: The Free Press, 1978).

11. On issue publics see, for instance, Bernard C. Cohen, "The Military Policy Public," *Public Opinion Quarterly* 30 (Summer 1966): 200-211.

12. Almond, p. 5.

13. Christopher H. Achen, "Mass Political Attitudes and the Survey Response," *American Political Science Review* 69 (December 1975):1218. Dean Acheson, "The

American Image Will Take Care of Itself," *New York Times Magazine*, 28 February 1965, p. 95, devalues "world opinion" for a similar reason. Opinion on international matters can be devalued "not because people do not know the facts—facts are not necessary to form [an] opinion—but because they do not know that the issues exist."

14. Robert Weissberg, *Public Opinion and Popular Government* (Englewood Cliffs, N.J.: Prentice-Hall, 1976), pp. 234-237, shows that this is usually a plus. See also Roberta S. Sigel, "Image of the American Presidency: Part II of an Exploration into Popular Vision of Presidential Power," *Midwest Journal of Political Science* 10 (February 1966):123-137. Using the split-ballot technique, Corey M. Rosen, "A Test of Presidential Leadership of Public Opinion: The Split Ballot Technique," *Polity* 6 (Winter 1973):282-290, found that the association of the president with a policy has a much greater effect on reducing opposition to a policy than increasing the numbers of those favoring a specific policy decision. It should be noted, however, that such findings may not be invariant. Lee Sigelman and Carol K. Sigelman, "Presidential Leadership of Public Opinion: From 'Benevolent Leader' to 'Kiss of Death'?" *Experimental Study of Politics* 7 (1981):1-22, found that an unpopular president—here Carter—can actually lower the support accorded an issue in the general public if he becomes associated with it.

15. John E. Mueller, *War, Presidents and Public Opinion* (New York: Wiley, 1973), p. 19.

16. Norman H. Nie, Sidney Verba, and John R. Petrocik, *The Changing American Voter* (Cambridge: Harvard University Press, 1979), p. 10. This effect is described more broadly as "instrumentation" in Donald T. Campbell and Julian C. Stanley, *Experimental and Quasi-Experimental Designs for Research* (Chicago: Rand McNally, 1966), p. 9.

17. Nie et al., p. 11. Here, for example, it is suggested that questions concerning "big government" in the 1950s were taken by respondents to refer to New Deal type social programs. By the late 1960s, however, this phrase came to be interpreted by the public as a reference to the U.S. military.

18. Lester Markel, "Opinion—A Neglected Instrument," in *Public Opinion and Foreign Policy*, ed. Lester Markel (New York: Council on Foreign Relations, 1949), p. 31.

19. Richard Rosenthal, paper presented to a colloquium at the Johns Hopkins University Psychology Department (May 1978). See also R. Gary Bridge, Leo G. Reeder, David Kanousc, Donald R. Kinder, Vivian Tong Nagy, and Charles M. Judd, "Interviewing Changes Attitudes—Sometimes," *Public Opinion Quarterly* 41 (Spring 1977):56-64. Tom Smith of the National Opinion Research Center has also suggested, in a personal conversation, that the order in which questions are asked may affect responses—possibly by giving information to the interviewee. Seymour Martin Lipset, "The Wavering Polls," *The Public Interest* 43 (Spring 1976):75, has argued that differing survey techniques (e.g., face-to-face versus phone interviews) may also lead to widely disparate results even when identical questions are employed.

20. Mueller, pp. 17-19.

21. Ibid., p. 2.

22. See Arrow.

23. Weissberg, p. 28.

24. An example of the vast differences in response that may arise out of this problem can be found in William L. Lunch and Peter W. Sperlich, "American Public Opinion and the War in Vietnam," *Western Political Quarterly* 32 (March 1979):23. They take note of three similar questions, asked in a two-day period by Gallup in 1944, which got widely varied results (though the number of persons interviewed is unavailable):

1. Do you think that in the years to come people will say the United States should have avoided getting into the war?
2. Do you think that in years to come people will say it was a mistake for us to have entered this war?
3. Do you, yourself, feel it was a mistake for us to have entered this war?

Questions 1 and 2 have society as a reference point; question 3 has the individual as its focus. The results are as follows:

Question	Yes	No	No Opinion
1	31%	54%	15%
2	26	60	14
3	14	66	9

25. This may make these individuals more susceptible to government ("national interest") persuasion on foreign policy issues. For a discussion suggestive of this see William A. Gamson and Andre Modigliani, "Knowledge and Foreign Policy Options: Some Models for Consideration," *Public Opinion Quarterly* 30 (Summer 1966):187-199.

26. Weissberg, p. 6.

27. Ibid., p. 149. In a somewhat similar vein, Murray Edelman, *The Symbolic Uses of Politics* (Urbana: University of Illinois Press, 1964), p. 39, argues, "It is not uncommon [for the government] to give the rhetoric to one side and the decision to the other."

28. Such, for example, was apparently the case with Taiwan in the late 1960s. Taiwan was reportedly allowed to take slightly damaged or used equipment from Vietnam for use in its own arsenal. In a further twist, the slightly damaged equipment, which had been acquired by the Nationalists at no cost, was repaired by the Chinese who then apparently sent the bill for this refurbishing to the U.S. Military Advisory Group on the island. See *NYT*, 29 March 1970.

29. Donald J. Devine, *The Attentive Public: Polyarchical Democracy* (Chicago: Rand McNally and Co., 1970), p. 67. Alan D. Monroe's work presents some interesting speculative evidence of the importance of the 50 percent level for policy-makers. See his "Consistency between Public Preferences," *American Politics Quarterly* 7 (January 1979):14-15.

30. Benjamin I. Page, "Policy Change and Public Opinion Change," Department of Political Science, University of Chicago, February 1979 (manuscript).

31. When using this directional method we shall adopt the conservative criterion, suggested by Page, of only taking opinion changes of six percentage points or more as significant. This allows us to be well within the .05 confidence interval when speaking of changes in the actual distribution of responses in the general public. In using this criterion, we assume a random stratified sample of approximately 1,500 persons and roughly evenly divided dichotomous survey items. The criterion for significance was increased to more than six percentage points when samples smaller than 1,500 were encountered, by multiplying the standard error for those smaller samples by 1.64 (the adjustment factor producing the six point criterion for 1,500 member samples). Once a trend is established it will be considered to have been reversed only when a significant opinion shift occurs in the opposite direction. On this method see Page, "Policy Change," and Shapiro, "The Dynamics of Public Opinion"(Ph. D. dissertation, University of Chicago, 1982), p. 15. This research design is similar to the separate-sample pre-test–post-test design in Campbell and Stanley, p. 53.

32. Mueller, p. 12.

33. See, for example, Bernard C. Cohen, *The Political Process and Foreign Policy: The Making of the Japanese Peace Settlement* (Princeton: Princeton University Press, 1957); Adam Przeworski and Harry Teune, *The Logic of Comparative Social Inquiry* (Wiley-Interscience, 1970); and Leo Spitzer, "The Presidency and Public Policy: A Preliminary Inquiry," *Presidential Quarterly* 9 (Fall 1979):443.

3

Sino-American Relations Preceding the Korean War

America's relationship with the People's Republic of China (PRC) was characterized, in its first two decades, by an unusually high degree of hostility. During this period American public opinion toward Communist China was also set in a generally negative posture. It is only within the past decade that Washington, and the American people, has come to accept the necessity and (at times) desirability of dealing with the Peking regime. This view, however, has been tempered by the United States' commitment to Taiwan—a commitment that seemed to place almost insurmountable obstacles in the way of a normalization of relations with the People's Republic.

Looking back to the first years of Sino-American relations, though, one must echo J. H. Kalicki's view that "there were few a priori reasons for the 1950s to be a decade of Sino-American hostility."[1] In spite of historical and ideological differences, there was much public expectation at the time of China's fall that a pragmatic willingness to deal with one another would develop in both Washington and Peking. The United States took the initiative in this respect, through a number of tentative steps that reflected its willingness to accept the newly forming Communist regime as the government of all China. While a mild reaction to the "loss" of China was beginning to be felt in American governmental circles by late 1949, most State Department officials recognized that China was never ours to lose and recommended the establishment of some form of diplomatic and trade relations with Mao's government.[2]

Reflective of this Washington mood was the fact that even after the Angus Ward incident in Mukden, plans for eventually recognizing the People's Republic of China were "pushed ahead."[3] Internal government documents perceived little in the way of organized public opposition to this course of action. "Among articulate observers," a 30 November 1949 study on American opinion prepared in the State Department reported,

there is no dominant trend either favoring or opposing U.S. recognition of the Communist regime. While the Ward Case has deepened already-held suspicions of Communist China, it does not seem to have basically altered the opinion situation.... The largest number of commentators still appear to expect eventual U.S. recognition.[4]

Advocacy of this "realistic" course toward the mainland was prominent in important newspapers such as the *Christian Science Monitor*, the *Wall Street Journal*, and the *Washington Post*.[5] The *New York Times*, no friend of such a policy, nevertheless conceded that "informed Senate quarters" believed Peking's diplomatic recognition "could be regarded as inevitable."[6] The seizure of American consular property in Peking and the February signing of the Sino-Soviet "Friendship Pact" did cause Washington to approach Asia in a more cautious manner.[7] Yet despite this hesitancy, the United States still seemed willing to work out a *modus vivendi* with the Chinese Communists.[8] One month after the Sino-Soviet pact was initiated, Dean Acheson, for example, could report to the San Francisco Commonwealth Club that the U. S. government was "entirely willing that Americans, in the future as in the past, should buy Chinese goods and sell American goods [to China]."[9]

Opinion in the general public during the winter of 1949-1950 was hostile to, but also apparently accepting of, the "liberation" of China.[10] The public, however, did feel that it was too early to recognize the new communist regime and opposed an exchange of ambassadors by a two-to-one margin—with the better informed college group somewhat more receptive to the establishment of *de jure* contacts.[11] Opinion, though still negative, was much more favorable on the question of opening trade relations with the Communists.[12] One close observer of public attitudes has argued that such a late 1949–early 1950 preference profile "revealed that the problem of China still seemed very remote to the majority of the American people."[13] This view of the opinion situation apparently was shared by Washington. As such, the executive branch did not perceive any great hindrance in moving America's Asian policy forward. Public attitudes, it expected, would eventually fall into place behind government policy, as "the results [of these negative polls] reflect the widespread distrust of dealing with any Communist regime—rather than considered opinion about relations with China."[14] A manifestation of this lack of "consideration" could be found in a September 1949 National Opinion Research Center poll which discovered that "our policy toward China" placed last in public interest among the five international items ranked in that survey.

The government, aware of this ebbing concern, repeatedly characterized public thought on China throughout 1949 and the early months of 1950 as "vague and uncertain."[15] The documents containing these characterizations seem to suggest that opinion was quite malleable since public attitudes had "not yet crystallized as to what should be U.S. policy toward a Communist China.''[16] In any case, it is clear that the public was not leading policy; Washington could not follow preferences it did not perceive to exist. The manner and speed with which America's policy toward China could be pursued was influenced by the overall negative opinion profile; the direction of policy, though, remained unaffected. Truman and Acheson would move slowly in the China area, giving opinion time to respond to their actions. They would not, however, abandon their long-term objectives. Press comment was seen in a similar "non-affecting" light, leading the Public Affairs Division at Foggy Bottom to conclude that most journalists were "conscious of treading [on] unfamiliar ground" and would be willing to take their cues from government "experts.''[17]

The public hostility which some Americans did display toward the communist Chinese was likely a "spillover" from the distrust most Americans had recently acquired toward the Soviet Union. Public and congressional acceptance of the Truman Doctrine required the portrayal of a monolithic communist menace. In this endeavor Truman was quite successful, leading the public to link the Asian communists with the on-going "international communist conspiracy.''[18] A "steadily increasing number of commentators," according to the State Department's *Monthly Survey* of American opinion, came to accept this government-proffered line.[19] This led a majority of the public who were aware of the Chinese civil war to view the Communists there as wholly dependent on the USSR. The *New York Herald Tribune* reflected the strength of this view when it stated on the eve of 1950 that "it would be the height of folly to deny or to minimize the great fact [of] ... the existence of a tightly linked chain of dictatorial power that runs from the Oder to the Pacific [coast of China].''[20] This sentiment became so widespread that one poll found a five-to-one majority agreeing with the statement that the Chinese rebels "take their orders from Moscow.''[21] Yet, even with this opinion frame, policy-makers apparently were confident that when the time came the public's view would shift just as it had toward the Yugoslavian communist state in the prior year. Current public attitudes were, after all, "probably not permanent," reflecting as they did "attitudes toward Russia more than attitudes toward China.''[22]

The Truman Administration did nothing to dispel the "monolithic" belief it had helped to foster. Far from challenging this view, it continued to reinforce it through statements charging that the Chinese communist leaders were so "thoroughly indoctrinated" by the Kremlin that they were "completely subservient" to Stalin's every whim.[23] As the Communists moved closer to total power, the State Department intensified its hectoring of China's new leaders. Thus, George Kennan, speaking in the summer of 1949 on CBS radio, could report to the American people that the Communists in China were "being utilized as a means of inducing them [the Chinese people] to accept a disguised form of foreign rule.''[24]

Given that a more sophisticated view of Asia existed in the halls of power, these rhetorical excesses should not be taken at face value. This becomes clear once internal government documents are examined. Much of America's policy toward China during 1949 and 1950 was informally following directives implicit in a number of National Security Council (NSC) memos. A May 1948 NSC paper stated, for instance, that America's policy decisions should be made "in terms of an evolving plan to lure a Communist China away from too-close relations with the Soviet Union."[25] Such a plan would represent "a recognition of realities rather than . . . a fruitless attempt to reverse or ignore the tide of events."[26] The policy chosen to pull the two communist giants apart was to accuse the Chinese leadership of subservience to the Russians "as a means of provoking them to behave more like nationalists."[27] This course of action was based on the belief made explicit in a December 1949 NSC memorandum that

if the Kremlin should attempt to extend to China the pattern of political and economic control and exploitation that has characterized its relations with its European satellites it is quite plausible that serious frictions would develop between the Chinese Communist regime and Moscow.[28]

Luring the People's Republic of China away from the Soviet Union could be accomplished in two ways. Either the entire Chinese leadership would pull back from the Soviets, or a split would develop between the more nationalistic elements of the Chinese Communist Party (CCP) and those holding to a pro-Soviet line. While pursuing both policies simultaneously, American officials had more hope in inducing a split in the CCP since "of Communist leaders and key men, only 30 percent are pro-Moscow. . . . "[29] By early February 1950 this had clearly become U. S. policy. On 2 February the Policy Planning Staff of the State Department began circulating a paper arguing that

the pressure of . . . [future political and economic] events will tend to inspire national-istically-inclined leaders in the CCP to break with those elements in the leadership who have sold themselves out completely to the Kremlin. . . . We should, of course, be ever on the alert for symptoms of such a break-away and should judiciously do all within our power to foster such a split.[30]

This "splitting" policy needs to be understood in terms of both strategic and domestic politics. During the 1948-1950 period, the Truman Administration was still oriented toward Europe and operating under severe budgetary constraints in its attempt to contain the Soviets. If China could be persuaded to follow an independent path in Asia, the United States could more plausibly fall back to its "island perimeter" and devote its limited defense resources to battling the Russians in Europe—a priority that found wide resonance within the general public.[31] A successful cleaving-off of China from the Soviet bloc, in other words, would "allow for a containment policy to operate within budgetary con-straints."[32] Subtle and well-connected commentators had, by early 1950, come to recognize this policy and to generally speak of it in positive terms. "Wrong as it may have been in the past, the State Department is now advocating the only feasible China policy for the future, which is to play for a sudden schism between China and Russia,'' wrote Ernest Lindley in mid-January.[33] In terms of domestic politics, the harsh rhetoric accompanying this policy of ''detaching'' pressure served to placate congressional critics and paper over differences between the more interventionist Defense Department and the longer term diplomatically oriented Department of State. The danger of such a policy, as even some contemporary observers realized, however, was that it might provide critics of America's actions in the Far East with ammunition to dissent from later China policies should all not go according to plan.[34]

America's China policy was also bound up in the Cold War battle for Europe in less ''tangible'' terms. Not only were military and economic factors perceived as important in consolidating the West's hold on a rebuilding Europe, but the psychological dimension of the problem was similarly accorded great weight. As George Kennan wrote in the first volume of his memoirs:

It was hard to overestimate, in those days of uncertainty and economic difficulty, the cumulative effects of sensational political developments. People were influenced ... not just by their desires as to what *should* happen but by their estimates of what *would* happen. People in Western Europe did not, by and large, want Communist control. But this did not mean they would not trim their sails and even abet its coming if they gained the impression that it was inevitable.... [I]t is the shadows rather than the substance of things that move the hearts and sway the deeds of people.[35]

Policy-makers, in other words, were concerned lest the precipitious collapse of the National government in China have ramifications upon the will of Western Europe to foreswear the communist alternative.[36]

Given these concerns, it was necessary to ''buy time'' in Asia while rebuilding Europe's economic and psychological backbone. This, as much as congressional pressure threatening to link passage of the European Recovery Program to the continuation of aid to China, kept the money flowing to Chiang's forces in the late 1940s. Public pressure does not seem to have been involved in this situation, as State Department documents show no sense of strong popular approval for a China aid package. Indeed, just the opposite picture was presented (backed by polls) in the analyses put out by State's Public Affairs Division.[37] Despite this, the president still clung to a course of limited aid to the Chiang regime. ''This course of action,'' the Secretary of the Army explained to the NSC in mid-1948,

would recognize the interest of Congress in continuing the ECA aid program as well as maintain, before the world, the semblance of adhering to announced U.S. policy toward China. *Such a course could not produce the favorable decision required in the short time available to the Chinese National Government; nevertheless, it would be in the nature of ''buying time'' until the overall world situation is clarified.*[38]

With the ''splitting'' policy still operative, and recognizing that there was no more time to be ''bought,'' the theme that ''China, with its long, proud history,

[was] becoming a mere dependency in the Soviet orbit'' was increasingly hammered home by government representatives in the first half of 1950.[39] Editorial
opinion closely tracked these governmental pronouncements. Reflective of this
was the *New York Times* reaction to the mid-February 1950 Sino-Soviet pact.
The *Times*, picking up the rhetoric of official Washington, described this agreement as one that showed that ''the Chinese Communists have sold out their
chance to be independent. On the face of it the price they got was impressively
low.... Mao gambled away China's chance for liberty by making itself a bed-
fellow of tyranny.''[40] Though American officials were genuinely concerned about
the possibility of secret protocols in the treaty, neither their actions nor more
closely held words indicate the pact to be decisive in their evaluation of the
mainland.[41] Their views were perhaps closest to those expressed in the conservative English weekly, *The Economist*. This pact, the news magazine offered,
''suggests that [for the time being] Peking will be for Moscow a friendly but
not a satellite capital.''[42] Interestingly, prior to full dissemination of Washington's negative public view of the treaty, several American news analysts commented along these English lines. Lowell Thomas, speaking on CBS radio hours
after the pact's revelation, stressed not a Chinese sell-out but ''that [the] Chinese
did win important concessions'' from Moscow. A day later Eric Sevareid, again
on CBS radio, reiterated this same point in noting that the treaty ''looks so good
for China that [the] immediate result is bound to be that American propaganda
trying to drive [a] wedge between China and Russia will become, at least for
[a] time, considerably less effective.''[43]

Throughout this entire period, Americans remained opposed to involvement
in the deteriorating East Asian situation. Polls consistently found at least a
plurality of citizens opposed to any type of intervention in the Chinese civil
war.[44] The China lobby, reflecting this fact, was in considerable disarray, as it
had ''not yet been able to catch the attention and sympathy of the American
people.''[45] This may have stemmed from the public's negative feelings toward
Chiang Kai-shek. The generalissimo was viewed in less than favorable terms by
a plurality of the total population and by a wide majority of those who had been
more closely following events in China.[46] This was in line with official pronouncements that had placed much of the blame for China's ''loss'' at the
doorstep of the Nationalist government and its leaders. ''The Nationalist Government,'' administration sources repeatedly stressed, ''was overthrown in China
not by force of arms. It [instead] collapsed from its own inherent weakness.''[47]

Both top Washington figures and the public they were leading seemed set
against further aiding the Kuomintang (KMT). Congressional Republicans, however, seemed much more favorably disposed to Chiang's cause. As early as
1947, these elected officials had begun to latch onto the failure of the Democrats'
Far Eastern policy as a club with which to score political points. Reflecting the
partisan coloration given to Asia, Senator Vandenberg, the apostle of biparti-
sanship, twice in early 1947 explicitly ruled out China as an area in which an
apolitical foreign policy would operate.[48] This contentious path was not entirely

Vandenberg's choice but resulted, in good part, from the executive branch's failure to consult with Congress on America's Asian policy.[49] Having been frozen out of the decision-making process, many Republicans felt little inhibition in challenging the administration over its Far East actions. Indeed, by the time Dewey was nominated in 1948, many expected a full frontal campaign assault upon America's failure in Asia.[50]

This, though, was not to be. Dewey's decision to base his front-running campaign on domestic issues and to speak out only occasionally on the need to "end . . . [our] tragic neglect of China" was largely responsible for this result.[51] The few comments Dewey did make on China failed to arouse much interest as attention on foreign issues during the campaign focused on the multiple crises occurring in Europe. Not seeking to highlight Truman's generally competent performance in these external events, Dewey chose to run on a plank generally supportive of a bipartisan foreign policy. Change in Asia would have to await his election.[52]

Dewey's surprise loss, however, made it certain that the China issue would continue to be a contentious one. Republicans, though disappointed in the small role America's China policy had played in the 1948 election, did not abandon hope in this issue's future utility.[53] With assistance from some pro-Chiang Democrats, the legislature consistently—and unsuccessfully—put pressure on the administration to alter its basic policy of disengagement. Notable among these congressional efforts was Senator Patrick A. McCarran's attempt to force action on a $1.5 billion China aid bill. This effort, which "did not meet [with] a sympathetic [public] response,"[54] was successfully countered by an Acheson letter to Senator Tom Connally—the pro-administration chairman of the Senate Foreign Relations Committee—which outlined results "which would almost surely be catastrophic" if the Senator's bill became law.[55] This letter, though, did not completely end congressional concern. Legislative interest again manifested itself in the summer of 1949 when twenty-two senators (including sixteen Republicans) wrote to the president seeking official assurance that the United States would continue to recognize the Nationalists. Truman's Secretary of State again indirectly responded to this senatorial challenge through a letter to Connally stating that the Foreign Relations Committee would be "consulted" prior to any recognition decision. A decision to recognize the new communist regime would depend on whether that government was in effective and popular control of the mainland, and whether it honored its international obligations. The State Department's pledge to contact Congress did not, however, satisfy all of the White House's opponents. Senator William Knowland, for example, commented that he expected what Acheson really meant in his letter was that he would shortly appear unannounced in the Senate chambers and state that "we have determined to recognize the Communist regime in China, we wanted to notify you before the statement was given to the press."[56]

Notwithstanding congressional sarcasm, most persons continued to expect that Peking's recognition was only a matter of time. While not all applauded this outcome, most felt it to be unavoidable. David Lawrence, lamenting the loss of the mainland in *U.S. News and World Report*, nevertheless accepted that "soon, it will be the painful duty of the United States to extend formal recognition to the Communist-controlled Government of China . . . as a common sense decision in diplomacy recognition is inevitable."[57] Chiang's supporters in Congress had struck neither fear into the heart of the State Department nor a responsive chord in the general public. Nor did "elite" opinion seem much dissuaded from eventually fulfilling our diplomatic "duty." Business representatives continually focused on the possibility of lost markets and the likelihood that western trade could wean the Chinese Communists away from their less lucrative ideological cousins.[58] The more generalized foreign policy "elite" seemed to hold to a similar position. In an admittedly less-than-rigorous poll conducted in February 1950, the Council on Foreign Relations found "uncertain acceptance" for the Peking regime among "720 men who are leading citizens in twenty-three cities." This group of attentive citizens favored recognizing the PRC by a nearly three-to-one margin provided the Chinese gave "acceptable guarantees covering American lives and property and agree[d] to carry out Chinese treaty obligations." An exchange of ambassadors was opposed by only a slight margin among these men even when the question suggested that this move might "encourage rather than discourage the further spread of Communism in Asia."[59]

The overall shape of American opinion, which Washington had helped to create, thus left a considerable amount of room for policy-makers to maneuver in East Asia. The State Department's opinion analyses repeatedly stressed this point, noting that despite a "vocal and influential minority," the majority of the public and the press supported the administration's stance. The clearest "command" emanating from the public, in reality echoing the Truman-Acheson policy, was for the United States to disengage from the decades-old KMT-CCP conflict. The administration resolved to take this track, expecting its problems with pro-Nationalist Congressmen to be cleared up in short order through an invasion of Formosa by the mainland's army. Along these lines, *Newsweek* suggested that the State Department would be greatly relieved "if Formosa fell promptly to the Communists, one way or another, and the Nationalist regime would [simply] vanish."[60]

Reflective of this stance was the State Department's late-December 1949 decision to send out—over Defense Department objections—a confidential guidance paper for overseas press and public affairs officers on how to deal with the impending collapse of all KMT resistance.[61] This memo, set in motion by the Nationalists' 8 December abandonment of the mainland, did not, however, remain secret for long. It was released through General MacArthur's Tokyo office in a manner Acheson later described as "more than clumsy blundering."[62] The publication of this guidance paper on 3 January led to an immediate congressional uproar among Nationalist supporters. To many it seemed that the State Department was conniving to drive the last nails into Chiang's already fast-closing coffin. Matters were made no better by an earlier New Year's Day article in the

Times outlining America's non-intervention policy in the Far East as explained to James Reston by a "responsible official." Nor could Truman have been very pleased to see the headlines being grabbed by former President Hoover's 2 January call for an American naval defense of Taiwan.[63]

To end this public agitation and to quiet the more secretive misgivings of Defense Secretary Louis Johnson, the president felt it necessary to make a formal pronouncement on American policy concerning China. His 5 January 1950 "United States Policy toward Formosa" statement was clearly in line with the disengagement sentiment prevalent in the public. (On the eve of the president's announcement a State Department opinion analysis had concluded that "most articulate commentators oppose U.S. military and naval intervention to protect Formosa.")[64] This declaration stated that the United States, in keeping with the Cairo and Potsdam agreements, considered Taiwan to be Chinese territory. Truman further noted that, given this condition, the American government saw no reason to consider supplying the Nationalist forces on Taiwan with arms. This was unambiguously stated when the president declared that the United States had no intention of "utilizing its armed forces to interfere in the present [civil war] situation. The United States Government will not provide military aid or advice to the Chinese forces on Formosa."[65] Secretary Acheson, in a private meeting with senators Knowland and Smith on the morning of Truman's announcement, reiterated the substance of the president's words and bluntly stated that he "did not believe it was in the interest of the American public to hazard a new war over Formosa."[66] Speaking publicly later in the day, the secretary again reinforced Truman's words noting that the United States saw Formosa as an unquestioned part of China and was "not going to quibble on any lawyers' words about the integrity of its position."[67]

Though papers such as the *Washington Post* did "quibble" over the status of Formosa, for the most part the public and press accepted the president's actions.[68] State's *Monthly Survey*, for instance, reported that Truman's words drew "widespread approval from press and radio observers and organization leaders ... indicating more support or acquiescence than criticism of the outline of policy laid down by the Administration."[69] A poll completed eight days after Truman's 5 January pronouncement discovered that support in the general public for this "non-intervention" policy also existed, as a five-to-three majority endorsed a "hands off" policy toward Formosa.[70] The American public may even have been losing interest in following the events that seemed certain to lead to the KMT's total defeat. Less than one month after Truman's declaration of U. S. policy, only 60 percent of the sample population had even heard of Formosa and only four-fifths of this group could "reasonably well" describe its current importance.[71]

Congressional criticism of Truman's actions was also surprisingly muted. Senate Democrats caucused on 17 January and then announced their unanimous support for the president.[72] Moderate Republicans such as Vandenberg expressed consternation over the president's continuing lack of consultation with Congress, but they expressed no real desire to get sucked into an Asian quagmire. Harder line Sinophiles in the Republican party also began to give up their hope of aiding Chiang in a return to the mainland. After all, Acheson had made it clear to them that "to all intents and purposes, all of continental China was now to be written off."[73] Instead, these men began to press the moral and strategic necessity of keeping Formosa in free hands. Senator Taft, speaking on 11 January, reflected this subtle shift away from a complete identification with Chiang's cause. Formosa, Taft stated,

is a place where a small amount of aid at a very small cost can prevent the further spread of communism. Such action does not commit us to backing the Nationalist Government in any prolonged war against the Chinese Communists. We can determine later whether we ever wish to recognize the Chinese Communists and what the disposition of Formosa shall be.... One thing is certain, if the Communists take over Formosa, we will have just as much chance of setting up an independent republic of Formosa as we have of returning the ... German provinces from Poland to Germany.[74]

The administration, confident that there was "almost no support" for the direction in which Taft's scheme might lead the United States, sternly rejected such arguments. It would oppose communist expansion into the remainder of Asia—to this end it began to lobby in Congress for funds to aid other Asian lands on 6 January —but to bankroll Chiang on Formosa would be "to deflect from the Russians to ourselves the righteous anger, and the wrath, and the hatred of the Chinese people."[75] Similar "deflection" concerns led Washington to also gently turn down requests for aid from Tibetan officials hoping to declare their independence.[76] Geopolitical concerns left little other choice; the United States did not want to appear imperialistic in Peking's eyes.[77]

In the months following the completion of the February Sino-Soviet pact, as congressional critics became somewhat less vociferous, qualms over the American policy of abandoning Formosa began to intensify in the Pentagon and among some State Department officials. The seemingly intransigent stance of Peking on questions involving U. S. property, and British diplomatic difficulties with the new regime, gave renewed impetus to those who felt "saving" Formosa did not automatically preclude relations with the mainland. Within the State Department, Dean Rusk and John Foster Dulles advocated such a "one China, one Formosa" policy course. Rusk, reflecting his feelings, wrote to Acheson on 30 May arguing against America's implicit policy of waiting for Formosa to fall. He protested that "it will not leave a good taste if we allow our political problems to be solved by the extermination of our war allies. That was the Russian solution of General Bor's Polish Army."[78] Dulles, for his part, wrote a note on 6 June suggesting both Chinas be included in the negotiations over a Japanese peace treaty.[79] Rusk and Dulles, aware of CIA estimates, knew time was growing short for Formosan independence plans.[80] A strategy was thus formulated whereby the Gimo would be approached, probably by Dulles in the course of his trip to Japan on June 15, with the word that (a) the fall of Formosa in the present circumstances was inevitable, (b) the U.S. would do nothing to assist the Gimo in preventing this, the only course open to the Gimo to prevent the bloodshed of his people was to request UN trusteeship. The US would be prepared to back such a move for trusteeship and would ready the fleet to prevent any armed attacks on Formosa while the move for trusteeship was pending.[81]

If Chiang refused such an offer, George Kennan suggested, then the United States should seriously consider the use of its own troops to occupy the strategically valuable island and to evict the generalissimo and any of his recalcitrant allies.[82] Realizing that such a scenario was unlikely, however, Rusk began to explore more subtle options—such as an internal coup—for the removal of Chiang.[83] All of these plans, though, proved stillborn, as Acheson remained true to his policy course. Dulles passed this word on to Nationalist Ambassador Wellington Koo at a mid-June meeting and, while expressing his own sympathy for the Kuomintang's predicament, could only offer the unreassuring words of advice that "God helps those who help themselves."[84]

Louis Johnson, Truman's Secretary of Defense, rightly considered Acheson the main impediment to plans for detaching Formosa from the mainland. Determined to do just this and, in the process, also undercut his bureaucratic rival, Johnson continually pressed for the right to sell Chiang's forces tanks and jets.[85] Toward this end, Johnson also instructed Paul Griffith, an assistant secretary of defense, to carry on an extended liaison with Ambassador Koo in order to coordinate pro-Nationalist activities. In the course of these contacts, Koo was provided with confidential information in an attempt to undermine Acheson's stance.[86] Truman, however, continued to follow the advice of his State Department and even warned Johnson not to meddle in this area of international policy. At a 3 June 1950 meeting between Koo and Griffith, the ascendency of Acheson's position could clearly be discerned. Griffith told Koo that though

the Secretary of Defense was always favorable to the Chinese cause . . . he [now] had to be discreet about it. Mr. Johnson has been told by the President to keep out of the Chinese question as it was one of foreign policy and therefore should belong to the State Department.[87]

The press in the spring and summer months appeared to adopt a position mildly supportive of the Acheson stance on Asia.[88] While there was little advocacy of aiding Chiang in a return to the mainland—that issue seemed settled— some influential voices did begin to call for aid to save Formosa. This minority of the press may have been influenced by the continuing "scolding" rhetoric emanating from Washington. Surely, critics reasoned, if the Chinese Communists were an extension of "international communism," there was little reason to abandon the "free territory" of Formosa to them with no hope of positive gain in return. Editorial sentiment along these lines frequently surfaced in the pro-Nationalist *New York Times*. A 23 April 1950 editorial argued, for instance, that

the Nationalist Government is actually more viable than it was six months ago. Its spokesmen have stated recently that with even modest economic assistance from the outside world they could hope to hold the island [of Formosa] almost indefinitely.... Since this government is the largest active, committed, military, anti-Communist force in East Asia its capacity to resist is of the gravest concern to all of the still free world.[89]

The presence of such sentiment in parts of the press, public, and Congress caused the administration to be unsuccessful in totally ending aid to Chiang's forces. The legislature was able to force the continuation of previously allocated aid through a number of actions, the most "spectacular" being the holding up of emergency funds for Korea in the House until the administration agreed to allow the remaining supplies to flow to Formosa. This move, which Republican Senate leaders labelled as "highly irresponsible," was justified by many Representatives on "logical" grounds. "What kind of policy for the Far East," asked Representative Donald L. Jackson, "would put economic aid into Korea which bears no relationship to our national defense, and at the same time, refuse a request to put aid into Formosa."[90] With only a relatively small amount of money involved, and the likelihood that the problem would "disappear" before it was all dispersed anyway, the administration allowed this round to be won by its Capitol Hill critics. To do otherwise would only have served to unnecessarily stir up the political waters in Washington.

The aid that was allocated to Taiwan, however, did show the true color of Washington's expectations. The Economic Cooperation Administration (ECA), for instance, focused exclusively on short-term, quick-return, projects—refusing to consider longer term investments.[91] Furthermore, in May $50 million in funds Congress had earlier appropriated for the "general area of China" were released for use, contrary to the lawmakers' original intent, in Indochina. This move was designed to bolster our French ally in the "China area," to show White House resolve in combating Asian communism, and to frustrate Chiang's hopes of receiving these funds. The bulk of the public apparently was responding to the president's policy, as a May Roper Poll found that only about one-quarter of the population indicated any further interest in aiding the generalissimo.[92] By mid-June, with the Communists massing their forces opposite Formosa and Koo warning U. S. officials of a possible July invasion, there was little doubt that the "adamant" Acheson would not be swayed from his policy course.[93] Philip D. Sprouse, intimately involved in the formation of America's China policy in these years, has acknowledged that

the U.S. was engaged [at this time] in what could be described as a withdrawing and disengaging operation with the prospect that by early 1951, with the Communists in possession of Formosa and the National Government no longer in existence [at least on

Chinese territory], the U.S. Government could seriously consider the question of recognition.[94]

The small amount of aid trickling to the Nationalists likely played a role in China's increasing hostility toward the United States in these months. This hostility was reinforced by America's ambiguous stand toward the China representation question at the United Nations. While most in the public continued to oppose "United States–United Nations recognition" of the People's Republic of China, there "remained a trend of feeling that eventually the Chinese Communists will be recognized and admitted to the UN."[95] Washington, again expecting the problem to clear itself up, did not wish to chance the political blame for "losing" the Nationalists' seat in the United Nations. To this end, the United States reportedly pressured a key Latin American state on the Security Council not to shift its vote in favor of admitting People's Republic of China early in 1950.[96] The speed and manner with which policy was pursued were, once again, influenced by the shape of public opinion—Truman did not want to risk moving too far in advance of the public. The course and destination of policy, however, remained unaltered. That America was not immovably opposed to Peking's eventual UN membership came through in the procedural stance it took in the world body. Dean Rusk, for example, told UN Secretary-General Trygve Lie in late January that

in a matter of several weeks seven members of of the Security Council will have recognized the Communist [Chinese] regime and when that happens a communist representative will be seated on a procedural vote. . . . [W]e would neither ourselves exercise the veto nor acquiesce in a veto by anyone else.[97]

As late as 31 May, Acheson could still be found reiterating this no-veto stance to an informal joint session of Congress.[98]

Matters in Asia in the first half of 1950 had not moved as rapidly as Truman and Acheson had expected. The Sino-Soviet alliance seemed to have solidified, yet the policy of splintering Peking from Moscow's orbit continued to be paramount at the State Department. Despite some concessions to congressional critics, the administration was successful in fending off attempts to embroil it in the one-sided-end game of China's civil war. Washington was steeled in this by its successful shaping of opinion in the prior two years. To accomplish this, the pace and presentation of policy had been altered, but not its overall substance and direction. The negative views of the public slowed the advance of American policy but did not derail it. In time, Washington believed, opinion would react to the reality of a slowly changing policy and accept the People's Republic of China into the world community. While still approaching the most sensitive China problems cautiously, Truman and Acheson now had little fear of a prolonged domestic backlash once Formosa fell. A relaxation of relations between America and China seemed just over the horizon. What followed, with the onset of the Korean War, however, was twenty years of hostility.

NOTES

1. J. H. Kalicki, *The Pattern of Sino-American Crises: Political and Military Inter-actions in the 1950s* (New York: Cambridge University Press, 1975), p. 13. This "for-ward-looking" statement can be instructively compared with Kenneth Young's words at a 1967 conference, "Since 1950 the relations between Peking and Washington and between the Chinese on the Mainland and the American people in general have been supercharged with hostile images and antagonistic motivations." See Young, *Diplomacy and Power in Washington-Peking Dealings: 1953-1967* (Chicago: University of Chicago Center for Policy Study, 1967), p. 25.

2. Kalicki, pp. 14-19; John Gittings, *The World and China, 1922-1972* (London: Eyre Methuen, 1974), pp. 163-179; *Foreign Relations of the United States* (hereafter *FRUS*), *1949*, vol. 9 (Washington, D.C.: State Department), pp. 12-15, 1251. See also Ely Kahn, Jr., *The China Hands: America's Foreign Service Officers and What Befell Them* (New York: Viking Press, 1976), pp. 202-203; Kenneth W. Rea and John C. Brewer, eds., *The Forgotten Ambassador: The Reports of John Leighton Stuart, 1946-1949* (Boulder, Colo.: Westview Press, 1981), pp. 309-312, 333-334; and Warren I. Cohen, "Ambassador Philip D. Sprouse on the Question of Recognition of the People's Republic of China in 1949 and 1950 (Document)," *Diplomatic History* 2 (Spring 1978), p. 216.

3. Ross Y. Koen, *The China Lobby in American Politics* (Chicago: Macmillan Co., 1960), p. 232.

4. *Special Report on American Opinion*, "US Attitudes on the Recognition of the Communist Regime in China" (30 November 1949), Records of the Office of Public Opinion Studies (State Department), 1943-1975. Office Files of H. Schuyler Foster (hereafter Foster Papers), National Archives, Washington, D.C., Box 33. See also the *Monthly Survey of American Opinion on International Affairs* (hereafter *Monthly Survey*) 103 (November 1949), Foster Papers, Box 12, where it is stated that "*the largest number of commentators, though shaken by the Ward case and deeply suspicious of Red China, did not discount the possibility or desirability of recognition at some time in the future*"(emphasis in original). The Foster Papers present an invaluable treasure trove for the opinion-policy analyst by providing some insight into how the executive branch perceived public opinion through the years.

5. William LaFeber, "American Policy-Makers, Public Opinion, and the Outbreak of the Cold War," in *The Origins of the Cold War in Asia*, ed. Yonosuke Nagai and Akira Iriye (New York: Columbia University Press, 1977), p. 56.

6. *NYT*, 7 January 1950.

7. "Communists Take U.S. Property in China," *Department of State Bulletin* (*DSB*) 22 (23 January 1950):119-123; *FRUS, 1950*, 6:270-275, 286-289.

8. Kalicki, p. 19; Warren I. Cohen, "Acheson, His Advisers and China, 1949-50," in *Uncertain Years: China-America Relations, 1947-1950*, ed. Dorothy Borg and Waldo Heinrichs (New York: Columbia University Press, 1980), pp. 15-51; *FRUS, 1950*, 6:321-322.

9. Dean Acheson, "New Era in Asia: U.S. Policy to Assist Free Peoples," *Vital Speeches of the Day* 16 (15 April 1950):356.

10. A. T. Steele, *The American People and China* (New York: McGraw Hill, 1966), p. 36.

11. Gallup poll, no. 433-K (July 1949), in George Gallup, *The Gallup Poll: Public*

Opinion, 1935-1970 (hereafter Gallup poll), 3 vols. (New York: Random House, 1972). Recognition was opposed by a 41 to 19 percent margin among the "informed" general public. Recognition among the college-educated group was opposed 54 to 32 percent. A later Gallup poll (no. 455-K, 2 June 1950) found similar results, with recognition opposed by a 40 to 16 percent margin among the 65 percent of the population who had a "correct conception" of the type of government ruling the mainland. A National Opinion Research Center (hereafter NORC) poll conducted in late January, which linked People's Republic of China recognition with Chiang's derecognition, found a 62 to 12 percent margin against this move. An early February 1950 Iowa poll found similar results. See *Monthly Survey* 106 (February 1950), Foster Papers, Box 12; and the *Weekly Summary of Comment on China* (hereafter "China Telegram") (February 8, 1950), Foster Papers, Box 26.

12. Gallup poll, no. 449-K (11 January 1950). Of the 76 percent of the population "informed," 29 percent favored trade relations with a communist China and 33 percent opposed this route. A May 1949 poll (no. 442-K) found trade relations opposed in the general public by a 46 to 34 percent margin.

13. Foster Rhea Dulles, *American Policy toward Communist China* (New York: Thomas Y. Crowell Co., 1972), p. 44.

14. "Public Opinion on US Policy toward China," (7 July 1949), Foster Papers, Box 33.

15. See, for example, *Special Report on American Opinion*, "Recent Opinion Regarding the Effect of the 'Loss' of China on US Foreign Policy" (22 April 1949); *Special Report on American Opinion*, "US Popular Opinion on China" (12 September 1949); "Recent Comment on Formosa" (9 December 1949); *Special Report on American Opinion*, "A Summary of Current American Attitudes on US Policy toward the Far East" (13 February 1950)—all in the Foster Papers, Box 33.

16. "American Public Discussion and Opinion on US Relations with China and Neighboring Countries" (26 September 1949), Foster Papers, Box 33.

17. Ibid.

18. On this point see LaFeber; Ralph B. Levering, *American Opinion and the Russian Alliance, 1939-45* (Chapel Hill: University of North Carolina Press, 1976); Michael Leigh, *Mobilizing Consent: Public Opinion and American Foreign Policy, 1937-1947* (Westport, Conn.: Greenwood Press, 1976); Thomas A. Paterson, "Presidential Foreign Policy, Public Opinion, and Congress: The Truman Years," *Diplomatic History* 3 (Winter 1979):1-18.

19. *Monthly Survey* 87 (July 1948), Foster Papers, Box 11.

20. Quoted in ibid., 104 (December 1949), Foster Papers, Box 12.

21. Gallup poll, no. 433-K (15 December 1949). Interestingly, this does not appear to have been General MacArthur's view. MacArthur accepted that the Chinese had parallel views with Moscow but felt they were not controlled by the Russians. See MacArthur's May 1951 testimony in *Military Situation in the Far East* (hereafter MacArthur Hearings), Hearings before the Committee on Armed Services and the Committee on Foreign Relations, United States Senate, 82d Cong., 1st sess., esp. pp. 144, 251, 300. Compare this with Marshall's statements, pp. 659, 704.

22. "Some Outstanding Features of American Opinion on China Policy, 1946-49" [1949], Foster Papers, Box 33.

23. Dean Acheson, "Total Diplomacy: To Strengthen United States Leadership for Human Freedom" (16 February 1950), in *America's Foreign Policy: Basic Documents,*

1950-1955, 2 vols., Document no. 2 (Washington, D.C.: State Department, 1957), pp. 6-7.

24. George F. Kennan, "The International Situation," *DSB* 21 (5 December 1949):324.

25. *FRUS, 1948*, 8:314-316.

26. "Outline of Far Eastern and Asia Policy for Review with the President" (16 November 1949). A copy of this was sent to the president, through the secretary of state. Declassified Documents Reference System (hereafter DDRS), 1975, 26 D.

27. Cohen, "Acheson", p. 21.

28. National Security Council memo no. 48/1, 23 December 1949. Reprinted in *Containment: Documents on American Foreign Policy and Strategy, 1945-50*, eds. Thomas H. Etzold and John Lewis Gaddis (New York: Columbia University Press, 1978), p. 257.

29. *FRUS, 1950*, 6:297.

30. Ibid., pp. 306-307.

31. See, for example, *Monthly Survey* 90 (October 1948), Foster Papers, Box 11.

32. Thomas H. Etzold, "The Far East in American Strategy, 1948-51," in *Aspects of Sino-American Relations since 1784*, ed. Thomas H. Etzold (New York: New Viewpoints, 1978), p. 108.

33. Quoted in *Monthly Survey* 105 (January 1950), Foster Papers, Box 12.

34. See, for instance, *The Economist* 158 (28 January 1950):187. There were signs throughout this entire period that a later vocal dissent might strike a chord in the public should the Truman-Acheson policy go awry. One sign of this appeared in a 23 December 1948 *Special Report on American Opinion* (Foster Papers, Box 33) on "China" based, in part, on an NORC poll. This winter poll found, in the words of State's analysts, that

aid from the U.S. is believed to be a decisive factor in the outcome of China's war. Should we stop sending aid to China, the Communists are likely to gain control say 72 percent of the respondents. But if we increase the amount only 23 percent think Communist control likely, while 41 percent say "unlikely" and 31 percent give no opinion. *In other words, a large portion of the public seems to feel we can stop the Communists in China by more aid, if we want to* [emphasis added].

A 12 September 1949 *Special Report* about "U.S. Popular Opinion on China" (Foster Papers, Box 33) reported that many also expressed disapproval of Washington when asked, "What is your opinion of the way our government has handled the China situation?" America's handling of this "situation" was disapproved by a 33 to 22 percent margin nationwide and by a 54 to 28 percent margin among those 36 percent who had heard of the White Paper. (The "uninformed group" disapproved of U.S. policy by only a 20 to 18 percent plurality, with fully 62 percent having no opinion on this question.) Finally, a memo from Foster (Box 33) to "Members [of] PA Information Policy Committee on [the] Far East" on 7 June 1950 noted that by a 32 to 20 percent margin a recent sample had agreed that "the Communists might not be in control of China now if our government in Washington had followed a different policy." The college subgroup agreed by a 53 to 28 percent margin with this statement.

35. George F. Kennan, *Memoirs: 1925-1950* (Boston: Little, Brown and Co., 1967), pp. 318, 351.

36. John H. Feaver, "The China Aid Bill of 1948: Limited Assistance as a Cold War Strategy," *Diplomatic History* 5 (Spring 1981):107-120.

37. See, for example, *Monthly Survey* 71 (March 1947), 74 (June 1947), 78 (October

1947), 79 (November 1947), 80 (December 1947), 82 (February 1948), and 83 (March 1948)—all in Foster Papers, Box 11.

38. "A Report to the National Security Council by the Secretary of the Army on Possible Courses of Action for the United States with Respect to the Critical Situation in China," NSC (16 July 1948), DDRS, 1979, 50A (emphasis added).

39. Acheson, "New Era in Asia," p. 155.

40. *NYT*, 19 February 1950. The *Times* often adopted a harsh stance in the 1950s on Far Eastern issues. Much of the responsibility for this can be traced to its main editorial writer on Chinese issues during this decade. Robert Aura Smith, from his accession to this post in 1949, was a firm supporter of Chiang Kai-shek. Praise of Smith, from a fellow hard-liner, can be found in Karl Lott Rankin, *China Assignment* (Seattle: University of Washington Press, 1964), pp. 184-185. When Smith was not writing these editorials, Otto Tolischus—another supporter of Chiang—was. Herbert L. Matthews, in his journalistic memoir, recalls that

the *Times'* editorial policy was consistently on the side of reaction, then [1949-1950] and throughout the 1950s, on the subject of the Far East. The reason was that our Asian editorials were written mostly by Robert Aura Smith and, for the remainder, by Otto Tolischus. Both men were extreme conservatives who believed McCarthy was doing some good.

See Matthews, *A World in Revolution: A Newspaperman's Memoir* (New York: Charles Scribner's Sons, 1971), p. 371.

41. See, for example, *FRUS, 1950*, 6:308, 311.

42. *The Economist* 158 (18 February 1950):363-364.

43. Quoted in "China Telegram," 15 February 1950 and 21 February 1950, in Foster Papers, Box 26.

44. Gallup poll, no. 441-K (27 May 1949) and no. 433-K (15 December 1948). See also a May 1950 Roper poll reported in Elmo Roper, *You and Your Leaders: Their Actions and Your Reactions, 1936-1956* (New York: William Morrow and Co., 1957), p. 175. See also NORC poll no. 155 (25 February 1948), NORC no. 156 (25 March 1948), NORC no. 157 (22 April 1958), NORC no. 166 (1 June 1949), and NORC no. 168 (11 August 1949). Of those polls, only NORC no. 157 showed the public favorable to sending supplies to Chiang's forces. Opinion expressed in this poll—worded identically to no. 166—however, had reversed itself by June 1949.

45. Koen, p. 89. Recognizing this, the Nationalist embassy engaged in certain ventures designed to generate support for its home regime. At this time, there was, for example, talk within the embassy of the need to "conduct a 'fear' campaign through all the press and radio media which will emphasize the dangers to this country [i.e., America] of the spread of Communism over China." See conversations between Norman Paige and Joseph Ku (Koo) on "Public Relation[s] Operations for Chinese National Government," 9 June 1949, the Wellington Koo Papers (hereafter Koo Papers), Columbia University, New York, Box 180.

46. Gallup poll, no. 466-K (19 September 1949). The general public felt unfavorable toward Chiang Kai-shek by a 35 to 21 percent margin. The informed population, here defined as the 36 percent of the sample group who had heard of the "White Paper," disliked Chiang by a 56 to 24 percent margin. An earlier NORC poll (late 1948) which asked, "In general, do you have a favorable or unfavorable impression of the present government of China, headed by Chiang Kai-shek," found the public about evenly split at that time (30 percent favorable, 28 percent not), though the college-educated group

disliked Chiang by a 48 to 32 percent plurality. See *Special Report on American Opinion*; "China" (23 December 1948), Foster Papers, Box 33.

47. Acheson, "New Era in Asia," p. 355; *The China White Paper, August 1949* (Stanford: Stanford University Press, 1967). The White Paper was originally issued as *United States Relations with China, with Special Reference to the Period 1944-1949* (Washington, D.C.: State Department Publication 3573, Far Eastern Series 30, 1949). The White Paper, according to State's Public Affairs Division, was well received by the "predominant group" of persons.

As in the past, the larger number of press and radio commentators have assented to the Government's conclusion that the present debacle in China was primarily due to the incompetence and decay of the Nationalist regime. They therefore argued that the "ominous result of the civil war was beyond the control of the U.S." and have found ample justification for the Department's policy of "no more aid to China now."

See *Special Report on American Opinion*, "Reaction to the China White Paper" (23 August 1949), Foster Papers; "Special Report for Ambassador Jessup Prepared in the Division of Public Studies: Current Opinion Situation Concerning China Policy" (16 August 1949), Foster Papers, Box 33; and *Monthly Survey* 100 (August 1949), Foster Papers, Box 12.

48. *Congressional Record*, 80th Cong., 1st Sess., vol. 93, pt. 2 (18 March 1947), p. 2167, and pt. 3 (16 April 1947), p. 3474.

49. H. Bradford Westerfield, *Foreign Policy and Party Politics: Pearl Harbor to Korea* (New Haven: Yale University Press, 1955), p. 241.

50. Koen, p. 89-90.

51. Westerfield, p. 367; LaFeber, p. 58. David Halberstam, *The Best and the Brightest* (New York: Fawcett Crest, 1972), p. 136.

52. *Monthly Survey* (July 1948), Foster Papers, Box 11; Robert A. Divine, *Foreign Policy and U.S. Presidential Elections: 1940-1948* (New York: New Viewpoints, 1974), pp. 210-276; Lewis McCarrol Purifoy, *Harry Truman's China Policy: McCarthyism and the Diplomacy of Hysteria, 1947-1951* (New York: New Viewpoints, 1976), p. 100.

53. Foster Rhea Dulles, p. 54.

54. *Monthly Survey* 95 (March 1949), Foster Papers, Box 11.

55. "Copy of Letter from Dean Acheson to Senator Connally, March 15, 1949, on $1.5 Billion Aid Bill (S. 1063)," Koo Papers, Box 164.

56. Quoted in Foster Rhea Dulles, p. 54; Westerfield, p. 360.

57. David Lawrence, "Recognition," *U.S. News and World Report*, 27 January 1950, p. 27. Walter Lippmann adopted a very similar stance. See "China Telegram," 14 January 1950, Foster Papers, Box 26.

58. Two respected journals of the financial community—the *Wall Street Journal* and the *Magazine of Wall Street*—held to this position. This position was also endorsed by the San Francisco Chamber of Commerce. Interestingly, the AFL was strongly opposed to any trade or recognition moves involving China. See *Opinions and Activities of American Private Organizations and Groups* 211 (24 October 1949), Foster Papers, Box 15; *Monthly Survey* 93 (January 1949), 102 (October 1949), and 103 (November 1949), Foster Papers, Box 12.

59. Joseph Barker, ed., *American Policy toward China: A Report on the Views of Leading Citizens in Twenty-Three Cities* (New York: Council on Foreign Relations, 1950).

60. Ernest Lindley, "The Storm over Formosa," *Newsweek*, 9 January 1950, p. 20.

61. Westerfield, p. 363; *MacArthur Hearings*, pp. 2577-2578.

62. Dean Acheson, *Present at the Creation: My Years in the State Department* (New York: W. W. Norton and Co., 1969), p. 350.

63. *NYT*, 3 January 1950; Westerfield, p. 364; Purifoy, p. 144. *Newsweek*'s 2 January 1950 edition (p. 10), carried news roughly similar in content to what Reston published.

64. "China Telegram" (4 January 1950), Foster Papers, Box 26.

65. Harry S Truman, "United States Policy toward Formosa," *DSB* 22 (16 January 1950):79.

66. *FRUS, 1950*, 6:260.

67. Dean Acheson, "United States Policy toward Formosa," *DSB* 22 (16 January 1950):81.

68. *Washington Post*, 10 January 1950. By 7 June the *Post* was calling for what it termed "dualism"—an American trusteeship over Formosa combined with the acceptance of Peking into the United Nations. See "China Telegram," 7 June 1950, Foster Papers, Box 26.

69. *Monthly Survey* 105 (January 1950), Foster Papers, Box 12.

70. NORC poll no. 273 (13 January 1950). But see Gallup poll no. 451-K, taken between 8 and 13 January 1950. This poll found that 24 percent of the 49 percent of persons "reasonably well-informed" on the problem of Formosa still wanted to aid Chiang in some way.

71. Gallup poll, no. 451-K (3 February 1950); no. 455-K (2 June 1950).

72. Westerfield, pp. 364-366.

73. *FRUS, 1950*, 6:258.

74. Quoted in Joseph W. Ballentine, *Formosa: A Problem for United States Foreign Policy* (Washington, D.C.: The Brookings Institution, 1952), p. 123.

75. Dean Acheson, "Crisis in Asia—An Examination of U.S. Policy," *DSB* 22 (23 January 1950):115; *NYT*, 6 January 1950. The idea that China was losing large portions of its territory to an imperialistic Russia became widespread as 1950 went on. This idea was pushed by Washington as another facet in its policy of breaking the Sino-Soviet alliance. A sign of the American public's acceptance of this view is a map included in a 15 August 1950 *Look* article ("Russia Today," pp. 28-29, by Richard Wilson) on Russia which places Sinkiang and Manchuria within the Soviet domain.

76. *FRUS, 1950*, 6:272-273, 285-286, 317-318, 331-333.

77. The Chinese Communists were not unaware of the rationale behind America's policy. See *New China News Agency* dispatch no. 273, January 1950.

78. *FRUS, 1950*, 6:351.

79. Ibid., p. 1211. See also ibid., pp. 1239-1241, 1280, 1327.

80. Ibid., p. 330; CIA Intelligence Memorandum no. 292 (11 May 1950), "Probable Developments in Taiwan, Reappraisal of ORE 7-50," DDRS, 1980, 399C.

81. *FRUS, 1950*, 6:348-349.

82. Warren I. Cohen, *The American Secretaries of State and Their Diplomacy: Dean Rusk* (Totowa, N.J.: Cooper Square Publishers, 1980), p. 46.

83. Rusk, for instance, requested a meeting with Hu Shih at the Plaza Hotel in New York on 23 June 1950 to ask about the "Free China" movement on Taiwan. Hu evidently took the conversation as one designed to test his interest in organizing opposition to Chiang's continued rule—a move he disavowed in his conversation with Rusk. See Koo Papers, Box 218, 24 July 1950 (Diaries).

84. "Notes of a Conversation" between Koo and Dulles, 12 June 1950, Koo Papers,

Box 180. Dulles told Koo that before the KMT could have any possible hope of aid it would have to prove it was willing to fight, since "the people of the State Department doubted that serious resistance would be offered in Formosa." Dulles had earlier (25 May 1950) told a Nationalist official that the American public was opposed to aiding the Nationalists since they appeared to lack the "will" to fight.

85. *FRUS, 1950*, 6:325-326, 351-352. In this period the United States allowed the Nationalists to buy certain types of weapons but did not offer them aid.

86. Cohen, *Dean Rusk*, p. 45; Nancy Bernkopf Tucker, "Nationalist China's Decline and Its Impact on Sino-American Relations, 1949-1950," in *Uncertain Years: China-America Relations, 1947-1950*, ed. Dorothy Borg and Waldo Heinrichs (New York: Columbia University Press, 1980), pp. 166-167.

87. "Notes of a Conversation" between Koo and Paul Griffith, 3 June 1950 (Koo Papers, Box 180). Griffith also told Koo that though Johnson would like to tour Formosa he had no hope of getting the trip approved by the president. He reported to Koo, in this vein, that in February General Bradley and the "chiefs of three services" wanted to visit Formosa when they were in the Far East. Truman flatly turned down this request.

88. State's *Monthly Report* for May 1950, 109, Foster Papers, Box 13, reported that "interest in aiding the Nationalists on their 'last stronghold' remains small."

89. *NYT*, 23 April 1950. As the *Times* editorial was being written, the Nationalists were in the process of losing control of Hainan island.

90. *Congressional Record*, 81st Cong., 2d Sess. (1950), p. 649; Westerfield, p. 366; Tang Tsou, *America's Failure in China, 1941-1950* (Chicago: University of Chicago Press, 1963), pp. 531, 538.

91. Rankin, pp. 69-75. This stance was perhaps unsurprising given the views of two of ECA's more recent administrators—Paul Hoffman and Roger Lapham. For their views see *Monthly Survey* 92 (December 1949) and 101 (September 1949), Foster Papers, Boxes 11 and 12.

92. Roper, p. 175. Twenty-six percent felt we had supported Chiang "longer than we should," 30 percent said we had supported him "just about as long as we should have," and 27 percent favored continued support.

93. Dulles told a closed conference of Republican senators on 12 June "that the attitude of President Truman, Secretary Acheson, and Under Secretary Webb, regarding China, remains adamant, but the attitude of Dean Rusk is less adamant." See memo from Chen Chih-mai to Ambassador Koo, 15 June 1950, Koo Papers, Box 180.

94. Letter from Philip D. Sprouse to Mr. Robert Blum, 8 February 1973, reprinted in Cohen, "Ambassador Philip D. Sprouse," p. 215.

95. *Monthly Survey* 108 (April 1950).

96. The nation pressured was reportedly Ecuador. See Robert Boardman, *Britain and the People's Republic of China, 1949-74* (New York: Harper and Row, 1976), p. 51.

97. Cohen, "Acheson," p. 41. Note, however, Tsou (pp. 525-526) reports that Acheson told Secretary Lie on 21 January that the seizure of America's consular property had stiffened U.S. opposition to the People's Republic of China's UN admission.

98. Tsou, p. 527.

4

Opinion and Sino-American Relations from the Advent of the Korean War to the Election of Eisenhower _____

The imminent fall of Formosa was not expected to lead to an immediate rapprochement with the People's Republic. The final defeat of Chiang's forces, however, would remove the major hindrance to an eventual reconciliation between the Pacific powers. With this in mind, *The Economist*'s American correspondent reported in early May that Washington's advocates of increased contacts with the mainland were "waiting hopefully for the fall of the last anticommunist bastion in China."[1] The U.S. government expected that once the civil war ended, future relations could be conducted in a relatively normal manner. "In general," a 30 December 1949 NSC memo argued, "it should be realized that it would be inappropriate for the United States to adopt a posture more hostile or policies more harsh towards a Communist China than towards the USSR itself."[2]

This policy of constrained normality, however, did not come to pass. The crossing of the thirty-eighth parallel by North Korean units on 25 June 1950 brought about a marked change in the moderate position that most Americans, and their government, had been taking toward events in Asia.[3] This shift in perceptions, though, was slow to evolve. The initial step in this change occurred on 27 June when Truman, responding to a suggestion by Acheson, interposed the Seventh Fleet between Taiwan and the mainland. According to Truman's *Memoirs* this action was taken in order to prevent the enlargement of "the area of conflict."[4] An unstated but equally important reason, though, was that "it would have been difficult to justify continued rejection of Republican pressures for United States assistance in the defense of Taiwan while seeking public support for the decision to intervene militarily in Korea."[5] This move, State's *Monthly Survey* reported, drew "less enthusiastic support than his decision on Korea, in the more limited attention accorded it. However, most of those commenting appear to have accepted the defense of Formosa as an integral part of America's defense program in Asia.''[6]

Whatever its motives, Truman's late June statement clouded the until-then clear future of Formosa. It was no longer argued that the island was an unquestioned part of the mainland; it was not stated that the determination of Taiwan's status had to ''await the restoration of security in the Pacific, a peace settlement with Japan, or consideration by the United Nations.''[7] The potential implications of America's new policy did not escape the Chinese Communists. They had been closely following the Formosan debate within the United States for over a year with growing concern. On 27 June their worst fears seemed to have been confirmed; one day later Peking issued a statement denouncing the American move into the Straits as ''armed aggression against the territory of China in total violation of the United Nations Charter.''[8]

American opinion in the summer and fall months of 1950 mirrored Washington's uncertainty over Taiwan's ultimate fate. A September NORC poll, though finding better than three-to-one approval for the president's Formosa policy among those with a view, discovered that fully 54 percent of the sample population were unable or unwilling to comment on this policy. The vagueness of public understanding about overall China policy remained a prominent feature of opinion throughout these months. Writing in early November, State's preference analysts were still noting that ''uncertainty and indecision on the part of the general public in regard to President Truman's present policy toward Formosa'' remained quite widespread.[9] This public vagueness reflected the caution with which the administration was approaching the China area. To protect Formosa and yet keep future channels open to the mainland as a way of preventing war was a delicate task—one that, at times, left the administration open to strong criticism for its seemingly inconsistent policy. ''It is difficult to believe,'' opined William Henry Chamberlain along these lines in the *Wall Street Journal*, ''that a policy—if it can be called that—of being on every side of every debatable issue at various times can lead to anything but failure, impotence and frustration.''[10]

One area where the public displayed none of this uncertainty, though, was in aiding Chiang militarily. Shortly after the Korean War began the public reversed itself and came to favor sending military supplies to Taiwan by a 48 to 35 percent plurality.[11] This increased acceptance of aiding the Nationalists stemmed, in large part, from a ''general increase of public willingness since the Korean War [began] to take positive action against Communist aggression wherever it may appear.''[12] Aiding the Nationalists did not, at least on the surface, preclude contact with the mainland. Public soundings, taken by State at this time, were in accordance with this governmental belief.[13] Simultaneous with this ''aid'' opinion shift, Washington geared up to send military equipment to Chiang's men. Protecting Formosa from communist aggression would be a priority item for both public and government, but if the mainland were to accept this new reality there was no reason America should rule out dealing with Peking.

Having implicitly moved to this ''one China, one Formosa'' stance, the White

House sought to aid the "free Chinese" and yet retain some East Asian maneuvering room. To this end, the aid slated for Taipei was neither massive in nature nor immediately promised, as had been true in the case of the Philippines and French Indochina.[14] Chiang and his forces would receive some defensive supplies, but nothing the mainland could consider a threat. In addition to these strategic hesitations, Truman's and Acheson's dislike of the generalissimo also played a role in the administration's cautious summertime decisions. Not only had Chiang failed in China, causing political problems for both men, but he had not been shy about intruding into American domestic politics. Pictures of Chinese children, in Nationalist-arranged demonstrations, holding up "Vote for Dewey" signs in the course of the 1948 campaign did little to endear Chiang to the Democratic President.[15] Behavior along these lines, from a man Truman felt had taken American aid and then "invested [this money] in United States real estate," set up a strong personal barrier to any large supply package.[16] Even after the post-Korea aid for Taiwan was approved, Koo was told by four pro-Chiang senators that "no chance [existed] for a really friendly policy toward Nationalist China on the part of the current Administration" due to "Truman's unfavorable attitude toward Chiang Kai-shek."[17]

This attitude, as well as the fear that Chiang would drag America into World War III if given half the chance, led the State Department to stress to Nationalist representatives the "very tentative" nature of America's defense commitment to them. If any large package of credits was to be considered for the island, it was intimated, Chiang would have to go. The Nationalists, for their part, reciprocated this pressure upon their bureaucratic enemies in Washington, seeking to ultimately tie the United States tightly to their cause. Unsurprisingly, this scenario led to bitter feelings between the two reluctant allies. As Dulles commented to Koo on 25 July, "he found it extremely strange that although Nationalist China and the United States were engaged in the same struggle against the Communist danger, they were hardly on speaking terms."[18]

In any case, by late July the Joint Chiefs of Staff (JCS) had reached the conclusion that Taiwan's defensive capabilities needed upgrading. Recognizing that the Seventh Fleet "may not be able to continue to participate in current operations in Korea and at the same time insure the denial of Formosa to communist forces," the joint chiefs urged that America's policy of withholding military aid from the Nationalists "be modified, as a matter of urgency, as to permit the granting of such aid." This recommendation was formalized as government policy in NSC 37/10 on 3 August 1950.[19] The State Department concurred in this policy shift and explained it to its charge d'affaires in Taipei in similar terms:

In the face of a very great Chi Commie build-up along the mainland coast, the Seventh Fleet may not be able to guarantee Formosa against a hostile landing. In this event forces on the island [would] have an important role to play in resisting this attack. In addition, it [would] not be in the U.S. interest for Formosa to fall by subversion or collapse on the island itself. Under the circumstances, it is our desire to furnish a prudent use of available appropriations, [granting] certain types of economic and military assistance to the authorities on Formosa.[20]

This aid, as noted, would be kept at a low level and the Nationalists on a short leash. Keeping open the possibility of relations with the mainland, and avoiding war with it, dictated such prudence. Truman's actions in late June, however, had ended America's hope of not seeming "imperialistic" in Peking's eyes. With this now the case, Acheson felt free to authorize Ambassador Henderson at the U.S. Embassy in India, on 22 July, to quietly "give assurances [to] Tibet re U.S. aid."[21]

The goal of avoiding war with Communist China was also pursued through continued prosecution of the State Department's "scolding policy." This insight can be gained from a review of Ambassador Koo's 25 July notes of a meeting with Dean Rusk. In the course of this meeting, Rusk told Koo that he could not accept that "men like Mao Tse-tung would be willing to carry out the orders of the Kremlin rather than work for the welfare of the Chinese people." Koo, perhaps surprisingly, agreed and added that "the Chinese Communist regime [was] divided [and that] ... Even among the Communist Party itself there were 100 percent Russian stooges and others who would go along with Russia only to a certain extent."[22] America's "scolding" rhetoric in this period, then, was evidently designed, at least in part, to strengthen the more nationalistic leaders in the communist hierarchy. Perhaps if a true nationalist (like Mao) could retain control, a civil war weary China could escape being dragged into a new conflict by the Kremlin.

In order to determine Formosa's legitimate defense needs, the joint chiefs recommended an on-site inspection of the island by U.S. officers. Without pre-clearance from Washington, General MacArthur responded to this suggestion by paying a two-day visit to Taiwan where he publicly told an ecstatic Chiang to "keep your chin up, [as] we're going to win."[23] State's Taipei representative reported back to Foggy Bottom that the "visit by MacArthur undoubtedly boosted morale on Formosa, especially of ranking authorities.... Authorities feel situation well cared for in the hands of MacArthur who will straighten out U.S. policy toward Formosa and Nationalist Government."[24] The Nationalists thus were placing their chips with the U.S. military in hopes of retaining power. MacArthur and Defense Secretary Johnson proved willing to take on this role as they consistently attempted to pull the United States into an alliance with Chiang in the months following June.[25]

This position contrasted to the State Department's arm's-length approach to the generalissimo, and its attempt to place the Formosa question before the United Nations. Acheson, who still had Truman's ear in this dispute, sought to internationalize the Taiwan problem as a way of keeping the island out of communist hands and retaining the possibility of future relations with the mainland. The public accepted the necessity of these internationalizing moves since to act otherwise might "embroil us in [a] war with Red China."[26] Contrary to the hopes of Chiang's boosters, the United States determined to

make no long-range commitments about continued recognition of the Nationalist Gvt as the Gvt of China, about the Chi[nese] seat in the UN, or, *particularly*, about U.S. support for attempts by the Nationalist Government to return to the mainland.

It was, this 14 August cable to Rankin emphasized, "not in the interest of the U.S. to restrict its freedom of action by indefinite commitments to the Chinese auth[oritie]s on Formosa as to our future policy."[27]

MacArthur's brief "morale boosting" inspection tour of Formosa was followed up three days later (on 4 August) by the arrival of a larger group of officers led by his deputy chief of staff, Major General A. P. Fox. Fox surveyed the island's defenses and set up a liaison staff with the Nationalists in order to improve the efficiency of inter-service contacts. The State Department, however, was concerned lest the existence of this extra channel back to Washington further limit its already constrained access to Nationalist officials. In response to this fear, State sought to step up its contacts with Chiang's men—Acheson going so far as to re-establish contact with Ambassador Koo after more than a one-year lapse.[28] Washington also finally authorized the first shipment of military aid to Taiwan in late August, and these supplies began to flow on 30 October.[29] This leisurely pace, however, perplexed the Nationalists. Rankin, reflecting this KMT concern, wrote to Washington on 9 November (after the first tentative contacts with People's Republic of China "volunteers" in Korea)[30] that

the critical situation resulting from Chinese Communist aggression in Korea makes it more urgent than ever that we be kept currently and fully informed of our government's policies and specific intentions as to military aid for the Chinese National forces on Formosa. I have raised these questions several times (for example, on August 18, October 9, October 19, and October 20), but so far our information is limited to one telegram from the Department about a shipment of ammunition and a navy report regarding radar.[31]

The pace of aid to Taipei reflected both U.S. supply needs in Korea and, more importantly, the administration's continued reluctance to become over-identified with the Nationalist cause.[32] With UN forces advancing on the Yalu, prudence dictated no warm embrace of Chiang. The Nationalists' American allies, however, did not read the situation in this manner and continued to press Truman and Acheson to adopt an avowedly pro-KMT policy—a policy that would preclude future dealing with Peking. Especially vocal in this regard were the publications of Henry Luce and the Hearst and the Scripps-Howard newspaper chains. These journals had plenty to write about as Washington's bureaucratic battles would occasionally flare into the open. Perhaps the loudest shot in this intramural government fire-fight involved a late August speech General MacArthur had prepared for reading at the Veterans of Foreign Wars convention in Chicago.

This statement, which the White House considered to have "imperialistic" overtones toward Formosa, was withdrawn upon Truman's orders once the president (by chance) learned of its existence. In this move, Truman had the State Department's support, though Defense Secretary Johnson dissented from this retraction sentiment. It proved impossible, however, to keep the speech out of print as pre-publication copies had already begun to circulate. *U.S. News and World Report*, a journal with close ties to the defense establishment, went to press with the full text of the address included in its 1 September issue. Once this material was public, *Time* felt free to weigh in with its analysis. The speech, Luce's magazine commented, should not have been ordered withdrawn as it had been written only "with the obvious intention of making military sense out of the Administration's strange, vacillating policy on Formosa."[33]

Truman, however, remained unmoved by the attempts to force Washington from a "one China, one Formosa" stance. The public, too, was not very exercised over the need to adopt a pro-Chiang, anti-Mao policy. To be sure, the Korean War had somewhat hardened public views on China, but State's opinion analysts did not see this as a long-lasting impediment to relations. Indeed, even in the face of the war State recognized that "a growing number of observers [had] shown a more sympathetic attitude toward admitting Peiping" to the United Nations.[34] This occurred since fears of Chinese intervention in Korea showed, in the opinion of the *Atlantic Monthly*, that "it has become increasingly absurd that 400 million Chinese are represented in the United Nations by a government which has lost all authority on the mainland of China."[35]

The President was bolstered in his diplomatic position by the public's acceptance of the view that, despite a war in Asia, Europe remained the area of primary concern for America. As State's *Monthly Survey* for August noted, "a majority of the public continues to feel that our security interests in Europe are more important than they are in Asia."[36] Officials encouraged this belief by warning that Korea conceivably could represent only a Soviet diversionary feint to the east. With such public perceptions behind him, Truman felt comfortable in commenting at a 31 August news conference that "it will not be necessary to keep the Seventh Fleet in the Formosa Strait if the Korea thing is settled."[37] The president's intention in making this statement was to counter the impression raised by MacArthur's withdrawn but published speech that the United States had vague unilateral territorial designs on Formosa. Despite fears in Taipei, Truman's words did not signal the future abandonment of Taiwan once hostilities subsided in Korea. At the very least, internal documents stated, "if the Seventh Fleet is withdrawn at some point in the future from its present mission, it is desired that the island be [left] in a substantially better position than it was on June 25."[38] The president made clear, in a nationwide radio and television address on 1 September, that he expected the future of Formosa to be settled peacefully through international action. "We do not want Formosa or any part of Asia for ourselves ... ," Truman reiterated; "Our purpose is peace not conquest."[39] Clearly the United States was not about to abandon Formosa; the same, though, could not be said with confidence about its Nationalist adminis-trators. In both these lines of policy, Washington expected the approval and acquiescence of most people despite the outcry of a "vocal minority."

This arm's-length stance toward the Nationalists did not, however, last beyond the massive 26 November attack by the People's Liberation Army (PLA) which turned back MacArthur's "Home by Christmas" Korean offensive. The idea of internationalizing the Formosa issue fell by the wayside as administration officials began to reassess their prior policy assumptions concerning China's degree of independence from Moscow. Dean Acheson, reflecting this change in thought, told English Prime Minister Attlee on 4 December that "the Chinese Communists were not looking at the matter [of Korea] as Chinese but as communists who are subservient to Moscow. All they do is based on the Moscow pattern, and they are better pupils even than the East European satellites."[40]

Though the policy of splitting the two communist giants remained operative, officials pushed their hopes for inducing a Moscow-Peking break far into the future. Each advance of Mao's troops added to the ranks of Chiang's potential allies in Washington. Truman, to his displeasure, found himself being drawn in this direction due to the PLA's actions. The president's disgust with the People's Republic overflowed on 30 November when, at a news conference, he raised the possibility of using atomic weapons in Korea.[41] The rapid shift at home was correctly read in Taipei as Rankin cabled to Washington that "rightly or wrongly I have the impression that we have been developing a fairly positive Formosa policy."[42]

After the Chinese crossing of the Yalu, backing for military aid for Taiwan became the majority position in this country as measured by a January 1951 Gallup Poll.[43] From late November on, American aid programs, and the United States' official presence on the island, also grew at an exponential rate.[44] As table 1 shows, by the middle of 1951, close to $100 million in aid had been allocated to the Nationalist government. The public was quite willing to help the "free Chinese," probably reflecting its increasingly hostile attitude toward Peking. Opinion soundings also showed that "overwhelmingly nationwide sup-port [existed] for continued recognition of the Nationalist Government and op-position to recognition of the Chinese Communists or their admission to [the] UN."[45] The American public came to view the People's Republic of China in such a negative light that by early 1953 KMT attacks on the mainland were backed by a four-to-one margin among the general population.[46] This was not surprising given that on at least seven different occasions during 1951 and 1952 a majority of the public told NORC interviewers that "United States airplanes should . . . bomb Communist supply bases inside China."[47] While actions on this scale did not take place, the United States did aid the Nationalists heavily in covert operations and also began to finally arm and train Tibetan rebels.[48]

Despite adopting closer ties to Chiang, Washington was still hesitant lest it get drawn into a war on China's mainland. Officials continued to recognize that they had to deal cautiously with Chiang since he retained his "vested interest

TABLE 1

FUNDS ALLOCATED TO NATIONALIST CHINA,
JUNE 1950 - DECEMBER 1951

	Thousands of Dollars, Cumulative Total
1950	
June	0
July	0
August	32,087
September	32,987
October	32,087
November	32,087
December	35,338
1951	
January	45,338
February	46,362
March	46,987
April	53,207
May	55,349
June	98,034
July	112,960
August	126,103
September	133,115
October	132,115
November	132,147
December	148,612

Source: Mutual Security Agency, Monthly Reports
(Reports and Analysis Branch, Division
of Statistics and Reports, 22 July 1952).

in World War III, which alone, he feels, might restore his mainland rule.''[49] Rusk, in early 1951, made America's cautions known to Ambassador Koo by pointing out that the State Department ''deprecated the idea of forcing the United States into a military alliance with the Nationalist Government by starting military operations against the Communists on the mainland. . . . the United States wanted no involvement in China's civil war.''[50]

This was America's position despite the fact that ''a vocal minority of commentators [see table 2] and a majority of the general public . . . favored such additional steps as greater U.S. aid to Chiang . . . which would enable him to carry the War against the Chinese Communists to the mainland.''[51] In writing this, however, State's opinion analysts were quick to point out that such attitudes ''more clearly represent 'public *willingness*' than 'public insistence' on a particular course of action.''[52]

American attempts to restrain Communist China were not limited solely to military means. Diplomatic efforts aimed at isolating the Chinese were also prominent. Under American prompting, for instance, the UN General Assembly in February 1951 branded China an aggressor in Korea. Three months later, the world body voted to have member states impose an embargo on strategic trade with the mainland. Containment was also pursued through a series of defense pacts signed with various Australasian states. On 30 August 1951 a bilateral defense treaty with the Philippines was initialed, and two days later the ANZUS (Australia, New Zealand, United States) pact was signed. This diplomatic tour de force concluded a week later with the concurrent signing of a peace and defense treaty with Japan.

The Japanese Peace Treaty negotiations provide an instructive example of the lengths to which America went during the war to deny international legitimacy to Peking. Throughout 1951 the British had been arguing that reality demanded the mainland be a signatory to the treaty. The United States, which had been leaning in this direction prior to the outbreak of hostilities, now strongly resisted such suggestions.[53] To deal with the People's Republic of China, the United States argued, was not to recognize reality but to flaunt it, as we would ''not [be] dealing with Peiping and Moscow separately but only with Moscow'' since the ''Peiping regime had no views of its own and . . . its views were those of Moscow.''[54] A compromise was reached with England whereby China would be neither mentioned in the treaty text nor invited to sign the completed document. This decision, which infuriated Chiang, was felt by the British to leave the question of which Chinese government to deal with solely up to Tokyo's post-occupation leadership. The United States, however, saw this concession as a mere formality and moved to have the Japanese deal exclusively with the Republic of China. The administration's position found resonance in the Senate, where a letter, signed by fifty-six senators, demanded that Japan have no dealings with the mainland. With this sentiment evident at home, Dulles had little difficulty in securing Prime Minister Yoshida's assent to dealing exclusively with the Nationalists.[55]

TABLE 2

PROMINENT MEDIA ADVOCATES OF GREATER AID
TO THE NATIONALISTS, MID-1951

Newspapers

Cincinnati Enquirer
Cincinnati Times-Star
Columbus (Ohio) Dispatch
Dallas News
Hearst Newspapers (16)
Houston Chronicle
Idaho Statesman
Knoxville Journal
Los Angeles Times
Manchester Union
Oakland Tribune
Portland (Maine) Press-Herald
San Diego Union
Scripps-Howard Newspapers (18)
Wheeling Intelligencer

Columnists

Constantine Brown
William H. Chamberlain
David Lawrence
Fulton Lewis, Jr.
Polyzoides
George Sokolsky
Walter Winchell

Magazines

American Mercury
Barron's
Christian Herald
Collier's
Fortune
Human Events
Life
Magazine of Wall Street
Reader's Digest
Saturday Evening Post
Time
U.S. News and World Report

Source: "Advocates of Strong US Support for Chinese
Nationalist Government (January 1-August 1,
1951)," Foster Papers, Box 33.

Note: List is intended to be representative, not
exhaustive. This report also lists twenty-
three senators (seventeen Republicans) and
eleven representatives (eight Republicans)
as prominent supporters of Chiang.

As has been suggested already in this book, the advent of Chinese intervention in Korea did not end the long-term effort to induce a split in the Sino-Soviet alliance. One should not, however, overlook the fact that "scolding" statements in this period also reflected the very real hatred in Washington of America's war-time enemy. This dislike, which may have first surfaced in Truman's late November 1950 news conference, was evident in the president's public statements throughout the war. On 19 December 1952, for instance, speaking before the National War College, the chief executive stated that

no one [should] think that this administration underestimates the effects of the Communist victory in China. We know that the capture of the great Chinese people by a clique of ruthless Communist fanatics was a tragic loss to the case of peace and progress.... We hope it will not be an irrevocable loss.[56]

The president's private correspondence makes clear that this display was not all show. Typical of his non-public sentiments was a 13 September 1951 letter sent to Supreme Court Justice William O. Douglas upon hearing of Douglas's advocacy of a Korean peace settlement predicated on Peking's recognition. The public's reaction to Douglas's words had been "almost completely unfavorable."[57] This was a feeling the president shared as he wrote Douglas that

as long as I am President, if I can prevent it, that cut throat organization will never be recognized by us as the Government of China and I am sorry that a justice of the Supreme Court has been willing to champion the interest of a bunch of murderers by public statement.[58]

Public harshness toward the People's Republic of China also sprang out of Washington's interest in building up support for the war. By early 1951 polls showed the extent of public disillusionment with the Korean adventure to be quite great.[59] In order to prosecute the war to its end, it was necessary to bolster the flagging morale of the public. By seeking to shape opinion in a negative fashion toward Peking, and by painting that nation's leadership as Soviet "puppets" (a view accepted by over 80 percent of the public),[60] Washington hoped to stiffen the resolve of the American people to carry on the war. Dean Rusk's 18 May 1951 "Slavic Manchukuo" speech, seen by many—despite State's denials—as indicating a reversal "of U.S. China policy toward greater support for Chiang and 'advocacy' of overthrow of [the] Peiping regime ... ," was designed, in part, to serve this morale-sustaining function.[61] So, too, was Dulles's statement from the same platform that "by test of conception, birth, nature, and obedience, the Mao Tse-tung regime is a creature of the Moscow Politburo, and it is on behalf of Moscow, not of China" that it is fighting in Korea.[62] Words such as these, opined the Scripps-Howard press three days later, showed that the "State Department has [finally] ended its six-year flirtation with [the] Chinese Communists."[63]

Making this "flirtation's" end clear to the public became increasingly important in the early 1950s as the need arose to combat the specter of McCarthyism. A policy of unrelenting rhetorical hostility toward the mainland had, in addition to its other benefits, political utility in repulsing the attack of these "primitives."[64] Partisan statements such as "Thanks to General MacArthur, Japan, who was our enemy is now our friend, while thanks to the State Department, China who was our friend is now our enemy" needed to be fended off.[65] If the idea that America had lost China gained credence at home, then a purge of Washington would be the problem's "logical" remedy.[66] MacArthur's recall in April 1951 and the congressional hearings that followed added wind to this idea's sails. In a December 1951 review of "U.S. Attitudes on China Policy," State's Public Affairs section laid bare the situation that faced the department:

The advent of the Korea conflict, the entry of Red China into the fray and the dismissal of General MacArthur [have] served as great spurs of public interest in the Far East. With the increased awareness of the region has come a heightened realization of the magnitude of the loss of China to Communism. *And there has developed an increased tendency* [among the public] *to agree with the vocal critics that U.S. policy "failed" or "erred badly" in dealing with China and that it is still confused at present* [emphasis in original].[67]

As the war continued this public impression grew stronger. With the war-borne necessity to keep up the verbal barrage against the Chinese, little else could be expected. The main visible effect of this phenomenon was to end the careers of several competent Foreign Service officers connected with past China policies. The secretary of state had apparently decided that his department could offer only token support to those who were besieged, as it was itself "under such assault from the outside that to propitiate its enemies it had to provide human sacrifices."[68]

The media, under the dual impact of harsh governmental statements and right-wing pressure, fell into an almost uniformly anti-Peking line. At times it even seemed that the press was outdistancing Washington in its anti-PRC stand.[69] In November 1950, following the first clashes with Chinese troops, the *New York Times* blasted Peking by arguing that "the Chinese Communists can hardly expect that, having failed to demand their way into the United Nations, they can [now] shoot their way into it by an assault on United Nations forces in the field."[70] Washington, by contrast, was still peddling a peaceful line, suggesting that it did not want war, and "if the Chinese Communist authorities or people believe otherwise, it can only be because they are being deceived by those whose advantage it is to prolong and extend hostilities in the Far East against the interests of all Far Eastern people."[71]

Throughout the war, though, the media generally moved in step with government rhetoric. Chinese servitude to Moscow and the "foreign" nature of China's communist leaders thus became standard bromides for U.S. editorial pages. As it became evident in Washington that a policy of containment toward the People's Republic of China would have to be undertaken following the cessation of hostilities in Korea, newspapers also began to reflect this assumption. It became obvious that a containment policy in the Far East, as in Europe, would be necessary since "bit by bit, the developments in East Asia have shown in Communist China the character of an international conspiracy."[72] Given this situation, it seemed obvious that Formosa deserved our future protection as it was the "best defense bargain we have ever had in Asia. . . . More than that, it is a force that is on our side and has been from the start."[73] The administration, aided by these media meanderings, was successful in instilling a great deal of hostility in the public regarding the mainland. With Americans being shot down by the Chinese this was not a difficult feat. The White House, though successful in keeping enough public support to continue the war, was poorly positioned for the upcoming elections. In instilling this hatred of the People's Republic of China the Democrats had, in many ways, played into the hands of those out of power. By early 1952 it seemed clear that anti-People's Republic of China stands would be "dynamite at the [electoral] polls" for those who could harness the issue.[74]

This dynamite, however, exploded in Democratic hands as Republicans were able to point to the Korean conflict as "dramatic evidence that once again Democratic policy has led to disaster in the Far East."[75] The State Department noted that its Far Eastern policies were "the major target for Republican [campaign] spokesmen, who usually contend that 'the surrender of China' and other 'mistakes' led to the Communist attack on Korea."[76] Eisenhower, in his presidential campaign, was also not above exploiting this theme—especially given his efforts to woo conservative backers of Taft and Harold Stassen to his side.[77] At his first "political" press conference on 6 June 1952, the general commented that "I do not know who is to blame for the loss of China. I do know that the dramatic triumphs of that period, if any, were claimed by the party in power. The party in power has to take some responsibility for any losses we have suffered."[78] By September Eisenhower had become even more explicit in his campaign rhetoric blaming both the outbreak of hostilities in Korea and the "abandonment" of China directly on the Democrats.[79]

The victorious Republican administration, which took office in early 1953, continued America's tough public stance toward China. If anything, the new president seemed even more negative vis-à-vis Peking than was his predecessor. One of Eisenhower's first acts in office was, for example, his "unleashing" of Chiang's forces—a move included in his initial State of the Union address.[80] Raising America's diplomatic representation in Taipei to the ambassadorial level, threatening the use of nuclear weapons in Korea, and placing "atomic missiles" on Okinawa were further outward manifestations of America's resolve under Eisenhower to oppose Mao's China.[81] Yet, in private, the new president remained unconvinced of the wisdom of totally isolating Peking.[82] Given this, his private actions did not always match his public words. The unleashing of Nationalist troops, for instance, was accompanied by Rankin's private "neutralization" (that is, re-leashing) of Chiang's men in Taipei.[83] This move was in line with Dulles's advice. As early as March 1952 the future secretary of state had written that

the present direction to the Seventh Fleet is bad for Nationalist morale and involves our assuming a defensive responsibility for Communist China which is inappropriate now that it is [an] adjudged aggressor in Korea. Chiang needs to be restrained, but we have ample means of doing so privately and without public humiliation.[84]

The weight of evidence seems to suggest that the incoming Republicans chose to continue the long-range geopolitical splitting policy of their predecessors. To this policy, though, was added the war-hardened conviction that America's actions toward Peking must be unyielding. Only this mode of behavior could finally convince the Chinese that America meant business in its containment policy. This behavior would hasten the day of the Sino-Soviet split since, as Chinese dependence increased on Moscow, the relationship might become too close for comfort. The Chinese might then, in Dulles's words, press "Russia for more than Russia would give."[85] This Republican policy implied that there would be little overall governmental effort to change the negative public opinion posture toward China in Eisenhower's initial years in office. Eisenhower and Dulles would, of course, welcome the collapse of the mainland's communist regime; such an eventuality, though, would not actively be courted. America's policy toward Peking, as a 19 November 1952 memo from Dulles to Eisenhower stated, would have as its goal the breaking of the "present ties between China and Moscow" and not the collapse of communism on the mainland.[86]

From time to time, Dulles's campaign statements in 1952 hinted at this theme. This position could also be discerned at his 15 January 1953 nominating hearings. In the course of these hearings, the secretary of state–designate made abundantly clear that breaking up the Soviet bloc did not necessarily portend the end of communism. Dulles told his Senate questioners that

. . . we must always have in mind the liberation of these captive peoples. Now liberation does not mean a war of liberation. Liberation can be accomplished by processes short of war. We have, as one example, not an ideal example, but it will illustrate my point, the defection of Yugoslavia, under Tito from the domination of Soviet communism. . . . [I]t illustrates that it is possible to [peacefully] disintegrate the present monolithic structure.

Dulles then went on to immediately link this statement to the situation in China and to point out that the Sino-Soviet alliance would not last as it was "an unholy alliance which is contrary to the tradition, the hopes, [and] the aspirations of the Chinese people."[87] As Dulles had told a Yugoslav delegate to the United Nations in mid-1952, Belgrade's "peaceful break-away [from Russia] showed a possibility that other countries, such as Czechoslovakia, Poland and China, might in due course peacefully resume effective control of their affairs."[88]

As the first Republican administration in two decades settled in to take office, American opinion on China stood at a very low point. This was both the result of government promptings and a natural reaction to a war-time enemy. This opinion posture would be reinforced in the early Eisenhower years as the government put into practice its post-war policy of unyielding ("splitting") pressure on the Communist Chinese.

NOTES

1. *The Economist* 158 (13 May 1959):1049-1950.

2. National Security Council memo no. 48/2, 30 December 1949. Reprinted in *Containment: Documents on American Foreign Policy and Strategy, 1945-50*, ed. Thomas H. Etzold and John Lewis Gaddis (New York: Columbia University Press, 1978), p. 273.

3. As late as a 23 June 1950 news conference, Dean Acheson was making clear America's resolve to maintain a "hands off" policy toward China. See J. H. Kalicki, *The Pattern of Sino-American Crises: Political and Military Interactions in the 1950s* (New York: Cambridge University Press, 1975), p. 36.

4. Harry S Truman, *Memoirs: Years of Trial and Hope*, vol. 2 (Garden City, N.Y.: Doubleday and Co., 1956), p. 334; Glenn D. Paige, *The Korean Decision* (New York: The Free Press, 1968), pp. 127, 149-151, 167. This move was one Johnson had taken credit for in conversations with Ambassador Koo. On 30 June, for example, he told the Nationalist emissary that "it had indeed been a hard struggle in the face of the determined objection of the State Department, but in the end he had won the fight. He asked Mr. Koo to tell Madam Chiang and Dr. Kung that he had kept his promise." See "Notes of a Conversation" with Louis Johnson, Koo Papers, Box 180.

5. Ralph N. Clough, *Island China* (Cambridge, Mass.: Harvard University Press, 1978), p. 8; H. Bradford Westerfield, *Foreign Policy and Party Politics: Pearl Harbor to Korea* (New Haven: Yale University Press, 1955), p. 307.

6. *Monthly Survey* 110 (June 1950), Foster Papers, Box 12. See also "China Telegram," June 28 and July 5, 1950, Foster Papers, Box 26.

7. *DSB* 23 (3 July 1950):5.

8. Allen S. Whiting, *China Crosses the Yalu: The Decision to Enter the Korean War* (New York: Macmillan Co., 1960), p. 58. As early as 15 March 1949 the Communists had announced their intention to "liberate" Taiwan in order to prevent the United States from using it as "a springboard for future aggression against China proper." See Congressional Quarterly, *China: U.S. Policy since 1945* (Washington, D.C.: Congressional Quarterly, Inc., 1980), p. 86.

9. *Monthly Survey* 114 (October 1950), Foster Papers, Box 12.

10. *Wall Street Journal*, 22 August 1950.

11. Gallup Poll, no. 458-K (12 August 1950).

12. *Special Report on American Opinion*, "Public Attitudes concerning Formosa," 26 September 1950, Foster Papers, Box 33.

13. See, for example, *Monthly Survey* 113 (September 1950), Foster Papers, Box 12.

14. Such a promise was made in Truman's 27 June interposition speech. By August the Voice of America had begun broadcasts to Indochina in another move designed to show expanded U.S. interest in the area.

15. *Life*, 8 November 1948, p. 51.

16. Warren I. Cohen, *The American Secretaries of State and Their Diplomacy: Dean Rusk* (Totowa, N.J.: Cooper Square Publishers, 1980), p. 53; *FRUS, 1950,* 7:180.

17. Koo Papers, 23 August 1950, Box 218 (Diaries).

18. "Notes of a Conversation" with John Foster Dulles, Koo Papers, 25 July 1950, Box 180; *FRUS, 1950,* vol. 6:356-357, 415, 418-419, 428. The Luce, Hearst, and McCormick publications were unmerciful in their attacks on Acheson in this period. On Luce see W. A. Swanberg, *Luce and His Empire* (New York: Charles Scribner's Sons, 1972), pp. 311-316. Typical of Luce publications was *Life*, which in its 24 July 1950 issue (p. 26) contained a complete page of editorials attacking the Truman-Acheson China policy and boosting Louis Johnson's position. *Life* argued that "Acheson would not only have let Formosa go to the Communists, he might have recognized the Communist government of China, if he could have got away with it—and he still might." *Life* also stated, "Let's keep the record straight about Formosa and the Nationalist government there because it is one of the keys to our success in the West Pacific. We need the Nationalist government as an all-out ally."

19. *FRUS, 1950,* 6:393, 413-414. The Defense Department was concerned at this juncture about a PLA troop build-up opposite Formosa and sought State's consent in allowing Nationalist bombings of these mainland troop concentrations. The State Department turned back these requests noting, "We are not at war with Communist China nor do we wish to become involved in hostilities with Chinese Communist forces . . . the action recommended would extend our involvement." See ibid., pp. 401-408.

20. Ibid., p. 436. Karl Lott Rankin, *China Assignment* (Seattle: University of Washington Press, 1964), p. 89, notes that this fear was based on the fact that the Seventh Fleet was stretched very thin due to the demands of the Korean War. "Not infrequently during the Korean War, no American vessel was seen within several hundred miles of Taiwan."

21. *FRUS, 1950,* 6:386. Aid, though, was delayed until 1951 due to disagreements with India and among Tibetan leaders. Another important policy step taken right after the outbreak of the war in Korea was the halt of oil shipments to China—presumably to prevent its trans-shipment to North Korea and to hamper any military moves China might be contemplating in the Taiwan area. American companies agreed to this move "voluntarily." The British, however, were more reluctant to bow to American pressure. See *Memorandum of Conversation between Secretary Acheson and British Ambassador Sir Oliver Franks,* "Oil to China," 13 July 1950, DDRS, 1979, 422A.

22. "Notes of a Conversation" with Dean Rusk, 25 July 1950, Koo Papers, Box 180; *FRUS, 1950,* 6:442.

23. *Time,* August 14, 1950, p. 22; Joseph W. Ballentine, *Formosa: A Problem for United States Foreign Policy* (Washington, D.C.: The Brookings Institution, 1952), p. 129.

24. *FRUS, 1950,* 6:411.

25. See Johnson-Acheson correspondence, ibid., pp. 325-326, 339, 331-352.

26. *Monthly Survey* 112 (August 1950), Foster Papers, Box 12.

27. *FRUS, 1950,* 6:438 (emphasis added).

28. Ibid., p. 415.

29. Ibid., pp. 414 (fn 4), 501. On 25 August Truman released $14,344,500 in funds for military aid for the Nationalists. The State Department approved the first shipment of military equipment to the island (worth $9,752,000) on 18 September 1950 with the

stipulation that "the aid to be furnished, pursuant to the recommendation of the National Security Council, should be designated to contribute to the defense of Formosa, and not develop the Nationalist military potential for a possible mainland invasion." Much of the aid allocated to Formosa at this time was apparently still economic in nature.

30. The public was also reacting in a relatively "unhurried" manner to the first Chinese attacks. State's "China Telegram" for 7 November (Foster Papers, Box 26) noted, for instance, that most in the public "doubted" that PLA intervention at such a late date "would seriously affect [the] outcome of [the Korean] struggle."

31. Rankin, p. 68. His concern may have been heightened by the 7 October 1950 People's Republic of China invasion of Tibet —an action made public seventeen days later.

32. See "Notes of Conversations" with Rusk, 19 September 1950, and with Dulles, 20 October 1950, in Koo Papers, Box 180.

33. *Time*, 4 September 1950, p. 9. The *Chicago Sun-Times* had received a pre-publication copy of the speech and—in order to meet its production deadline—asked the State Department if the hour of public release of the speech could be changed. This was the first Washington had heard of this speech, and three days later it was ordered withdrawn as it seemed (to the White House, at least) to imply that the United States had territorial designs on Formosa. However, *U.S. News and World Report*, relying on the previously stated release date, went to press with the statement. The issue containing the speech was dated 1 September 1950 (pp. 32-34) and in the mail as early as 26 August. See also *MacArthur Hearings*, p. 2386, and *FRUS, 1950*, 6:451-462, where Johnson, alone among top advisers, disagrees with the withdrawal action. On *U.S. News*' defense establishment ties see Franz Schurmann, *The Logic of World Power: An Inquiry into the Origins, Currents and Contradictions of World Politics* (New York: Pantheon Books, 1974).

34. *Monthly Survey* 113 (September 1950), Foster Papers, Box 12; "Current Public Concern on Foreign Policy Matters" (23 August 1950), Foster Papers, Box 20.

35. "The United Nations," *Atlantic Monthly*, October 1950, pp. 19-20.

36. *Monthly Survey* 112 (August 1950). A 20-25 August 1950 Gallup Poll (no. 460-TPS) asked whether it "is more important for the United States to (A) try to keep the rest of Asia from falling under Russian control, or; (B) try to stop Russia from taking over Western Europe?" While 48 percent of the respondents thought both goals "equally important," those expressing a preference "favored" Europe by a 31 to 8 percent margin. A National Opinion Research Center poll in the same month found that the public believed that if a choice had to be made, it would be more important—by a 51 to 17 percent margin—to oppose an invasion of Europe than Asia.

37. *Public Papers of the Presidents of the United States* (hereafter *Public Papers*), *1950* (31 August) (Washington, D.C.: U.S. Government Printing Office, 1965), p. 606.

38. *FRUS, 1950*, 6:436.

39. *Public Papers, 1950* (1 September), p. 613. Truman's speech was in line with the continuing attempts to split Peking from Moscow. The president noted in his talk that "only the Communist imperialism, which has already started to dismember China, would gain from China's involvement in the war."

40. "U.S.-U.K. Washington Conversations, 1st Meeting," 4 December 1950, DDRS, 1975, 29E; see also *FRUS, 1950*, 6:601; Truman, *Memoirs*, 2:339.

41. *Public Papers, 1950* (30 November), p. 295.

42. Rankin, p. 79.

43. Gallup poll, no. 469-K (29 January 1951). Military aid was favored by a 54 to 32 percent spread.

44. Clough, p. 10.

45. "Advocates of Strong U.S. Support for Chinese Nationalist Government (January 1-August 1, 1951)," Foster Papers, Box 33.

46. Gallup poll, Special Survey (9 February 1953). These attacks were favored by a 65 to 14 percent margin.

47. NORC, no. 302 (18 April 1951), no. 307 (24 May 1951), no. 312 (27 August 1951), no. 313 (20 October 1951), no. 320 (14 March 1952), no. 327 (30 June 1952), and no. 329 (28 August 1952).

48. Rankin, pp. 99, 157; Ely Kahn, Jr., *The China Hands: America's Foreign Service Officers and What Befell Them* (New York: Viking Press, 1976), p. 241. In 1951 Truman reportedly approved an attack by 10,000 Nationalist troops, who had fled to northern Burma in 1949, into China. These troops received a large amount of covert aid channelled through the CIA, despite the fact that only months before the Chinese intervention in Korea the Truman Administration had been trying to remove these troops from Burma as an unnecessary provocation to both Burma and the People's Republic of China. See Thomas Powers, *The Man Who Kept the Secrets: Richard Helms and the CIA* (New York: Pocket Books, 1981), p. 101. Secret support for the Tibetans continued up through the early portion of John Kennedy's term. See David Wise, *The Politics of Lying: Government Deception, Secrecy, and Power* (New York: Random House, 1973). With the end of the hostilities in Korea in sight, the United States again attempted to dislodge the Nationalist troops from Burma. See "Notes of a Conversation" with Walter Bedell Smith (6 March 1953) and with Walter Robertson (30 September 1953), both in Koo Papers, Box 187.

49. John Foster Dulles, untitled note, 31 March 1952, John Foster Dulles Papers (hereafter Dulles Papers), Princeton University, Princeton, N.J., Box 60.

50. "Notes of a Conversation" with Dean Rusk, 18 January 1951, Koo Papers, Box 184.

51. "Advocate of Strong US Support for Chinese Nationalist Government (January 1–August 1, 1951)," Foster Papers, Box 33.

52. "Notes on Current Attitudes," 28 May 1951, Foster Papers, Box 1.

53. *FRUS, 1950*, 6: 1211, 1239-1241, 1280, 1327.

54. "Notes of a Conversation" with Dulles, 31 May 1951, Koo Papers, Box 184.

55. See Koo, "Notes of a Conversation" with Dulles, 28 May, 31 May, 2 August 1951 (Box 184). See also Michael A. Guhin, *John Foster Dulles: A Statesman and His Times* (New York: Columbia University Press, 1972), pp. 59-62; Louis L. Gerson, *The American Secretaries of State and Their Diplomacy*, Vol. 12: *John Foster Dulles* (New York: Cooper Square, 1967), pp. 92-93; Hungdah Chiu, "China, the United States and the Question of Taiwan," in *China and the Taiwan Issue*, ed. Hungdah Chiu (New York: Praeger Publishing, 1973), p. 156.

56. *Public Papers, 1952* (19 December), p. 1091.

57. *Monthly Survey* 125 (September 1951), Foster Papers, Box 12.

58. Letter reprinted in *Off the Record: The Private Papers of Harry S Truman*, ed. Robert H. Ferrell (New York: Harper and Row, 1980), p. 218.

59. By early 1951 the public felt entering the war had been a mistake by a 47 to 38 percent plurality (Gallup poll, no. 469-K, January 1951) and felt America should pull out by a 66 to 25 percent majority (ibid.). This poll also asked a question about which area in the world America should be most concerned about falling under Russian dom-

ination. While 28 percent felt America should be equally concerned about both Asia and Europe, 49 percent favored Europe exclusively as compared with only 9 percent who took this position toward Asia. On disillusionment with the Korean War, see also John E. Mueller, *War, Presidents and Public Opinion* (New York: Wiley, 1973).

60. By an 81 to 5 percent margin the public believed that China had entered Korea "on orders from Russia." See "Gallup Poll on Red China and UN," 28 December 1950, Foster Papers, Box 33.

61. Dean Rusk, "Chinese-American Friendship," *DSB* 24 (28 May 1951):846-848; "China Telegram," 23 May 1951, Foster Papers, Box 27.

62. John Foster Dulles, "Sustaining Friendship with China," *DSB* 24 (28 May 1951):844.

63. Quoted in "China Telegram," 23 May 1951, Foster Papers, Box 27.

64. Dean Acheson, *Present at the Creation: My Years in the State Department* (New York: W. W. Norton and Co., 1969), p. 354.

65. This statement, attributed to Senator McCarran, was repeated by Senator Bridges in the course of the May 1951 *MacArthur Hearings*, p. 689.

66. Norman A. Graebner, *The New Isolationism: A Study in Politics and Foreign Policy since 1950* (New York: The Ronald Press, 1956).

67. "A Summary of U.S. Attitudes on China Policy, 1949-1951" (7 December 1951), Foster Papers, Box 33.

68. Kahn, p. 242.

69. Between 1945 and 1950 a group of private experts on China generally critical of Chiang reviewed twenty-two of thirty works dealing with China in the *New York Times Book Review*. During the 1952-1956 period, no book reviews for the *Times* were written by these scholars. Similarly, the *New York Herald Tribune* had these same experts write thirty of their thirty-five book reviews on China in the years 1945-1950. During the later period these authors again reviewed no works for this paper. See Robert P. Newman, *Recognition of Communist China?: A Study in Argument* (New York: Macmillan Co., 1961), pp. 11-12.

70. *NYT*, 5 November 1950.

71. *Public Papers, 1950* (16 November), p. 712.

72. *NYT*, 4 January 1953.

73. Ibid., 4 May 1952.

74. Claude A. Buss, *The People's Republic of China and Richard Nixon* (Stanford: Stanford University Alumni Association, 1972), p. 78.

75. Ronald J. Ciardi, *The Korean War and American Politics: The Republican Party as a Case Study* (Philadelphia: University of Pennsylvania Press, 1968), p. 102.

76. *Monthly Survey* 137 (September 1952), Foster Papers, Box 12.

77. Graebner, p. 99; Ciardi, pp. 206-245; and Robert A. Divine, *Foreign Policy and U.S. Presidential Elections, 1952-1960* (New York: New Viewpoints, 1974), pp. 10-35.

78. *NYT*, 7 June 1952.

79. Divine, *1952-1960*, p. 70.

80. *NYT*, 1, 3, and 8 February 1953. The *Times*, like most of the press, was supportive of this move.

81. Graebner, p. 129; Sherman Adams, *Firsthand Report: The Story of the Eisenhower Administration* (New York: Harper Brothers, 1961), pp. 48-49, 102, 118. Eisenhower also reportedly pressed the Nationalists to beef up their garrison on the Tachen Islands as a deterrent to communist attack.

82. The journalist Robert T. Donovan, in *Eisenhower: The Inside Story* (New York: Harper and Row, 1956), p. 134, has written that Eisenhower

was not convinced that the vital interests of the United States were best served by prolonged non-recognition of China. He has serious doubts as to whether Russia and China were natural allies. He speculated on whether Soviet interests lay primarily in Europe and the Middle East rather than in the Orient. Therefore, he asked, would it not be the best policy in the long run for the United States to try to pull China away from Russia rather than drive the Chinese ever deeper into an unnatural alliance.... Confronted, however, by the hostile conduct of the Chinese Communists and the intense antipathy to Red China among the American people, Eisenhower never in the years under consideration here (1953-1955) made any moves to change this policy of non-recognition.

The story of how Donovan got close enough to top officials to write his "official unofficial political biography of Eisenhower" is contained in Wise, pp. 103-105. Donovan has recently (*NYT*, 16 September 1982) revealed that at a private dinner for Republican businessmen in 1956 Eisenhower "lectured his guests on the need to recognize China." Donovan has recalled, "Ike gave such a cogent argument on how foolish it was to pretend that such a large country did not exist . . . that he carried the evening with his arguments."

83. Rankin, p. 155.

84. Dulles, untitled note, 31 March 1952, Dulles Papers, Box 60.

85. Dulles, untitled memorandum to Eisenhower of meeting with Koo and George Yeh, Nationalist Minister of Foreign Affairs, 19 November 1952, Dulles Papers, Box 58.

86. Ibid.

87. Hearings before the Committee on Foreign Relations, U.S. Senate, *On the Nomination of John Foster Dulles*, 15 January 1953 (Washington, D.C.: Government Printing Office, 1953), p. 5.

88. Dulles's untitled memorandum to Eisenhower of conversation with Dr. Ales Bebler of the Yugoslav UN delegation, 24 June 1952, Box 60. It is also interesting to note that in the spring of 1950 Dulles's book, *War or Peace* (New York: Macmillan Co., 1950), was published. This book contains an interesting passage on the question of China and the United Nations which seems to hint that Dulles was not the commensurate hard-liner some made him out to be. In a revealing passage Dulles (p. 140) noted that "if the Communist government of China in fact proves its ability to govern China without serious domestic resistance, then it, too, should be admitted to the United Nations." His changed view, once in office, may have reflected his desire to first "split" the Chinese away from the Russians before allowing them in the world body.

5

Opinion and Sino-American Relations in the Eisenhower Years _____

The end of the Korean War found China apparently interested in integrating itself into the world community. Such a hoped-for integration would have the latent purpose of securing certain Chinese international objectives (for example, the return of Taiwan to the mainland, admission to the United Nations) that had seemed tantalizingly close prior to the start of the war. Washington, however, opposed the notion of accepting the Peking regime as the legitimate representative for all of China. America continued to display an unyielding hostility toward the mainland in the hope of forging too tight an embrace between the Chinese and Russians, which would, it was believed, eventually lead to a rupture in Sino-Soviet relations. This Eisenhower Administration policy occasionally saw the light of day. State officials, at times, did publicly enunciate their view that "a relationship of dependence on the senior partner as complete as we can make it will not make the embrace any more congenial for the Soviet partner or the Chinese Communist junior partner."[1]

As in earlier years, China continued to be painted as "subservient to Moscow and international communism."[2] A ready audience existed for such pronouncements since "the overwhelming weight of opinion in the United States holds that the Chinese Communist regime is a willing and subservient tool of the Kremlin and opposes any steps toward [a] relationship with the regime."[3] With this view prevailing, it was not surprising that polls early in Eisenhower's term showed that most Americans favored the arming of Chiang's forces for an attack on the mainland. The public also felt by an 83 to 14 percent margin that all allied trade with the People's Republic of China should be halted.[4] Though the American people had apparently accepted the government's rhetorical image of China, not all Washington officials were totally convinced by their own words. Certain appointed officials, however, were close to Chiang's supporters in Congress and argued for an even tougher American response toward the mainland—one designed to bring about the communist regime's ultimate demise. While Dulles would have welcomed such an occurrence, this was secondary to his primary Far Eastern objective of breaking the Sino-Soviet alliance. That the secretary chose to stay with this course during his first years in office is not surprising given the dynamic situation which seemed to arise out of Stalin's death and the first tentative public cracks that appeared in the Peking-Moscow "monolith."[5]

Similar to the Truman-Acheson years, the policy of rhetorical hostility Eisenhower and Dulles followed toward the mainland was over-determined. Conditions at this time in the French-fought and American bankrolled Indochina war were quite fluid and seemed to dictate a non-conciliatory stance toward Peking.[6] This was the case as American field commanders and diplomats openly worried in the latter stages of the Korean War over a Chinese turn to the south. Such a concern evidently played a role in Chiang's rhetorical unleashing in early 1953.[7] Dulles publicly implied as much when he told a March 1953 meeting of the Advertising Council that

Korea and Indo-China are two flanks. There is a large force [i.e., Communist China] in the center.... It is necessary, I believe, to create some sort of threat in the center to hold and pin them down and then there is a better chance of getting some success on the two flanks.[8]

Though the fear of large-scale Chinese intervention began to ease somewhat in late 1953, Washington's words remained full of bluster.[9] The need to bolster France's resolve, as well as to build support in Congress and among the American people for increasing U.S. involvement in Indochina, dictated such a reaction. When America finally agreed—under strong allied pressure[10]—to the inclusion of the People's Republic of China at an Asian peace conference, one further strut in the structure impelling a tough rhetorical position was added. Washington now felt it had to counter the Soviet-fostered impression that the mid-February agreement to include China in the talks implied that a degree of diplomatic recognition was being accorded Peking. U.S. officials repeatedly stressed that this was not the case; Geneva was to be an "international conference" and not a "Big Five" parley.[11]

The need to counter this "Big Five" impression grew as the 26 April conference date approached. The public was not opposed to such talks, as a March poll had shown and government opinion analysts had stressed, yet the State Department worried lest the American gesture be incorrectly interpreted.[12] Concerns of this nature led to increasingly harsh statements about the mainland in the first half of 1954. Typical of these pronouncements was Alfred le sense Jenkins's (State's main Chinese Political Affairs officer) accusal of the CCP as being "slavishly subservient to Moscow" and, therefore, having "betrayed the powerful Chinese longing to stand up straight."[13] Perhaps the most extreme of these statements, though, was reserved for the secretary himself to make. Speaking before a congressional committee on 19 March, Dulles made "clear" the kind of alien and uncaring rulers now imposed on China:

In a country like China there are every year, I suppose, a million people or more—I do not know how many millions, nobody knows, who are going to die anyway of starvation. Whether they die of starvation or die on the field of battle may not seem of great moment to them. In fact, there are some reasons why they might prefer to have them die on the field of battle where they become heroes fighting the terrible imperialists rather than have them die of starvation as a demonstration of incompetence and heartlessness and ruthlessness of their own government.[14]

This statement was, of course, also part of the general campaign to justify a strong stand in Indochina. Only if the Chinese knew that their entrance into this fray "would result in grave consequences which might not be confined" to Southeast Asia could America be relatively certain that these millions of lost souls would die on barren rice fields and not Asian battlefields.[15]

As France's Indochina military condition continued to worsen, America's need to portray an interventionist China to justify its own contemplated moves grew. This was in spite of the fact that internal documents recognized that even if China had wanted the Viet Minh to stop fighting "it is by no means certain that they could achieve it."[16] On 29 March Dulles publicly revealed that America was considering the use of force to buttress France's declining military fortunes. Speaking before the Overseas Press Club, the secretary justified the possibility of "united action" by noting that Peking had "largely stepped up their support of the aggression which I have described in that area. Indeed, they promote that aggression by all means short of intervention."[17] One week later, Dulles chronicled this Chinese involvement in greater detail, charging that

the rulers of Communist China train and equip the troops of their puppet Ho Chi Minh. They supply these troops with large amounts of artillery and ammunition. They supply military and technical guidance in the staff section of Ho Chi Minh's Command, at the division level and in specialized units such as the signal and engineering corps, artillery units, and transportation.[18]

Despite this litany of Chinese sins, military, allied, congressional, and public misgivings led to the abandonment of the military option for Indochina and its downgrading to a mere negotiating ploy in Geneva.[19] The army had no interest in another limited Asian land war, nor were our allies enamored of the idea of fighting a ground war with only American air and naval support. Congress, for its part, was quite unenthusiastic about the contemplated intervention. The *Christian Science Monitor*, for instance, reported that, "the Administration's poll takers on Capitol Hill [have found] . . . that there were no more than five men at the most to be found in all of Congress who were positive and unequivocal in their approval of quick and decisive [military] action."[20] Melvin Gurtov, in a study of the *Congressional Record* from June 1953 to July 1954, found that of the thirty-five speeches or insertions into the record on intervention into Indochina, only three favored such a move without reservation.[21]

Congress's sentiment was in line with opinion in the public. Despite administration efforts, most Americans remained opposed to a southern replay of Korea. Washington's efforts to bolster public support for an armed U.S. intervention apparently had not had sufficient time to make an appreciable impact on the populace. The introduction of American troops into Asia's "rice bowl" was opposed by better than three to one in the general public, while the more likely air and naval response was opposed by a five-to-three majority.[22] Even such conservative journals as the *Wall Street Journal* and the Scripps-Howard press opposed getting involved in Southeast Asia since "America would be inviting [a] calamity if it took up a losing colonial war."[23] A March ad hoc committee composed of representatives from the military, diplomatic, and intelligence sectors of government had recognized this public reluctance and suggested that the

NSC take cognizance of [the] present domestic and international climate of opinion with respect to U.S. involvement and consider the initiation of such steps as may be necessary to ensure worldwide recognition of the significance of such [military] steps in Indo-China as part of the struggle against Communist aggression.[24]

Despite this effort to bolster support for erecting a military barrier to Chinese "aggression" in Indochina, a May poll found the public still lacking in enthusiasm for another Asian adventure. When asked what the United States could hope to gain from fighting in Vietnam, most persons did not frame their responses in the containment terms the government was encouraging, and roughly half of those interviewed volunteered that the United States could expect to gain "nothing" from such an involvement.[25]

Washington's increased interest in a military solution had grown out of its extremely pessimistic assessment of the likely outcome at Geneva. Six days after Dulles's 18 February agreement to attend the peace conference, the State Department's Policy Planning Staff (PPS) prepared a negative assessment of the chances for a successful result from the multi-nation meeting. This paper argued that the most likely outcome—a partition formula—would be seen "as the ultimate sell-out" by our non-communist Asian allies and would, in all likelihood, eventually lead to a Sino-American war in Vietnam.[26] Two weeks after this memo began circulating, the State Department's office in charge of Southeast Asian affairs offered forth an even more pessimistic outlook on the upcoming talks. This report argued that "any formula of coalition or a territorial division, any procedure of elections or plebiscite would be powerless to defer" a Viet Minh victory.[27] Many in Washington, believing this to be the case, felt that "it may be better for us for the conference in Geneva to end inconclusively than to put our signature to a partition or 'sell-out' of our Asian allies."[28]

Given America's overall policy background there should be little (retrospective) surprise, then, at Washington's continued negative portrayal of Peking, nor at the hostility the United States displayed toward the Chinese once the Geneva conference began. The State Department continued to make clear that the inclusion of the People's Republic of China in the talks in no way legitimized the Peking regime.[29] Edwin W. Martin, deputy director of State's Office of Chinese Affairs, stated, "Does our agreement to sit down at Geneva with representatives of the Peiping regime mean that our policy on China has changed or is about to change?... The answer is definitely no."[30] John Foster Dulles was even more blunt in explaining China's presence at the conference. The secretary noted, "We do not refuse to deal with it where occasion requires.... It is, however, one thing to recognize evil as a fact. It is another to take evil to one's breast and to call it good."[31] America's unyielding stance was publicly reflected in Dulles's refusal to shake Chou En-lai's outstretched hand at the conference, or even to look at him in the meeting room.[32] It was, one observer later commented, the "most bizarre performance of his Secretaryship."[33]

Intransigence on both sides led to the failure of the Korean portion of the conference. Dulles, as prearranged, left Geneva after just nine days, saying the meeting had gone "just as we expected."[34] Continued American interest in the talks, however, was shown by Under Secretary Smith's assignment to lead the delegation in the secretary's absence. The moves the United States undertook in the next few months were designed to deter any possible progress in the talks since this might lead to a lessening of the People's Republic of China's diplomatic isolation. A top secret 3 May memorandum prepared in Geneva laid bare these tactics which would

... in the first instance be directed toward influencing the course of negotiations to the end that no agreement will be reached which is inconsistent with the basic U.S. objectives. Toward this end, the U.S. should ... Endeavor to stimulate the Communists to the adoption of harsh negotiating tactics and inflexible positions. The Working Group is preparing detailed suggestions of fruitful ways of playing on Communist and particularly Chinese Communist sensitivities.[35]

The press was generally supportive of the United States' diplomatic posture at Geneva. This stance, the *New York Times* argued, was justified since the Communists were not really interested in negotiations. The conference for them was merely one more step in their long-range "preparations ... for taking over Eurasia."

Despite American roadblocks, the Indochina portion of the Geneva conference was able to make impressive progress as China took several conciliatory steps designed to keep the session from collapsing. The progress in Geneva raised the possibility that "if a truce is arranged there will be great pressure, not only from France but from many other countries ... for admitting Peiping to the United Nations."[36] Adding fuel to this speculation was the 5 June 1954 advent of "informal talks" between American and Chinese representatives at Geneva over the problem of foreign nationals detained in each country. These talks, arranged by England, were raised to a higher and more formal level in July. The United States, publicly at least, continued to make clear that these low-level talks "in no way implied United States accordance with any diplomatic recognition of the Red China regime."[37] They were, rather, a "necessary evil" designed to free Americans held in China. In addition to this, they could be—and were—used as evidence by America that it was not the intransigent party in the Sino-American dyad. There was little public pressure on the State Department to act contrary to its obstructionist course. The *Monthly Survey* put out shortly after the completion of the Geneva accords noted that "the Administration position on Communist China, and its program for mutual security aid to friendly [Asian] nations, continues to receive general approbation."[38]

China's concessions in Geneva were part of an overall "peace offensive" whose shape became clear with time. On a June trip to Peking, ostensibly for consultations over the Indochina peace talks, Foreign Minister Chou En-lai paid formal visits to both India and Burma. These visits each concluded with the issuance of a joint communiqué stressing peaceful coexistence. The portents of an end to China's diplomatic isolation clearly seemed to be in the air, increasing the possibility of Peking's gaining a seat in the United Nations. Such a possibility caused great concern among Chiang's supporters in Congress and a resolution was readied calling for U. S. withdrawal from the world body should China gain admittance. This course of action, though, was not favored by the general public. A mid-July poll found that only 25 percent of the survey population would recommend U.S. withdrawal from the United Nations, whereas 59 percent felt America should accept the will of the majority on the "Chirep" question.[39]

Eisenhower also made clear his displeasure with this resolution, arguing—in a view widely echoed in the press—that it would inhibit the successful conduct of foreign policy.[40] In any case, Eisenhower noted that there was little chance that the United States would allow such a development to come to pass. Speaking at a 7 July news conference, the president stated that his administration saw the question of China's admission to the United Nations as a "moral one." Given this view, he was "completely and unalterably opposed under present conditions to the admission of Red China into the United Nations." The president continued, in a statement that would often be repeated in substance and tone over the next fifteen years, that

today we have Red China going to Geneva, and instead of taking a conciliatory attitude about anything, it excoriated the United Nations. As a matter of fact, at Geneva it demanded a repudiation of the United Nations position. On top of that, Red China is today at war with the United Nations. They were declared an aggressor by the United Nations in the assembly [over Korea]; that situation has never changed. They are occupying North Korea; they have supported this great effort at further enslavement of the peoples in Indochina; they have held certain of our prisoners unjustifiably, and they have been guilty of the employment of the worst possible diplomatic deportment in the international affairs of the world.

How can the United States, as a self-respecting nation, doing its best and in conformity with the moral standards as we understand them how can we possibly say this government should be admitted to the United Nations.[41]

A Gallup poll released nineteen days after the president spoke showed that most Americans also saw the issue as a "moral one" from which there could be no backing down; admission of the People's Republic of China to the United Nations was opposed by a seemingly unbridgeable gulf of 78 to 7 percent.[42]

Eisenhower's policy toward Chinese admission to the United Nations was not, though, a continuation of the Truman-Acheson position. Appending the president's remarks on 8 July, Dulles told a packed news conference that the United States would now "invoke the veto if necessary" to keep Peking out of the world body.[43] Furthermore, while side-stepping the withdrawal issue, the secretary argued that the representation question was an important substantive matter. It therefore had to be decided by a two-thirds margin in the General Assembly, were the issue to come to a vote.[44] When this matter finally did reach the floor for debate—seven years later during Kennedy's first year in office—this "important question" policy came into prominence as America's chief strategy to retain Taipei's seat in the General Assembly.

Behind Eisenhower's moral concern, and Dulles's more tactical stance, also lay certain domestic political imperatives. Opinion as harshly set as that against China—even if led there by government actions—presented no real incentive to cross it without advance preparation. Few would want to stand against a public that by a 59 to 26 percent majority favored *not* improving relations with the mainland.[45] Evidence of this deep public displeasure with Peking was not hard to find. A September 1954 NORC poll, for instance, discovered that, for the fifth time since 1951, majority support existed for "giving the Chinese Nationalist government on Formosa all the help it needs to attack the Chinese Communists on the mainland."[46] The 1954 elections were on the horizon and, true or not, these polls seemed to back up the "common wisdom" that there was "no surer road to career suicide [in politics] than to be connected in any way with any form of 'appeasement,' real or imagined of communism."[47] In this vein, one contemporary political commentator surveying the pre-election landscape noted,

The Republicans have been increasingly nervous and defensive about Indochina. In 1952 they made profitable use of the charge that the Democrats had "lost China," and they fear now that the Democrats, in their turn, will raise the cry of "weakness" and "indecision" in Indochina.[48]

With few public or policy reasons to alter its course, Washington held to its negative China trajectory. This occurred despite the late July completion of the Geneva accords and the subsequent release of six jailed Americans by the People's Republic of China. The administration ruled out the sincerity of any conciliatory mainland gestures, suggesting that they were mere tactics by which "subversion, infiltration and propaganda" could be more effectively pursued.[49] Within a week of the prisoner release, it became clear that no quick reciprocal action could be expected from Washington. This week included a Chinese-American aerial clash off the mainland's coast and a warm reception given to touring South Korean President Syngman Rhee who, before a joint session of Congress, argued (with no takers) for a war of liberation against the mainland.[50] Reviewing this spate of events, the *Times* agreed with Washington's public assessment of the Asian situation—there was "no truce in Red China's war on the minds and bodies of men."[51]

American resolve at this time was further highlighted by discussions with the Republic of China over a mutual defense pact and the impending formation of the South East Asian Treaty Organization (SEATO). These dual discussions form the background against which the People's Republic of China began its shelling of Quemoy and Matsu islands in September 1954. U.S. public opinion, perhaps in partial reaction to the killing of two American advisers on the first day of shelling (and reflecting previous government shaping actions), rallied to Taipei's defense and favored its aid in the struggle with the Communists by a three-to-one edge.[52] "Antipathy to Communist China is keen," commented State's opinion analysts.[53] Washington responded to these mainland provocations by increasing its rate of weapons delivery to the Nationalists, including sophisticated Sabre-jet fighters designed to give the KMT mastery over the coastal skies. Furthermore, discussions concerning the defense pact with Taiwan were accelerated as the White House repeated its pledge to defend Formosa from invasion. While publicly equivocating, privately officials were also leaning toward including Taiwan's coastal islands under America's defense umbrella. This was a move the press approached cautiously, reflecting its "desire to avoid provocative action which might cause war."[54] Washington, seeking to contain the Chinese Communists, took the opportunity provided by this crisis to step up its plans to aid the non-communist states of Indochina. By January 1955 an aid program, for example, was in place for the Diem regime in South Vietnam.

Eisenhower, despite his unfailing support for the Nationalists, was not anxious to see this "vest pocket" war expand. This concern led him to pressure Chiang—despite objections from most members of the joint chiefs—to cease bombing runs over the mainland.[55] Nor would the president agree to Senator Jenner's request that the United States issue a statement to the effect that it would "never, under any circumstances, recognize the Peiping government."[56] Over a year earlier, in turning down a similar request, Eisenhower had explained that we should "just think back to 1945 when Germany was our deadly enemy; who could have foreseen that in only a few years it would become a friendly associate?"[57] The president held to this position despite Peking's November disclosure that it had jailed eleven American airmen—secretly held since the Korean War—as spies. Though Eisenhower rejected congressional calls for a blockade of the Chinese coast in response to this act, the atmosphere between the two nations grew even more bitter than it had been.[58] Reflective of this was a November NORC poll which found recognition of the mainland opposed by an 82 to 5 percent margin.[59] "Certainly this [airmen outrage]," thundered editorial pages across the country, "should end any further talk of admitting Communist China to the United Nations."[60]

The tangible outcome of the first Straits crisis, even taking into account the Nationalist loss of the Tachens (exchanged for a secret U.S. pledge to defend Quemoy and Matsu), was less than favorable to the People's Republic of China.[61] This was the case as ties between Taipei and Washington were tightened through the passage of the Joint Formosa Resolution and the accelerated approval of the mutual defense pact in Congress. These measures enjoyed wide public support which helped account for the way they "breezed" through the legislature despite some unspoken Democratic misgivings.[62] Little was to be gained from bucking the executive-fostered hostility toward the mainland so prevalent in the land. State, at this juncture, also contemptuously rejected Peking's offer to allow the relatives of imprisoned Americans to journey to the mainland for visits.[63] The Chinese Communists, Washington argued, had to be opposed on all actions, conciliatory in appearance or not, since they had been "charged by world communism with special responsibilities for Communist enslavement of the rest of Asia."[64] Logic such as this led the public to favor "all out" support for Quemoy and Matsu by a three-to-two spread among those aware of the crisis and with a position on it.[65]

By early February the possibility that the United States might have to engage in an "all out" defense of the small coastal islands began to abate. The *Wall Street Journal*, for instance, told its readers that the "new challenge to Red China isn't as drastic—or risky—as it sounds."[66] Writing from Washington on 1 February, James Reston supported this view, reporting that

President Eisenhower put the so-called Formosa crisis in better perspective today by insisting emphatically on reducing the size of the United States Army.... Officials do strange things here, but the President does not cut the army and the Secretary of State does not go off fishing in the Bahamas if they think the Republic faces a test of military strength with more than [a] half-billion Chinese.[67]

With tensions declining, the United States agreed to allow China to participate in a UN debate on the Far East. Henry Cabot Lodge, Jr., the American delegate, made clear, however, that this participation would be similar to that of a guilty party being brought to court.

China, to the professed delight of the American delegation, turned down this offer. Despite the rejection, Peking did show an increased interest in contacts with America. After having failed to move the United States with the stick, the People's Republic of China apparently determined to once again try a more moderate track. As early as February, Chou En-lai was passing word through diplomatic channels of China's desire for greater contacts with America.[68] Peking may have been influenced to move in this direction by a hint of change within the United States. *Times* columnist C. L. Sulzberger noticed, for instance, that "now that the gamble of unseating China's Communist regime has long since failed there is much interest in reports that at least some American opinion is openly discussing [the] grant of recognition to Peiping as a means of easing tension."[69] Some of the impetus for this view may have grown out of the words of the administration itself. The president's January call for a cease-fire in the Straits led to speculation over a future "two-China" policy. *Life* argued against such a notion, editorializing that "the Formosa government is one of the few real obstacles to the Communist drive in Asia. Unless we are willing to envision and intend the Communists' ultimate downfall, as Chiang does, then the Formosa alliance is a fraud."[70] Speaking at a 19 January 1955 press conference, though, the president refused to rule out an explicit "two Chinas" policy for America. This was, Eisenhower told assembled reporters, "one of the possibilities that is constantly [being] studied."[71]

Dulles's private statements in this period similarly showed an underlying flexibility. He recognized, as he told Ambassador Koo, that "facts spoke louder than words. There already existed two Chinas, just as there were two Germanies, two Koreas, and two Viet-nams, although the United States had no intention to recognize Communist China on the mainland."[72] The secretary also displayed this flexible tendency when he told Anthony Eden on 24 February 1955 that

Under the circumstances we feel that we have gone as far as is prudent in making concessions [such as giving up the Tachens]. If the Chinese Communists, while retaining their claims to Formosa, would give assurances that they would not seek a verdict by force, then the situation would be different.[73]

Dulles, though, would not alter his policy under communist pressure nor lightly abandon his tactics designed to break the Sino-Soviet alliance.

Though Dulles's private thoughts did not surface,[74] the president's, from time to time, did. Eisenhower's sentiments, clearly not of the "rollback" genre, helped to spur speculation that America's Asian policy was undergoing a "fundamental review." Papers such as the *Wall Street Journal* "conceded that any peaceful settlement [in the Far East] inevitably involves the two-China principle."[75] It was predicted by some news analysts that the administration would take the lead in making it "politically 'safe' to speak of negotiating with the [Chinese] Communists."[76] Though, given Dulles's "splitting" stand, not all of Washington's actions bespoke of a moderating policy, press sources continued to discern a relaxation in America's Asian stance.[77] Evidently journalists were not alone in positing such movement; the Committee of One Million against the Admission of Communist China to the United Nations, which had officially disbanded in August 1954, announced its reorganization as it felt it had to once again counteract the "influential voices" talking about an eventual reconciliation with the People's Republic of China.[78] As one of these "voices" may have been the president's it is not surprising that—unlike in 1953—this group was apparently unable to set up an appointment with Eisenhower in order to get a reorganizational boost.[79]

The less strident era of People's Republic of China foreign policy, which began in early 1955, has come to be known as the "Bandung Phase" after the Indonesian site of the April 1955 Afro-Asian conference. The Bandung conference occurred at a time when war clouds seemed to again be gathering in the Formosan Straits. Chiang had added to these tensions by implying on Edward R. Murrow's "See It Now" March 1 television program that he expected air and sea support from America when he launched his "final counter-attack" on the mainland. Though the president sought to counter this impression a day later, stating that the United States would "not . . . be a party to an aggressive war," tensions continued to simmer. These tensions finally spilled over in late March when Admiral Carney (chief of naval operations) left the impression during a private dinner with newsmen that war with China was less than a month away.[80] Despite another disclaimer by the president, concern over the Far East rose. "Out of the strategy conferences in Washington and into the headlines across the U.S.," *Time* reported, "boiled an urgent question: Will the U.S. soon be at war again?"[81]

The public was apparently quite worried about a flare-up in the Taiwan region. By mid-April better than a four-to-one majority of those surveyed felt America should meet with Russia and Communist China "to see if a peaceful solution can be worked out in the Formosan dispute."[82] Chou En-lai seemed to be accommodating such views when he offered China's once-spurned hand to America at the Afro-Asian conference. Speaking on 23 April, Chou stated that

the Chinese people do not want war with the United States of America. The Chinese Government is willing to sit down and enter into negotiations with the United States Government to discuss the question of relaxing tension in the Far East, and especially the question of relaxing tension in the Taiwan area.[83]

The initial State Department reaction to Chou's words, taken with Dulles out of town, was a curt two-paragraph statement effectively rejecting the offer.[84] Henry Luce's *Time* applauded this response as showing a recognition of the fact that "in the Red lexicon relaxing tensions means lulling the non-Communist forces to sleep while the Communists build up their strength."[85] With Dulles's return to Washington, though, the department began to reconsider its initial statement. Along these lines, the secretary granted that "there may be a realization [in Peking] of the fact that a real peacefulness, instead of just talk about peace while carrying on war, was from their standpoint the best policy."[86] These words found some resonance in the public. "Against the recent background of 'deep anxiety' over the possibility of war in the Formosa Strait," State's 3 May opinion survey reported, "Premier Chou En-lai's offer to negotiate directly with the U.S.— together with the U.S. Government's 'positive' response—has rekindled the hope for peace."[87]

In making known his interest in negotiations, Dulles was reflecting a number of policy trends. The surface policy of defusing war prospects in the Far East and getting the jailed Americans in China released was one facet. In addition to this, it is clear that U.S. policy—though still negative—was continuing its early 1955 inch toward a less hostile posture vis-à-vis the Chinese Communists. These talks would both signal a minor moderation in America's China stance and help to undercut allied arguments for a more drastic relaxation of U.S. policy in the Far East. These talks would also be useful in blocking Soviet efforts at including the People's Republic of China as a member of the ''Big Five'' at an upcoming international conference. Dulles, in a 1 July 1955 draft memorandum on how to deny ''Great Power Status to Communist China,'' wrote in this obstructionist vein,

Probably the best solution is for the U.S. to have some direct talks with the Chinese Communists which will slightly increase the scope and level of the talks now being held at Geneva with reference to citizens of the two countries held by the other.[88]

Small signs of Washington's moderating policy continued to appear throughout the summer. America, for example, did not waver in making known its willingness to negotiate with Peking and even went so far as to hint that an exchange of theatrical companies might be possible in the near future.[89] More quietly, the United States backed off its previous pledge to the Nationalists to definitely help defend Quemoy and Matsu, seeking instead a KMT withdrawal from these islands.[90] Opinion, responding to Washington's public moves, was trending in a direction generally supportive of the government's actions. An early May poll found, for instance, that 70 percent of the public felt ''it would be a good idea . . . for U.S. representatives to reach an agreement [with China] on some of the problems in Asia.''[91] Opinion, furthermore, became somewhat less negative concerning China's eventual admission to the United Nations.[92] Events in East Asia were being mirrored in Europe as significant progress was made on the Austrian Treaty with the Soviets. Noting this dual decline in world pressure, Dulles granted that there were ''small but perhaps significant signs'' of a more forthcoming attitude among both communist giants.[93] China, in an attempt to keep this forward momentum going, began to allow the Americans it was holding to receive mail from the Red Cross.[94] On Memorial Day China took the even more significant step of releasing four of these prisoners.

By 11 July the administration had determined to go through with these talks. The announcement was made on 25 July that one week later ambassadorial-level discussions with China would commence in Geneva. While the public remained widely opposed to recognizing Peking, this statement was greeted by a chorus of reactions that were ''favorable, if not completely optimistic.''[95] Certain congressmen and journalists even began to speculate on the imminency of a meeting between Chou and Dulles.[96] A National Opinion Research Center poll completed in late August found such a meeting to be favored by an overwhelming 82 to

10 percent gap among those surveyed.[97] Expectations that such a meeting was just around the corner had been heightened by the release of eleven more American prisoners as a Chinese show of good faith as the negotiations began. The State Department, though, was not anxious for public expectations to get ahead of its slowly changing policy. This was characteristic of Dulles's "management" of public opinion throughout the 1950s. Though encouraging some changes in attitude, the secretary sought to keep such alterations relatively shallow so that he would not later face the possibility of public pressure to move faster in adjusting policies than strategic conditions warranted. State, therefore, publicly cautioned that while the talks "might mark the beginning of a new phase of Chinese Communist relations with the rest of the world . . . one swallow does not make a summer."[98]

One reason Dulles sought to moderate any abrupt opinion shifts was that the policy of splitting the Sino-Soviet alliance through pressure on its "junior member" had not been abandoned. This, plus the fact that elections were once again in sight, led the United States to stall in the Geneva negotiations. *U.S. News and World Report* speculated, along these electoral lines, that Washington would continue its attempt to diplomatically isolate China until after November 1956 when it might institute a "two China" policy.[99] Whatever the motivations behind America's unyielding negotiating stance, one official has granted that such policies were designed "to foil and frustrate China's ploys for . . . agreements and rapprochement with the United States."[100] Eisenhower publicly hinted at such a negotiating posture when he told reporters in mid-August that the change they discerned in America's East Asian policy was "far more apparent than real."[101] The U.S. representatives at Geneva were clearly uncomfortable with this unresponsive posture. The chief American translator at these talks has made this apparent in describing a 1955 conference room scene where Chinese Ambassador Wang repeatedly pressed for wider "people to people" contacts. Ambassador Wang, wrote this military officer, "taunted us with being afraid of facts and the truth. There was little that could be effectively said in rebuttal. In fact, there was nothing; we took refuge in silence."[102]

As a result of these tactics, the talks in Geneva began to bog down. This was especially true after the 10 September agreement on repatriation was reached, thus seeming to satisfy America's immediate reason for meeting with the People's Republic of China. While most observers approved of continuing the talks, a few (like Hearst's *New York Mirror*) did argue for ending the discussions, declaring that "no more good" could come out of them.[103] Increasing the acrimony, as winter fell on Washington, was what America considered to be Chinese foot-dragging in carrying out the September repatriation agreement. The *New York Times* characterized this mainland behavior as "hold[ing] . . . Americans as hostages in an attempt to blackmail the United States" into better relations. By December the conflict at the talks began to break into the open, leading the *Times* to argue that "the basically dishonest position of the Chinese has made the Geneva talks almost impossible from the beginning."[104] Public accusations between capitals apparently had some effect on the public as those favoring a foreign ministers' meeting fell from 82 percent of the population to 74 percent, with a concomitant rise in those opposed to such a move.[105]

Despite rising United States–People's Republic of China acrimony, it was increasingly coming to be accepted in articulate circles that U. S. policy was not designed to "liberate" the mainland. The *Des Moines Register* bluntly recognized this, stating, "You might as well talk about the fabled White Russian taxi drivers of Paris 'liberating' the Soviet Union."[106] Acceptance of this view led to the belief that American policy toward China really was altering beneath a relatively immobile façade. By mid-March 1956 *Newsweek* reported that a sense of inevitability over the need for a change in relations with Peking had settled on our nation's capital. There "is a growing conviction in Washington," this news journal reported, "that Red China can't be kept out of the United Nations much longer and that the U.S. might as well accept the inevitable gracefully."[107] Many expected, though, that any far-reaching policy change would have to accommodate itself to the American electoral cycle. This was believed to be the case as concern "over Communist China's expanding influence in Asia" became a prominent "theme in campaign oratory."[108] Taken as a reflection by much of the press of this short-term immobility was Dulles's strong public rejection on 12 June 1956 of another Chinese offer to hold a foreign ministers' meeting. This occurred despite the fact that a mid-year poll found a continuing 80 to 14 percent majority in favor of such a meeting.[109] Peking similarly received a chilly response from Washington to its renewed offer of allowing American newsmen to report from behind the "Bamboo Curtain."

U.S. intransigence, though, reflected more than electoral politics. With the Soviet bloc cracking under the weight of "de-Stalinization," there seemed little reason to alter America's pressure on the Far East in any major way. Actions by Peking in 1957 also precluded any large American policy changes, as the Communist Chinese once again shed their conciliatory stance toward the United States. This was due to a number of domestic and international factors. Among the most important of these were the failure of the "Hundred Flowers" campaign on the mainland, past U.S. intransigence at the Geneva talks, and Russian rocketry successes which may have convinced Mao that "the forces of socialism [were now] overwhelmingly superior to the forces of imperialism."[110] Interestingly, just as this tougher Chinese line was taking shape, certain prominent Americans began to call for a re-examination of U.S. China policy. Senator Green, chairman of the Foreign Relations Committee, for example, said in mid-February that China "is a great country and organized, and I do not myself see why we should recognize these other Communist countries and withhold recognition of China."[111] On 19 February, in response to this statement, Secretary Dulles stated that consideration of Peking's recognition in the near future would be "premature, to say the least."[112]

Calls for relaxing trade restrictions with the mainland also began to become more frequent among business leaders. Among those calling for a change were

Henry Ford II and U.S. Chamber of Commerce president John S. Coleman.[113] Press response to these pronouncements was generally favorable, with the *Wall Street Journal* editorializing early in 1957 that such sentiments raised the "question of whether the United States is not perhaps already too inflexible regarding Red China. We do not know the answer, but we are sure that a policy which precluded any change in our attitude ever, would be unwise."[114] Statements by these industrial heads were in line with increasing acceptance by the general public of trade with the Chinese Communists. In early 1957 State's opinion analysts, recognizing this, wrote that "the trend of opinion over the past few years appears to be in the direction of increased popular willingness to continue, or approve, [Chinese-American] non-strategic trade."[115] While responses to surveys focusing on commerce between the enemy nations varied widely depending on question-wording, evidence from identically phrased items does show a clear trend over time toward greater approval for U.S. (and allied) trade with the mainland.[116]

Scholars advocating a Far Eastern policy change also began to find a wider audience for their views. John K. Fairbank, for instance, argued in the April 1957 *Atlantic Monthly* that a re-evaluation of our Asian stance was necessary since "waiting for the enemy to fall on his face is not a policy."[117] The noted theologian Reinhold Niebuhr also contributed to this public debate, writing,

Our opposition to the entrance of China into the United Nations is the consequence of a fiction of which we have been prisoners as a nation for decades.... Sooner or later we will be forced to accept the Communist conquest of China as an ineluctable fact and admit Communist China to the United Nations.[118]

Even an ambitious young Massachusetts senator commented that America's policy toward Peking was "probably too rigid" though, at present, there were still "compelling reasons for non-recognition."[119] *Time* unhappily noted this upsurge of discussion and charged that

a more-or-less concerted effort to stimulate debate on a "realistic," i.e., more lenient, U.S. China policy, if not to propagandize actively on its behalf—has indeed suddenly blossomed from public forums and periodical presses since last winter.[120]

Tentative government steps had encouraged this flowering of debate. The United States, in response to England's importunings, publicly eased up on its opposition to allied loosening of the strict embargo directed at the mainland. Washington also lessened its opposition to newsmen's traveling to China—though in a somewhat ambiguous manner.[121] The president, further, became more outspoken in his advocacy of eventually opening trade relations with the People's Republic of China since "the Yankee . . . is a fine trader, and we got to be a great country by trade."[122] These actions, and others, such as a hint that Chinese Communist athletes might be invited to compete in the 1960 Winter

Olympics in California, led the Council on Foreign Relations' annual summary of international events to conclude that "beneath the official surface, the substance of Chinese-American relations was plainly altering in 1957."[123] These "alterations" may also have been spurred on by the "savage" 24 May 1957 anti-American riots in Taipei. This outburst led to widespread calls for a policy review, even "from some of the Nationalist Government's staunchest supporters in Congress."[124]

It, however, must again be stressed that the shifts that had occurred in American policy since the Korean War, while real, were minor. A policy of public toughness and private resolve remained primary for Washington. The still-pending break in the Sino-Soviet alliance, refusal to yield to an "aggressor," and concern with our Asian allies all contributed to this policy continuity. Not surprisingly, then, American resolve continued to display itself in a number of ways. Prominent among these was the May 1957 announcement that Matador tactical missiles would be placed on Taiwan, and the attempt by Dulles to downgrade the Geneva talks due to their fruitless nature.[125] The policy of rhetorical toughness also continued to be visibly pursued. This action not only served to bolster our allies' resolve, but also helped to eliminate the possibility of too rapid a change in public opinion. The upsurge in debate that *Time* had taken note of needed to be channeled and moderated, lest the possibility arise that State's overall harsh policy would become a future political liability for the in-office Republicans. Self-interest guided State's attempt to moderate alterations in the public's preferences, since if the idea of a "new China policy" gained sufficient adherents, Dulles might eventually be forced to abandon his splitting efforts before they had fully borne their strategic fruit.

To foreclose this possibility, as well as to reassure nervous nations around China's periphery,[126] it was decided that the secretary should make a major policy address on East Asia. The forum chosen for this was a June 1957 conference of San Francisco businessmen. The perceived necessity to control the volume of public discussion, and to calm our allies' frayed nerves, is evident in a pre-speech memo Walter Robertson sent to Dulles:

Recent statements by Senators Green, Fulbright, Humphrey and Magnuson have caused speculation throughout Asia as to our China policy and have given particular concern to our Asian allies. Off-the-cuff statements by the President in his press conferences have also been interpreted to indicate a pending shift in policy. Your speech, therefore, will be scrutinized with the keenest interest for evidence of a wavering policy. Obviously any chink in your armor will be exploited to the greatest possible extent.[127]

With this in mind, the secretary told the gathering of West Coast entrepreneurs that communism in China was only "a passing and not perpetual phase. . . . If we believed that this passing would be promoted by trade and cultural relations, we would have such relations."[128] Not coincidentally, *Time* reported just prior to this speech that State Department sources had revealed to it that Dulles would not waver in applying pressure on the mainland since this "tough policy, which puts strains on the Moscow-Peiping alliance, is more likely to create [a] disruption" than a "more lenient" policy.[129]

Despite occasional rhetorical countermoves, Washington's stance toward China continued to inch in a moderate direction; what was necessary for policy-makers, however, was to prevent opinion from getting ahead of these glacial governmental shifts. Since Korea, policy had altered slowly with regard to China and opinion had largely tracked these movements. By 20–25 August 1958, support for the People's Republic of China's admission to the United States had reached an all-time high of 20 percent—though this still meant it was opposed by better than a three-to-one margin in the general public.[130] The government, to this point, had been quite successful in maintaining "control" over the outlines of popular attitudes on China. It should be noted, however, that even though opinion was led in this era, without alterations in it such policy changes as did occur likely would have been impossible.

On 23 August, as this Gallup UN poll was being conducted, the mainland renewed its shelling of the offshore islands after a lull of more than three years. By 25 August the United States had determined to defend these Nationalist outposts, even if this necessitated the use of nuclear weapons.[131] Throughout this crisis the administration attempted to sway the public behind its position.[132] In this effort, however, it had at best moderate success. Though opinion was still negative toward the mainland, the passage of time—and U.S. actions since the Korean War—had undercut the argument of holding these coastal islands no matter what the risks.

It is one thing for this country to undertake the defense of Formosa itself, although the passing years are taking our Formosa policy also further from reality. But it is something else again to act as though the Nationalists are on their way back to China and that these islands are priceless pawns to be held at any cost, including a war,

commented the *Wall Street Journal*. Given the prevalence of this iconoclastic sentiment, it is not surprising that both a Trendex and an Iowa poll found support for an active U.S. defense of the offshore "outposts" falling short of a majority. Similarly, the *Journal* interviewed 180 people and found only about half of this group in favor of America's acting to repel an attack on Quemoy or Matsu. The seventy persons opposed to this move generally felt, as did a *Journal* editorial, that the islands were "of no intrinsic significance for American interest."[133] The "attentive public" also had doubts over the wisdom of U.S. policy at this time; letters, telegrams, and phone calls to the State Department and Capitol Hill widely opposed risking war over these supposed Nationalistic "strongholds."[134]

With the public hesitant over America's course in Asia, it is not surprising that this issue eventually took on a partisan coloration. As one Washington wag put it,

We are told by the candidates of the Grand Old Party that unless we defend Quemoy and Matsu everything that is precious in the vast blue reaches of the Pacific will be lost, including honor. The Democrats, lost in Alsopian gloom, reply that we must get out of there quickly or be engulfed by at least 600,000,000 Communist Chinese.[135]

Editorial opinion in this country generally reflected the split in the public. Whereas the *Detroit Free Press* argued, "If the islands are not defensible or worth defending, why not just say so, pull out, and forget the demands that Red China first agree to [a] ceasefire," the *Spokane* (Washington) *Spokesman-Review* suggested, "It never pays to submit to blackmail even for the sake of two little islands."[136] There was, though, a definite trend for more prestigious newspapers to argue against American involvement in the defense of Quemoy and Matsu. The *Christian Science Monitor*, *New York Times*, *Washington Post*, and *St. Louis Post-Dispatch* all expressed strong reservations over U.S. actions in the Far East.

In spite of these public reservations, the administration did not waiver in its determination. Defending the islands remained policy even though officials privately conceded to one another that, as regards the status of the "offshores," they did "not feel we have a case which is altogether [logically] defensible."[137] As in past crises, officials expected that citizens would rally to their side were war to break out. In such a situation, Washington reasoned, the normal "rules" of opinion would not apply.[138] With most of the public hostile to Peking, the probability of electoral difficulty arising from the decision to defend these islands was judged, in any case, to be minor given the stakes involved. The United States backed up its announced position by sending Sidewinder air-to-air missiles to the Nationalists and providing KMT artillerymen with new eight-inch howitzers capable of firing tactical atomic shells.[139] Tensions in the Straits area, however, began to abate with Chou En-lai's 6 September call for talks in response to American urgings. The successful Nationalist running of the Quemoy blockade eight days later, and the resumption of ambassadorial talks in Warsaw on 15 September, helped to further contain tensions. By early October the danger of war ended with the People's Republic of China's announcement of a unilateral seven-day cease fire. Chiang's late October disavowal of force to "reunify" China, announced under American pressure, effectively closed this chapter of Sino-American relations. It also led to speculation, denied by State, that the United States had finally accepted the existence of both Chinese regimes. "The question of whether the United States is headed toward a two-China policy is [now] largely one of semantics and it does not matter what the policy is called," concluded the *Washington Post*.[140]

With the passing of this crisis, Washington again took some minor steps toward reducing tensions with Peking. Opinion was of a nature where small policy moves did not seem likely to provoke a negative political reaction. The reticence the public had displayed in the just-finished Straits crisis seemed to buttress this interpretation. Reflecting Washington's decision to test the waters with Peking, America's Warsaw negotiators received new latitude to approach their Chinese counterparts over increased contacts. These diplomats were allowed to modify America's stance on the newsman issue until their proposal "became virtually identical with the original Peking proposal of 1956."[141] The policy of pressure, though, also remained in place. It was now, however, cast in a more reactive than active mode. The United States would not yield to Chinese aggression, but it would be more open to testing Peking's intentions. Part of the impetus for this change came from Christian A. Herter's interest in making his own mark on foreign policy. Herter, who officially took over from a terminally ill Dulles early in 1959, was not shackled by an over-identification with the previous secretary's harsh rhetoric toward China. Immediately upon Herter's swearing in, State announced that it had validated the passports of thirty-three journalists for travel to the mainland and expected that the Attorney General would waive restrictions on Communist Chinese newsmen who wished to enter American territory.[142]

Herter also benefited from a more moderate Congress than had faced Secretary Dulles. The 1958 mid-term elections had decimated the ranks of congressional Republicans, with some of the most vocal pro-Nationalist advocates not returned to office. This led to a decline in Capitol Hill pressure for every Foggy Bottom speech on Asia to include a ringing moral denunciation of the mainland. This slight change in legislative atmosphere was reflected in an early 1959 speech given by freshman Senator Clair Engle. Engle had won Senator Knowland's seat when "the Senator from Formosa" had retired to run (unsuccessfully) for governor of California. The newly elected legislator, in a floor speech widely praised by his colleagues, wondered

why our policy in China should be any more sacrosanct than our policy in Europe.... I am convinced that our China policy needs critical reexamination. I am prepared to dispute the premise that our present policy is adequate and that nothing about it should be changed.[143]

Despite its significant moderation since the early 1950s, it should be underlined that opinion in the public and the press (see table 3) still remained quite negative toward the mainland. With the Chinese increasingly unresponsive at Warsaw, and America unwilling to ease its "splitting pressure" too much, there was little incentive in Eisenhower's final years for public attitudes to undergo any major alterations. Peking's suppression of the Tibetan revolt, border skirmishes with India, and its imprisonment of Bishop James Edward Walsh on espionage charges all contributed to the relative stasis of opinion. Indeed, if anything, the general public's opinion about China seems to have drifted downward in 1959 and 1960.[144] The most important effect of Chinese actions in this period, though, was to produce

TABLE 3

PRESS OPINION TOWARD CHINA AT THE CLOSE
OF THE EISENHOWER YEARS

(a) Opposed to US-UN Recognition or 'Softer' Policy

Albany Knickerbocker News
America
Army-Navy-Air Force Journal
Birmingham News
Bloomington Pantograph

Boise Statesman
Chicago American
Chicago Sun-Times
Chicago Tribune
Cincinnati Enquirer

Cleveland Plain Dealer
Columbus (Ohio) Dispatch
Dallas News
Flint Journal
Ft. Worth Star-Telegram

Hearst Newspapers
Honolulu Star-Bulletin
Houston Chronicle
Houston Post
Human Events

Indianapolis Star
Jackson Clarion-Ledger
Los Angeles Times
Manchester Union Leader

Memphis Commercial Appeal
Nashville Banner
National Review
Newark News
New Bedford Standard Times

New Orleans Times-Picayune
New York News
Oakland Tribune
Philadelphia Bulletin
Philadelphia Inquirer

Portland (Me.) Press-Herald
Richmond Times-Dispatch
St. Louis Glove-Democrat
St. Paul Pioneer Press
Salt Lake City Tribune

San Diego Union
Saturday Evening Post
Savannah News
Scripps-Howard Newspapers
Spokane Spokesman-Review

Washington Star
Wheeling Intelligencer
Wichita Eagle

(b) Advocates of 'Change'

Atlanta Constitution
Boston Herald
Charlotte Observer
Christian Century
Christian Community

Christian Science Monitor
Commonweal
Dayton News
Denver Post
Des Moines Register

Nation
New Republic
New York Post*
Norfolk Virginian-Pilot
Portland Oregonian

Providence Journal*
Racine Journal-Times
Raleigh News and Observer
The Reporter
Rochester Democrat and Chronicle

Table 3 *continued*

Harrisburg Patriot	St. Louis Post-Dispatch
Little Rock Gazette	San Francisco Chronicle
Louisville Courier-Journal*	Topeka Capital
Madison Capital Times	Wall Street Journal
Milwaukee Journal	Washington Post
Minneapolis Star	

Source: Special Report on American Opinion: "Public Attitudes toward Communist China, 1958-1960" (24 May 1960), Foster Papers, Box 33.

Note: List refers only to those with explicit editorial policy. List is meant to be representative, not exhaustive.

*Denotes explicit newspaper advocate of a 'Two China' policy.

in America a picture of a Red China possessing increasing might and increased willingness to employ it at the expense of the free world. As a result, the feeling that Red China is an acute "danger" to U.S. interests has become more general and acute.[145]

This impression was not totally inaccurate, as Mao reportedly told *Izvestia* in June 1959, "We do not want conciliation with the U.S.A. The United States must submit to us [in Asia]. Otherwise, we do not wish to enter into negotiations with them."[146]

The Eisenhower years closed with opinion still generally negative toward the mainland. The public had moderated its views of the People's Republic of China somewhat, in response to government actions and the fading of Korean War memories. These opinion changes, however, were not great. Without these preference changes, though, policy doubtless would not have even made the miniscule progress it had by 1960. It should also be stressed that a public so hostile to major policy changes (even if led there by Washington) presented a powerful brake on any contemplated policy alterations. This was not a great hindrance to the Republicans given their policy of harsh "splitting" pressure. Public attitudes would, however, present a problem for Eisenhower's Democratic successor.

NOTES

1. Walter P. McConaughy, "China in the Shadow of Communism," *DSB* 30 (11 January 1954):42.

2. Ibid., pp. 40-41.

3. "Summary of Current American Attitudes on Foreign Policy," 29 January 1953, Foster Papers, Box 1.

4. A 15 March 1953 Gallup poll found better than 60 percent approval for giving the Nationalists ships "to blockade the coast of Communist China" and planes to "bomb Communist China." The poll that found 83 to 14 percent disapproval of allied trade was an NORC survey conducted in May 1953. Fifty-six percent of those responding also reported that we should "insist" our allies halt this trade. See *Special Report on American Opinion*, 23 March 1953, Foster Papers, Box 1, and ibid., 10 June 1953. See also *Monthly Survey* 145 (May 1953), Foster Papers, Box 12.

5. See, for instance, Harry Schwartz, "The Testing of the Moscow-Peking Axis," *New York Times Magazine* (1954), pp. 10, 36. See also *NYT*, 8 February 1953, 18 July 1954, 13 October 1954, 12 December 1954; and Louis Fisher, "China and Russia: Allies or Rivals," *Reader's Digest*, July 1954, pp. 103-107.

6. Between 1951 and late 1953 the United States paid for 40 percent of the war's cost. By late 1953 this had grown to 60 percent, and it grew to 78 percent by mid-1954. See Melvin Gurtov, *The First Vietnam Crisis: Chinese Strategy and United States Involvement, 1953-1954* (New York: Columbia University Press, 1967), pp. 24-25.

7. See Dulles's testimony in *Executive Sessions of the Senate Foreign Relations Committee* (Historical Series), 83d Cong., 1st sess., 1953 (Washington, D.C.: Government Printing Office, 1977), pp. 139-144, and his untitled note of 31 March 1952, Dulles Papers, Box 60.

8. Quoted in Gurtov, pp. 27-28.

9. Everett F. Drumright, deputy secretary for Far Eastern affairs starting in November 1953, has written to Gurtov (p. 176, fn 47), "I do not believe that [Dulles] or other high officials of State or the Pentagon seriously entertained the idea there would be direct Chinese intervention. Sometimes statements are made for political rather than realistic reasons."

10. The United States was, at this time, trying to encourage the establishment of an integrated European Army. A treaty with this goal in mind had been signed on 27 May 1952 with Germany, Belgium, France, Italy, Luxemburg, and the Netherlands. There was great difficulty encountered, though, in putting this treaty into effect. U.S. maneuvering in diplomatic circles was designed to show American concern for allied interests, thereby easing the necessary parliamentary ratifications of the treaty. This concern was especially acute with the French, whose National Assembly finally rejected the treaty on 30 August 1954. With the creation of this army as a prime goal, it is not surprising that the United States acquiesced to allied calls for China's inclusion at the Geneva talks. See Michael A. Guhin, *John Foster Dulles: A Statesman and His Times* (New York: Columbia University Press, 1972), pp. 215-219, and *FRUS, 1952-1954*, 16:418-419, 466.

11. *FRUS, 1952-1954*, 16:424-425, 433, 496-497, 532-534. An early December 1953 NORC poll found that 79 percent of the survey population favored a new "Big Four" meeting. Among this 79 percent, the extension of an invitation to China to attend a "Big Five" parley was opposed by a 41 to 31 percent margin. See "Recent Opinion Polls Relating to Communist China," 23 December 1953, Foster Papers, Box 33. This

document notes that "the December survey results provide confirmation of the long-held popular antipathy to Communist China and to any move which would aid the Peiping regime or which could be interpreted as U.S. approval of it."

12. Gallup poll, no. 528-K (12 April 1954). By a 58 to 25 percent margin the public felt it a "good idea" for America to agree to meet the Chinese Communists in Geneva. See also State's *Monthly Review* 154 (February 1954), Foster Papers, Box 12, and *Special Report on American Opinion*, "Public Attitudes toward Meeting with Communist China at the Geneva Conference," 25 March 1954, Foster Papers, Box 33. The *Special Report* notes a poll finding only 49 to 41 percent approval for this move. It goes on to state, however that "both before and after the Foreign ministers' meeting in Berlin, American opinion has supported the announced policies of the United States regarding Communist China. . . . All of these policies are upheld by the great majority in the press, in Congress, among National organizations, and among the general public."

13. Alfred le sense Jenkins, "Present United States Policy toward China," *DSB* 30 (26 April 1954), p. 624.

14. Senate Committee on Foreign Relations, *Hearings on Foreign Policy and Its Relation to Military Programs* (19 March, 14 April 1954) (Washington, D.C.: U.S. Government Printing Office, 1954), p. 31.

15. John Foster Dulles, "Korean Problems," *DSB* 29 (14 September 1953):342.

16. *FRUS, 1952-1954*, 16:423. See also ibid., p. 549. This view, though, was not universally held within the administration. See, for example, ibid., p. 438.

17. John Foster Dulles, "The Threat of a Red Asia," *DSB* 30 (12 April 1954):540.

18. John Foster Dulles, " 'Not One of Us Alone': A Mutual Security Program for 1955," *DSB* 30 (19 April 1954):582.

19. *FRUS, 1952-1954*, 16:349.

20. *Christian Science Monitor*, 29 April 1954.

21. Gurtov, p. 145.

22. Gallup poll, no. 530-K (17 March 1954); no. 531-K (14 June 1954). If America was to get involved in an Indochina war with the People's Republic of China, roughly 30 percent of the population reported that it would favor bombing mainland cities, about 50 percent of those surveyed were opposed to this action.

23. See *Monthly Survey* 156-157 (April–May 1954), Foster Papers, Box 12.

24. *FRUS, 1952-1954*, 16:479.

25. This response was given by 48 percent of the population in two separate May surveys (Gallup poll, no. 530-K [14 May 1954]; no. 531-K [16 June 1965]). In each of these polls, less than one-third of the respondents saw any possible gain in fighting in Indochina.

26. *FRUS, 1952-1954*, 16:422. See also ibid., pp. 471-481 where it is predicted, in late March, that Indochina's fall would lead to pressure on the Mideast and Europe and to Japan's ultimate "communization."

27. Ibid., p. 438.

28. Ibid., p. 424.

29. Ibid., p. 96.

30. Edwin W. Martin, "Considerations Underlying U.S.-China Policy," *DSB* 30 (12 April 1954), p. 543.

31. John Foster Dulles, "Berlin Foreign Ministers' Report" (24 February 1954), in *American Foreign Policy: Basic Documents, 1950-1955*, 2 vols. (Washington, D.C.: State Department, 1957), p. 88.

32. Edgar Snow, *The Other Side of the River: Red China Today* (New York: Random House, 1961), pp. 93-94. Dulles, on 25 April 1954, was asked by journalists in a background briefing whether there was any possibility he would meet with Chou before returning to the United States. The secretary responded, "Not unless our automobiles collide." See *FRUS, 1952-1954* 16:564.

33. Quoted, without attribution, in Foster Rhea Dulles, p. 144.

34. Ibid., pp. 144-145. Upon arriving home, Dulles told a nationwide radio and television audience on 7 May 1954 that "what started as a civil war [in Vietnam] has now been taken over ... by international Communism for its own purposes. Ho Chi Minh, the Communist leader in Vietnam, was trained in Moscow and got his first revolutionary experience in China." See *FRUS, 1952-1954*, 16:721.

35. *FRUS, 1952-1954*, 16:674-675.

36. *NYT*, 11 July 1954.

37. "Discussions concerning Americans Detained in Communist China," *DSB* 30 (21 June 1954):950. The Chinese may have had more to talk about than was generally conceded at the time. On the problems encountered by detained Chinese students in the United States see William L. Ryan and Sam Summerlin, *The China Cloud: America's Tragic Blunder and China's Rise to Nuclear Power* (Boston: Little, Brown and Co., 1968). See also Kenneth Young, *Diplomacy and Power in Washington-Peking Dealings 1953-1967* (Chicago: University of Chicago Center for Policy Study, 1967), pp. 37-38.

38. *Monthly Survey* 159 (July 1954), Foster Papers, Box 12.

39. Gallup poll, no. 534-K (9 August 1954). The December 1953 *Monthly Survey* (152) reported, in the context of its discussion on China, that 84 percent of people surveyed in a poll conducted by NORC felt the United States should go along with majority opinion at the United Nations. It should be noted, though, that this question referred to no specific country.

40. *Monthly Survey* 158 (June 1954), Foster Papers, Box 12; "China Telegram," 8 July 1954, Foster Papers, Box 29. This is a case Eisenhower had also made a year earlier. On 27 May 1953, the Senate Appropriations Committee had reported out a bill with a rider on it barring any financial contribution to the United Nations should mainland China be admitted. Senator Styles Bridges told reporters that only three of twenty-three committee members had voted against this rider. Eisenhower, when publicly asked about this bill, gave a noncommittal answer (see *Public Papers, 1953* [5 March], p. 88). In private, according to his memoirs, the president, however, told certain members of Congress on 2 June that the UN rider "could seriously hamper me in the conduct of foreign affairs." A compromise was reached whereby a non-binding resolution was, instead, offered to Congress. See Dwight D. Eisenhower, *The White House Years: Mandate for Change, 1953-1956* (Garden City, N.Y.: Doubleday and Co., 1963), pp. 214-215. Eisenhower's description is a retrospective one and may, as such, contain errors. In fact, Eisenhower does not correctly recall the nature of his news conference remarks on this question. The press, at the time, was generally making the same kind of arguments that Eisenhower reported making in private. On this, see *Monthly Survey* 145 (May 1953), Foster Papers, Box 12.

41. *Public Papers, 1954* (7 July), p. 618.

42. Gallup poll, no. 533-K (26 July 1954). Similar results were also found in a Gallup poll released in early August (no. 534-K). See also a 25 November 1953 NORC (no. 349) question which asks, "Would you approve or disapprove of letting Communist

China become a member of the United Nations?'' That poll found 74 to 12 percent having no opinion and 6 percent giving conditional (''depends'') answers.

43. ''Chinese Representation in the United Nations,'' *DSB* 30 (19 July 1954):75-89; *NYT*, 9 July 1954. On 1 July, Senator Knowland threatened to resign as floor leader and lead the fight to take the United States out of the United Nations should China be admitted. The minority leader, Lyndon Johnson, made a statement similar in tone. See *U.S. News and World Report*, 9 July 1954, p. 35.

44. Koo and Dulles had discussed this ''important question'' tactic as early as 24 November 1953. Koo Papers, Box 190.

45. September NORC poll cited in *Special Report on American Opinion*, ''Popular Attitudes on Asian Defense Questions,'' 30 November 1954, Foster Papers, Box 33.

46. Ibid.; NORC nos. 302 (18 April 1951), 312 (27 August 1951), 320 (19 March 1952), 363 (10 September 1954), and unnumbered (24 May 1951).

47. *NYT*, 11 July 1954. See also ibid., 14 February 1954, where A. M. Rosenthal commented that ''if any public figure in the United States ever comes out flatly for going the way to Communist Chinese membership [in the United Nations] he will have to be prepared to retire or be entirely sure that the administration has decided that the time had come to admit Peiping.'' These words were prompted by some comments by Arthur H. Dean, the U.S. Panmunjom negotiator, over China. Dean, it should be noted, published an article in *Foreign Affairs* in the spring of 1955 advocating recognition of Peking. See Arthur Dean, ''United States Foreign Policy and Formosa,'' *Foreign Affairs* 33 (April 1955):360-375.

48. *NYT*, 11 July 1954.

49. Ibid., 2 August 1954.

50. *Monthly Survey* 159 (July 1954), Foster Papers, Box 12.

51. *NYT*, 3 August 1954, 27 July, 29 July 1954.

52. Gallup poll, no. 537-K (6 October 1954). In this poll taken between 16 and 21 September, 10 percent were found to favor the United States' bombing the mainland in reaction to this crisis, 31 percent favored U.S. forces' aiding in repulsing an attack on Formosa, 28 percent favored only sending supplies, and 21 percent felt the United States should not get involved. Ten percent had no opinion on this issue. A September Minnesota poll found 50 to 30 percent opposition to ''joining forces with Chiang Kai-shek to fight against Chinese Communists if they try to capture the island of Formosa.'' See ''China Telegram,'' 22 September 1954, Foster Papers, Box 29.

53. *Special Report on American Opinion*, ''Popular Attitudes on Asian Defense Questions,'' 30 November 1954, Foster Papers, Box 33. This report also cited an October NORC survey which found 48 to 17 percent approval ''of our government's policy toward the Chinese Nationalist government on Formosa headed by Chiang Kai-shek.'' Approval of government policy rose to 52 to 9 percent, in response to the same question, by December. Thirty-nine percent had no opinion or knowledge of U.S. Formosa policy. See *Special Report on American Opinion*, ''Some Current Popular Attitudes on Far East Questions,'' Foster Papers, Box 33; NORC, no. 365 (26 November 1954). Reflective of the public hostility to China were two *Reader's Digest* articles that appeared during the crisis. See G. S. Gale, ''Six Hundred Million Puppets'' (December 1954), pp. 97-99; and Irwin Ross, ''Red China: The World's Biggest Dope Peddler'' (February 1955), pp. 121-124.

54. ''China Telegram,'' 13 October 1954, Foster Papers, Box 29. On arms deliveries see *NYT*, 30 November 1954.

55. *NYT*, 8 October 1954.

56. Sherman Adams, *Firsthand Report: The Story of the Eisenhower Administration* (New York: Harper Brothers, 1961), p. 128.

57. Eisenhower, *Mandate for Change*, p. 214.

58. *Wall Street Journal*, 1 and 2 December 1954. Dulles, though, did say a blockade might be a future possibility.

59. NORC, no. 365 (26 November 1954); *Special Report on American Opinion*, "Some Current Popular Attitudes on Far East Questions" (undated, early 1955), Foster Papers, Box 33; *Monthly Survey* 164 (December 1954), Foster Papers, Box 12.

60. *NYT*, 25 November 1954.

61. "Notes on a Conversation" with Walter S. Robertson, 22 January 1955, Koo Papers, Box 195.

62. A mid-March 1955 poll found 73 to 18 percent approval for Congress's actions on the joint resolution. See *Monthly Survey* 167 (March 1955), Foster Papers, Box 12; and NORC, no. 370. An Iowa poll in early February found 55 to 19 percent support for Congress's giving "President Eisenhower the authority to do whatever is necessary to defend Formosa against the Chinese Communists." See "Current Farmer Opinion on Formosa," 9 February 1955, Foster Papers, Box 33.

63. "U.S. Position on Red Chinese Offer to Families of Prisoners," *DSB* 32 (31 January 1955):192; "Department Not Issuing Passports for Visits to Communist China," *DSB* 32 (7 February 1955):214.

64. Alfred le sense Jenkins, "China and the Stakes in Asia," *DSB* 32 (3 January 1955):5.

65. Gallup poll, no. 544-K (27 March 1955). See also NORC poll (10 September 1954), no. 363. Less than "all out" support might "facilitate and encourage the bloody liquidation by the Chinese Communists of [the] free Chinese on Formosa," according to Dulles. See his speech in *American Foreign Policy: 1950-1955* (29 March 1954), p. 2378. See also *Monthly Survey* 167 (March 1955), Foster Papers, Box 12. This survey contains a poll that found a 46 to 34 percent margin in the general public against "working out a truce in the Formosa area, if it meant letting the Chinese Communists have the islands of Quemoy and Matsu which are near the mainland of China."

66. *Wall Street Journal*, 28 January 1955. This was written in the context of an item noting that a seventy-five-plane wing of the U.S. Air Force had just been rotated to Formosa.

67. *NYT*, 3 February 1955.

68. Kenneth T. Young, *Negotiating with the Chinese Communists: The United States Experience, 1953-1967* (New York: McGraw-Hill, 1968), pp. 41-44.

69. *NYT*, 2 February 1955. Among articles in this vein was Barbara Ward Jackson, "War Won't Solve the Formosa Crisis," *Look*, 3 May 1955, pp. 90-96.

70. Quoted in *Monthly Survey* 165 (January 1955), Foster Papers, Box 12.

71. *NYT*, 20 January 1955; *Public Papers, 1955*, p. 190. The president's remarks, in keeping with the practice of the time, were allowed to be quoted only indirectly in the press.

72. "Notes of a Conversation" with Dulles, 10 February 1955, Koo Papers, Box 195.

73. "Paper to Be Used in Conversation with Eden," 24 February 1955, Dulles Papers, Box 90.

74. He continued to push the hard line. Dulles, for instance, told the Advertising

Club of New York on 21 March 1955 that "the aggressive fanaticism of the Chinese Communist leaders presents a certain parallel to that of Hitler. Also, it contrasts to the past tactics of Soviet Communism." "Remarks to the Advertising Club of New York," 21 March 1955, Dulles Papers, Box 90.

75. *Wall Street Journal*, 1 February 1955.

76. *NYT*, 10 February 1955.

77. Ibid., 1 March 1955.

78. Ibid., 12 April 1955. Planning for a revival of the dormant group began as early as 2 February 1955. See Stanley D. Bacharach, *The Committee of One Million: China Lobby Politics, 1953-1971* (New York: Columbia University Press, 1976), p. 183.

79. The evidence on this point is somewhat unclear; see Bacharach, p. 108. While the group did not meet with Eisenhower, it is possible they did not seek such a gathering. This, of course, could also be a reflection of how they perceived the attitude of the White House.

80. O. Edmund Clubb, "Formosa and the Offshore Islands in American Policy, 1950-1955," *Political Science Quarterly* 74 (December 1959):517-531; *NYT*, 26 and 27 March 1955, 3 April 1955. The president, in mid-March, likely added to these tensions when in the course of a news conference he implied that tactical nuclear weapons might be employed against China if a large-scale conflict broke out in Asia. See J.H. Kalicki, *The Pattern of Sino-American Crisis: Political and Military Interactions in the 1950s* (New York: Cambridge University Press, 1975), pp. 149-151.

81. *Time*, 4 April 1955, p. 13.

82. Gallup poll, no. 546-K (1 May 1955).

83. Statement reprinted in Richard Moorsteen and Morton Abramowitz, *Remaking China Policy* (Cambridge, Mass.: Harvard University Press, 1971), p. 103. See also *NYT*, 25 April 1955, and *Selected Documents of the Bandung Conference* (New York: Institute of Pacific Relations, 1955).

84. "Chinese Communist Intentions in Formosa Area," *DSB* 32 (2 May 1955):738.

85. *Time*, 2 May 1955, p. 19. "Prior to Secretary Dulles' press conference, commentators viewed Chou['s] offer to negotiate with U.S. with a good deal of 'skepticism,' " noted State's 27 April 1955 "China Telegram," Foster Papers, Box 29.

86. *American Foreign Policy, 1950-1955*, p. 2501. Dulles explained his actions to a worried Koo on 5 May, telling him that "the United States had always hoped for a cease-fire in the Formosa Strait.... He did not know how sincere was the proposal made by Peiping's representative at Bandung to negotiate with the United States, but he wanted to learn the real meaning and purpose of Peiping in making such a proposal." "Notes of a Conversation" with John Foster Dulles, 5 May 1955, Koo Papers, Box 195.

87. *Monthly Survey* 163 (3 May 1955), Foster Papers, Box 12.

88. "Estimate of Prospect of Soviet Union Achieving Its Goals," Paper IV, 1 July 1955, Dulles Papers, Box 90.

89. *NYT*, 30 July 1955.

90. "Notes of a Conversation" with Walter S. Robertson, 5 May 1955, Koo Papers, Box 195; untitled cable from Robertson to Dulles (no date [1955]), DDRS, 1980, 402C; M. H. Halperin, "The 1958 Taiwan Straits Crisis: A Documented History" (Memorandum RM-49000-ISA, December 1966), DDRS, 1979, 26B. Halperin argues that Eisenhower never promised to defend Quemoy and Matsu if the Tachens were evacuated. He implies it was Dulles's idea and the president overruled it. However, the cable from Robertson to Dulles states that the "Gimo clearly understands President has *altered his*

earlier decision and will not use U.S. military forces in defense [of Quemoy and Matsu]." The United States instead began pressing Chiang to leave Quemoy and Matsu in exchange for the United States' interdicting the shipping of all war-related materials along the Chinese coast from Swatow to Wenchow. The Gimo, according to Robertson, "offered his humble apology for not being able to go along with proposal [to] give up Quemoy-Matsu which would be 'surrendered to Communists which would endanger support of overseas Chinese and his own people.' " See also Robertson's cable to Dulles (no date, 1955), DDRS, 1980, 402A.

91. *Monthly Survey* 164 (1 June 1955).
92. Gallup poll, no. 547-K (4 June 1955).
93. *NYT*, 6 May 1955.
94. Ibid.
95. Young, p. 54; *Monthly Survey* 171 (1 August 1955), Foster Papers, Box 12.
96. See *NYT*, 27 July 1955.
97. NORC poll, no. 376 (29 August 1955).
98. Comment by Dulles at 2 August news conference. See *DSB* 33 (15 August 1955), p. 262.
99. *U.S. News and World Report*, 15 July 1955, p. 10.
100. Young, p. 113.
101. *NYT*, 19 August 1955.
102. Robert B. Ekvall, *Faithful Echo* (New York: Twayne Publishers, 1960), p. 101.
103. *Monthly Survey* 173 (5 October 1955), Foster Papers, Box 12. Herbert Hoover, Jr., the under secretary of state, explained to Koo on 26 September 1955 that

he did not think it would be a wise policy for the United States to terminate these bilateral talks in Geneva now. It was the United States' intention to continue them until the Communists themselves saw the futility of going further with them and asked to stop them. In that event, the whole world would know that the responsibility for ending these talks rested with the Communists and not with the United States.

See "Notes of a Conversation," Koo Papers, Box 195. State also wanted to avoid any crisis at this time due to Eisenhower's heart attack, and thus felt it best to continue the talks. Robertson to Koo in ibid.

104. *NYT*, 11 September, 18 December 1955.
105. NORC poll, no. 382 (26 January 1956).
106. Norman A. Graebner, *The New Isolationism: A Study in Politics and Foreign Policy since 1950* (New York: The Ronald Press, 1956), p. 253.
107. *Newsweek*, 19 March 1956, p. 29.
108. *Monthly Survey* 185 (20 October 1956), Foster Papers, Box 12. China's admission to the United Nations was opposed in the planks of both parties, the Republicans promising to oppose such seating in order to uphold "international morality." See Dulles Papers, Democratic and Republican Platforms, Box 108.
109. NORC, no. 390 (26 June 1956). Dulles, though, is reported to have talked to his friend Dean Rusk (then at the Rockefeller Foundation) about how a change in relations—if it were to ever come—could be presented to the public. See Warren I. Cohen, *The American Secretaries of State and Their Diplomacy: Dean Rusk* (Totowa, N.J.: Cooper Square Publishers, 1980), p. 85.
110. John Gittings, *Survey of the Sino-Soviet Dispute: A Commentary and Extracts*

from the Recent Polemics, 1963-1967 (New York: Oxford University Press, 1968), p. 82.

111. Quoted in Congressional Quarterly, *China* (Washington, D.C.: Congressional Quarterly, 1980), p. 111. Green later toned down the nature of his remark. In October 1957 Dean Acheson also called for a review and revision of America's China policy since "Chiang Kai-shek is not going to live forever." See *The New Republic*, 21 October 1957, p. 6.

112. Dulles's news conference in *DSB* 36 (11 March 1957):405.

113. *Time*, 10 June 1957, p. 20. In September, 175 business leaders "counter-at-tacked" by making known their opposition to trade with Communist China. See *Monthly Survey* 196 (2 August 1957), Foster Papers, Box 13.

114. "China Telegram," 6 February 1957, Foster Papers, Box 30.

115. *Special Report on American Opinion*, "Popular Attitudes on Trade with Red China," 19 February 1957, Foster Papers, Box 33.

116. Examples of identical polls that showed opinion shifts include a January 1956 and a mid-March 1957 NORC poll: "As you may know, our government does not let American businessmen sell any such goods to Communist China now. Would you approve or disapprove of changing this to let Americans trade with Communist China, if such trade does not include war materials?" January 1956 opinion was 61 to 32 percent against such trade; March 1957 opinion showed 55 to 35 percent disapproval of this proposition. When the government's current policy was not mentioned, the public was about evenly split. This is shown by a July 1956 and a January 1957 NORC poll: "Now a question about Communist China. Would you approve or disapprove of Americans carrying on trade with Communist China, if this trade did not include war materials?" The July 1956 poll showed 55 to 40 percent disapproval of this proposition while the later poll showed only 47 to 46 percent disapproval. A 9 June 1957 Minnesota poll found residents of that state opposed trade by a 46 to 44 percent margin. A later, May 1958 survey in Oregon found 35 percent of the population in favor of easing the embargo. Polls by newspapers in Portland and San Francisco both showed majority support for trade. However, a 14 December 1957 Roper poll found the public opposed to any trade with the People's Republic of China by a 53 to 32 percent margin. This finding was almost opposite another (differently worded) NORC question asked in October 1955 which found 55 to 39 percent approved of trade, "if this trade does not include war materials." See *Monthly Survey* 174 (1 November 1955), Box 12; *Monthly Survey* 201 (3 January 1958), Box 113; "China Telegram," 13 May 1958, Box 30; "China Telegram," 27 May 1958, Box 30; *Special Report on American Opinion*, "Recent Popular Attitudes on Some Issues Relating to Communist China," 25 April 1956, Box 33; *Special Report on American Opinion*, "Popular Attitudes on Trade with Red China," 19 February 1957, Box 33; and *Special Report on American Opinion*, "Recent Public Opinion Polls on U.S. Relations with Red China," 3 April 1957, Box 33—all in Foster Papers. See also NORC nos. 340 (14 May 1953), 353 (9 March 1954), 372 (23 June 1955), 376 (29 September 1955), 390 (26 June 1956), 401 (28 December 1956), and 402 (18 March 1957).

117. John K. Fairbank, "China: Time for a Policy," *Atlantic Monthly*, April 1957, p. 35. Professor Edwin Reischauer also raised his voice, at this time, in advocacy of a new China policy.

118. Reinhold Niebuhr, "China and the United Nations," *Journal of International Affairs* 11 (May 1957):187-188.

119. *Monthly Survey* 199 (1 November 1957), Foster Papers, Box 13.

120. *Time*, 10 June 1957, p. 20.

121. Paul S. Holbo, *United States Policies toward China: From the Unequal Treaties to the Cultural Revolution* (Toronto: Collier-Macmillan, 1969), p. 94. Regarding newsmen, the State Department eased restrictions on journalists who wished to travel to China in August 1957—one year after the official Chinese offer. Dulles, however, explicitly ruled out granting reciprocal privileges to Chinese newsmen. While some professed to see progress toward better relations in this move (e.g., Richard P. Stebbins, *The United States in World Affairs, 1957* [New York: Harper and Bros., for the Council on Foreign Relations, 1958], p. 228), the Far East correspondent of the *Chicago Daily News*, Keyes Beech, cabled from Hong Kong that "in the opinion of the correspondent [here], the Dulles statement authorizing them [i.e., journalists] to travel to China was deliberately contrived to leave the Reds no choice but to refuse." See *Time*, 9 September 1957, pp. 89-90. State's hand also may have been forced by constant press criticism of its early blanket refusal to allow newsmen to travel to China. The 7 January 1957 *Time* (p. 65) reported that three journalists had entered China. Though the State Department did revoke their passports, its reaction was relatively mild since it "was not eager to start a war with the U.S. press on its right to gather news." In late December 1957, the United States also reversed its position on another issue, allowing the mothers of three Americans held in China to travel to see their sons. See *NYT*, 2 January 1958, and Foster Rhea Dulles, *American Policy toward Communist China* (New York: Thomas Y. Crowell Co., 1972), pp. 169-173.

122. *Public Papers, 1957* (28 June), p. 442. See also *Time*, 17 June 1957, p. 15, where Eisenhower is quoted as stating, "Frankly, I am of the school that believes that trade in the long run cannot be stopped. You are going to have either authorized trade or clandestine trade." Some of the impetus for this rhetorical shift arose from America's allies who were pressuring the United States to ease the Korean War trade restriction list. Rather than cause alliance problems (some countries already were taking unilateral steps), the United States acquiesced in this move while expressing great "disappointment." See Robert Boardman, *Britain and the People's Republic of China, 1949-74* (New York: Harper and Row, 1976), pp. 92-109. As early as 8 December 1955 Dulles was considering allowing the allies to trade with China, lest America's actions be divisive. See "The U.S. Position on China Trade Controls," Office of Naval Intelligence in Collaboration with the Politico-Military Policy Division, Office of the DCNO Plans and Policy (9 April 1956), DDRS, 1980, 366A. See also Stebbins, *The United States, 1957*, pp. 60-62.

123. Stebbins, *The United States, 1957*, p. 229. Such actions, State's *Monthly Survey* (198, 2 October 1957, Foster Papers, Box 13) stated in a similar vein, led a number of "observers to the conclusion that U.S. policy toward China has undergone some modifications. While agreeing that technically the United States has in no way modified its policy of non-recognition, some commentators see definite signs of a more 'flexible' attitude."

124. *Monthly Survey* 194 (3 June 1957), Foster Papers, Box 13.

125. Dulles's 9 January 1958 testimony in *Executive Sessions of the Senate Foreign Relations Committee Together with Joint Sessions with the Senate Armed Services Committee* (Historical Series, vol. X), 85th Cong., 2d Sess. (1958) (Washington, D.C.: U.S. Government Printing Office, 1981), pp. 5, 21.

126. *Executive Sessions* (Historical Series, vol. IX), 85th Cong., 1st Sess. (1957) (Washington, D.C.: U.S. Government Printing Office, 1979), pp. 415-416. Such a con-

cern likely also stood behind the 11 August 1958 public issuance of a harsh "guidance paper" sent to embassies. See "U.S. Policy on Nonrecognition of Communist China," State Department release, no. 459 (11 August 1958), reprinted in *DSB* 39 (8 September 1958):389.

127. Memo from Walter S. Robertson to John Foster Dulles, "Suggested Changes in Your Draft Speech on Communist China" (undated, 1957), Dulles Papers, Box 121.

128. *Time*, 8 July 1957, p. 9. Even this June speech, and the news conference that followed it, were seen as showing hints of flexibility by some members of the press. Dulles, for instance, stated that, "when it comes to having diplomatic and official relations with a regime . . . if any regime conducts itself respectably in the field of foreign affairs, then our attitude would be responsive to that." The secretary also noted, "Our policies are readily adjustable to meet the requirements of changing conditions. . . . But there are occasions when not we but others, should provide the change." See the *New Republic*, 15 July 1957, pp. 4-5.

129. *Time*, 10 June 1957, p. 20.

130. Gallup poll, no. 603-K (26 September 1958).

131. Halperin, pp. 113-114.

132. Reflective of these efforts were government statements such as Dulles's 4 September background briefing with newsmen and the president's 11 September speech. See "U.S. Reviews Chinese Communist Aggressive Actions in Taiwan Straits Area," *DSB* 39 (22 September 1958):445-447; "Communist Threat to Peace in Taiwan Area" (Eisenhower speech), *DSB* 39 (29 September 1958):481-484; "Secretary Dulles' News Conference of September 9," *DSB* 39 (29 September 1958):485-493; and Halperin.

133. The Trendex poll found defense of these islands favored by a 46 to 33 percent margin. See "China Telegram," 16 September 1958, Foster Papers, Box 31. The Iowa poll found 43 to 34 percent support for actively aiding the Nationalists, "after being reminded 'President Eisenhower has indicated [the] U.S. will help [the] Chinese Nationalists defend Quemoy and Matsu against Red China.' " See "China Telegram," 21 October 1958, Foster Papers, Box 31. A Gallup poll (no. 604-K, 26 September 1958) found that by a 91 to 6 percent margin the public favored working out a solution in the United Nations before "we get more involved in a military way in the fight over these two islands"; *Wall Street Journal*, 5, 7, and 8 September 1958.

134. The "China Telegram," 23 September 1958, Foster Papers, Box 31, reported that the State Department had received 626 letters in a recent week on the coastal islands (up from 138). "Of these, 322, individually written, expressed opposition to U.S. involvement, 73 favored giving U.S. help to Chiang and 65 urged UN solution of [the] crisis." See also *Monthly Survey* 210 (2 October 1958), Foster Papers, Box 13, where it is noted that State and congressional mail is "substantially opposed" to defending Quemoy and Matsu.

135. *NYT*, 26 October 1958.

136. Both quoted in *Time*, 13 October 1958, p. 16.

137. Dulles memo quoted in Halperin, "The 1958 Taiwan Straits Crisis . . . ," p. 102.

138. See, for example, ibid., pp. xiv, 232-234, 248-290, 391. This was largely the same attitude as had guided U.S. actions in the first Straits crisis, when it had more public support. See "Notes of a Conversation" with Walter S. Robertson, 5 May 1955, Koo Papers, Box 195. Robertson told the Nationalist ambassador that though he had doubts that the public favored "getting involved in war with Communist China on account of the Matsu and Quemoy islands," this would not be a great hindrance to action. "If

he [i.e., the President] should decide to join in the defense of the island in an emergency, public opinion in the United States would support it, and so would its [that is, America's] allies.''

139. Hungdah Chiu, "China, the United States and The Question of Taiwan," in *China and the Taiwan Issue*, ed. Hungdah Chiu (New York: Praeger Publishing, 1973), p. 171; Halperin, pp. v, vi, xi, 113-114. The use of atomic weapons against the mainland, if war broke out, evenly (42 to 41 percent in favor) divided the public according to Gallup poll, no. 604 (26 September 1958). Among other responses to this crisis, the United States put off a 55,000-man troop reduction in the armed forces.

140. *Monthly Survey* 212 (3 December 1958), Foster Papers, Box 13.

141. Young, p. 16.

142. Herter, on 22 May, also lifted the U.S. ban preventing Canadian trucks from carrying Chinese goods over U.S. highways. See *Far Eastern Economic Review* 26 (4 June 1959):774.

143. *Congressional Record* 105, 7, 86th Cong., 1st Sess. (21 May 1959), p. 8760. This change in legislative atmosphere was traced to the views of many new congressmen. The Tufty News Service asked the eighty-one newly elected members of the House "whether the U.S. should recognize Red China." Of the forty-five responding, sixteen said "yes," twenty said "no," and the rest gave "qualified answers" indicating approval of U.S. recognition under some circumstances. See "China Telegram," 22 December 1958, Foster Papers, Box 31. The Senate's "Conlon Report" on Asia was a further sign that Congress was willing to entertain new ideas over China. See "United States Foreign Policy in Asia," study no. 5, *United States Foreign Policy: Compilation of Studies*, 87th Cong., 1st Sess., Senate Document no. 24 (Washington, D.C.: U.S. Government Printing Office, 1961), pp. 391-551.

144. Evidence for a slight negative bias in public attitudes arises from the Minnesota poll. A 4 December 1960 poll found that Minnesotans were against allowing trade by a 54 to 35 percent margin. In August 1958 opening trade relations with the People's Republic of China was favored by a 49 to 37 percent margin. The 4 December 1960 poll also found a 10 percent increase (from 59 to 69 percent) in those opposed to the admission of China to the United Nations. (Nationwide, opinion on the Gallup UN question appeared stable between 1958 and 1961.) "Elite" opinion may not have participated in this slight downward drift. A poll the Foreign Policy Association took in 1960 among 4,600 persons in twenty-two states participating in its discussion program found a 47 to 31 percent margin of approval for "Peiping's UN entry if Peiping will make important concessions, such as a renunciation of the use of force." A similar plurality favored Peking's recognition, and 61 percent favored an independent Taiwan. These results, though, may have been affected by the wording of the questions and, as such, should be viewed cautiously. See "China Telegram," 19 April 1960, Foster Papers, Box 31.

145. *Special Report on American Opinion*, "Public Attitudes toward Communist China" (24 May 1960), Foster Papers, Box 33. This view also had some following in academic circles. See Robert C. North, "The Challenge of Communist China," World Politics 1 (October 1960):156-164, esp. p. 159.

146. W. W. Kulski, *The Soviet Union in World Affairs: A Documentary Analysis, 1964-1972* (Syracuse: Syracuse University Press, 1973), pp. 353-354. Kulski suggests that one reason for China's tougher diplomatic stand in this era was to deflect rising "two-Chinas" talk in foreign policy circles in the United States *and* the Soviet Union.

6

Opinion and Policy on China in the Democratic Sixties _____

The presidential election of 1960 was one of the closest in American history. Prior to the campaign, it was widely expected that November's key issues would cluster around foreign policy concerns.[1] Despite this expectation, though, America's China policy did not play a major role in the race. For a brief time Kennedy's advocacy of abandoning Quemoy and Matsu, in the televised debates with Nixon, did threaten to become a major issue. In later debates, however, Kennedy moved to a less-exposed limb and his position became largely indistinguishable from Nixon's more "pro-island" stance.[2] With the blurring of these differences, the islands, as *Time* put it, "float[ed] back out of the center of U.S. debate and back to their rightful place in ambiguity along the China coast."[3] Mr. Nixon's promise to veto China's UN membership garnered only scattered electoral applause, as both candidates made known their strong opposition to the mainland's admission to the world body until it "changes its aggressive policies."[4] The failure of the China debate to ignite sustained interest among the electorate led to speculation that the time was rapidly approaching when a rapprochement with the mainland could be attempted. With Kennedy's election this speculation grew, as it was known that Chester Bowles, a key advisor to the president-elect, favored such a course of action.[5] "Mr. Kennedy's election," John K. Fairbank told a Connecticut audience two weeks after the fact, "presumably marks the burial of the unreal and divisive issue of 'Who lost China?' "[6]

Kennedy's appointment of Adlai Stevenson as UN ambassador and Dean Rusk as secretary of state also seemed to augur well for a future bid to Peking. Rusk, it was reported, personally favored setting up *de facto* relations with the mainland until opinion could be brought around to accepting full diplomatic recognition.[7] Stevenson's hopes for a new Asian policy were a matter of public record due to a January 1960 article he had written for *Foreign Affairs*.[8] *"The general tendency"* among the press and public, reported State's *Monthly Survey*, *"is to anticipate a 'more flexible' United States posture [on China] during the Kennedy Administration."*[9] Contrary to expectations, though, the president was in no mood for any "spectacular" initiatives directed at China. Opinion shaped in the crucible of the Korean War, and hardened into place in the Eisenhower-Dulles years, would not "allow" such gestures so early in Kennedy's term. The president, if he was interested in these actions, would have to spend time preparing the public to accept them. Such moves, however, were ruled out both by political realities and by America's strategic policy. In the Kennedy years, the United States would continue its policy of firmness, though mixing it with more of an expressed willingness to accept China if she mended her ways. The change in the mainland's behavior, however, would have to come first. A continuing policy of toughness would not only deliver the final blow to the cracking Sino-Soviet alliance but would also make clear to Peking (and the American public) that containment remained a high priority for a Democratic White House pursuing a "counter-insurgency" foreign policy.[10] Only if Washington made China realize that its aggressiveness would be counter-productive would the mainland moderate its policies and be "persuaded that a peaceful existence with its neighbors represents the best hope for us all."[11] Kennedy, for the near future, though, was

not optimistic that the Chinese Communists [were] at all desirous of paying the price they would have to pay—at least in relaxing their aggressive intentions—by entering into harmonious relations with us or by meeting conditions for admission to the UN.[12]

The cause for this presidential pessimism lay in China's increasingly strident world posture, growing out of economic, ideological, and military concerns. This Chinese attitude, evident in the late 1950s, became more pronounced as the new decade began. China's "Hate America" week in the summer of 1960 was picked up by much of the press as a symbol of Peking's hostility to the West. Even respected liberal journals that advocated improved relations with the People's Republic, such as *The Christian Century*, believed that China

is the most dynamic, disruptive and dangerous force in world affairs.... Unlike Russia, China is led by men who believe that wars can be won. Some of China's leaders are reported to be prepared to sacrifice half their people if by doing so they could "win" a war, on the ground that theirs would still be the most populous nation on earth. Such a position may be insane, but unfortunately we have learned that a nation's policy cannot be ignored just because it is widely at variance with reality. Hitler taught us that particular lesson.[13]

With this image broadly accepted, the new president faced little media pressure to alter America's existing China policy. If anything, the opposite was true. Expressing a certain amount of chagrin, the *Baltimore Sun* observed along these lines that if the Maoist "doctrine" of intransigence and war "became the standard Communist line everywhere, the depressing result would be that Mr. Khrushchev, the hobgoglin of the American way of life, would be the man we would be rooting for.''[14] This widespread belief in Chinese inflexibility, while somewhat overstated, was not without a basis. "It is better," Peking informed its cadres early in 1961, "to maintain a frozen relationship between China and the United States, with a continued impasse for many years [than to compromise].''[15]

In spite of presidential reluctance, many of Kennedy's mid-level appointees hoped for a new beginning in United States China policy. To this end, State's Policy Planning Staff prepared a classified "think paper" outlining several low-level initiatives that could be pursued in East Asia.[16] The preparation of this paper was not out of line with opinion, as a February 1961 poll found a majority of persons favoring taking "steps to improve our relations with Communist China.''[17] As this paper germinated in State's bureaucracy, though, the president made clear to the secretary of state that he did not want to read in the press that any major policy shifts involving China were under way.[18] Some probing for signs of People's Republic of China moderation was acceptable, but any display of American flexibility would have to be minor and taken within the context of the overall harsh policy stance. As such, these small gestures were to have a dual nature. They were to be pursued as much to test Chinese diplomatic intentions as to backstop Washington's rigid stance. A magazine cover story on Dean Rusk in late 1961 stated this very simply: American "diplomatic flexibility toward Communist China [is] designed to win support from world opinion for a tough determination to contain Chinese expansionism even at the risk of war.''[19]

The March 1961 Warsaw meeting between ambassadors Beam and Wang Ping-nan shows the dual nature of American-Chinese contacts during the Kennedy years. The United States, testing the waters, placed proposals on the table designed to open American borders to People's Republic of China newsmen. Peking, however, refused to discuss these matters until the United States agreed to abandon Taiwan to its fate. This display of Chinese inflexibility was prominently played up by Washington as the president, playing to a skeptical audience, announced in ringing terms that "we are not prepared to surrender" to Red China. Observers congratulated the president on this stance, some arguing that this mainland action should conclusively end any talk of Sino-American détente.[20] This episode seems to have definitively proved to the president the need to maintain America's unyielding posture toward the mainland; signs of Chinese moderation did not yet exist. Discerning this, the *Wall Street Journal* wrote of Kennedy's first two months of foreign policy that "essentially what he is [now] following is the old Eisenhower-Dulles approach of firmness in dealing with the Communists.''[21]

Among the options mentioned in the PPS paper was an American initiative to establish relations with Mongolia. The idea behind this Bowles-inspired plan was to make clear that the United States could accommodate itself to well-behaved Asian communist states—hopefully the end result of American toughness toward China. Under Secretary Bowles was more successful in pushing this plan than he might otherwise have been, due to many top government officials being distracted by events in Berlin.[22] While it was unclear how Peking viewed this action, congressional critics of closer relations with the mainland suspected that what was "really meant by a U.S. mission in Outer Mongolia would be the thin edge of a wedge designed ultimately to push Red China into the United Nations."[23] This Capitol Hill interpretation was backed up by press reports, which speculated "that Mongolia will be recognized as a first step [in improving relations with China], that entry to the UN on politically impossible terms will [then] be offered to Peking, and that these two steps will constitute a 'softening up' of American public opinion" toward the People's Republic.[24]

When Kennedy did focus his attention on this gesture, he may have seen it in a different light. In 1960, the vote on delaying debate on the "Chirep" issue at the United Nations had been won by a bare margin. "Since the majority by which we have been able for ten years to bar Communist China has shrunk to eight nations," commented one weekly, "it now seems likely that China will enter next year."[25] Concern that Taiwan would lose its UN seat to Peking greatly troubled Kennedy. Betraying this worry, he told UN Ambassador Stevenson that Peking had to be kept out of the world body since "if Red China comes into the UN during our first year in town . . . they'll run us both out [of office]."[26] The Mongolian issue became a hostage to the "Chirep" politics. With journals warning of a coming "Far East Munich" in his term, prudence on People's Republic of China admission to the United Nations seemed the best course to follow for the first Democrat in the White House since the "loss" of China.[27] Kennedy believed, as *Business Week* did, that despite his election, "in American politics . . . there is perhaps no more complicated and emotional issue than the subject of Communist China."[28] If China were to enter the United Nations, even against U.S. opposition, this would necessitate a prior period of "softening" to gain the public's acceptance of this distasteful event. Time for persuasion would be needed, lest the "losing" administration face the possibility of electoral repercussions for Taipei's defeat. As the *New York News* warned, "Shadow boxing or half-heartedness on Stevenson's and the Government's part [at the United Nations] would be swiftly detected by most Americans and the Kennedy Administration would have to answer for it at the 1962 and '64 elections."[29]

Time, though, was just what the new president lacked. The "Chirep" vote was only months away, and altering opinion in that short a period—even if otherwise unopposed—was not a live possibility. Attempting to lead opinion over the short run on the "Chirep" question was always difficult for Washington, but for a Democrat—with liberal credentials—it would be next to impossible without incurring severe political damage. The United States also, after all, was opposed to China's UN admission; to act otherwise would reward its intransigence.[30] More importantly, though, the "China Lobby" would not let such a "softening" period pass unchallenged. State's *Monthly Survey* focusing on June pointed this out by noting that

an *intensive effort* was launched this month to mobilize American opinion against the reported "new US approach" to the China problem by sources which are opposed to a change in the status quo. Spearheading the drive were many prominent Republicans. Former Vice President Nixon called upon President Kennedy to "shoot down" the "trial balloon suggesting two Chinas in the UN."[31]

Nor, if he had wanted, could Kennedy have solely attended to altering opinion on China. Seeming U.S. retreats on Cuba and Laos, and "embarrassments" in Berlin, the Congo, and Vienna and on nuclear arms testing, made it imperative for the young president to show resolve on other issues. With the widespread *"mood of concern* about the course of U.S. foreign policy in the wake of a series of 'defeats' for the U.S. and 'triumphs' for the Russians," the president could not lightly afford to expend his resources aggravating this overall impression by favoring People's Republic of China entrance into the United Nations.[32] This was especially the case as many journalists hammered home the theme that "what action is taken [in foreign policy] appears to be in the direction of making concessions" to our Communist enemies.[33]

It seems likely that, throughout 1961, Washington's actions toward the Far East were affected by an opinion profile it had not helped to shape.[34] The feint toward Mongolia would not only serve to "soften" this opinion profile but, more importantly, would provide the administration with leverage over the Nationalists, who were sending a high-level delegation to Washington in late July. Washington needed this leverage as Nationalist China seemed bent on its own destruction at the United Nations—a destruction, the White House expected, for which it would ultimately be blamed. In order to prevent the Nationalist ouster, America needed the votes of a substantial number of African states. These nations were determined that newly independent Mauritania be admitted to the world organization. The Soviet Union, however, made it clear it would veto this membership bid unless Mongolia was also inducted into the "community of nations." Taipei, considering Mongolia both a lost province and a Soviet puppet, refused to accept this demand, setting the stage for the needed African votes to line up against it in retaliation. At the July and August meetings Washington, in effect, would seek to keep Taiwan from committing diplomatic suicide. The White House would do this as it still opposed entrance of a hostile China into the United Nations and because it expected the suicide to be ruled—in the press and public—a murder by its own hands.

Some in the administration, though, advocated not "trading" with the Nationalists during their Washington stay, but moving in a more direct manner to save Taipei's seat. Ambassador Stevenson, for example, favored undertaking a campaign designed to end with both Chinas in the United Nations. With the support of Harlan Cleveland, the assistant secretary for international organizations, Stevenson presented his plan to the president arguing that it would both ease tensions in the Far East and allow Taiwan to retain a degree of international legitimacy. He suggested promulgating the line that

The reason why the U.S. Government is considering a change of strategy on the Chinese representation question in the UN is that we face probable defeat on the moratorium if it is pursued at the coming 16th General Assembly. In light of this, we have been considering the best strategy to protect our interests and those of Nationalist China.... We want to avoid in particular the real possibility of a replacement of Nationalist China by Communist China in the UN.... No decision has been taken. However, the best strategy would appear to be to insist upon the continued membership of Nationalist China while providing for the possible concurrent representation and membership of Communist China.[35]

The president, adept at reading political trends, told Stevenson that his plan would be acceptable only if Taipei and Capitol Hill went along with it. These conditions were, of course, impossible to fulfill. While Kennedy was opposed to allowing a belligerent China into the United Nations, he would likely have been more receptive to his ambassador's idea (as a way of guaranteeing Taipei's representation) had he not feared a domestic political backlash. He did not wish to be perceived as the second Democrat in as many tries to "lose" China. "Even the possibility that the U.S. might back a proposal at the UN which would contemplate Red China's membership, without jeopardizing free China's," wrote State's analysts in early July, "has set off a chorus of disapproval" in the press and public.[36] In what must have been a particularly pointed blow at Adlai Stevenson's notion, the entire Illinois Republican House delegation, as well as Chicago's *News*, *Sun Times*, and *Tribune* newspapers, came out in opposition to any hint of such a plan.

Conditioning Stevenson's notion on Taipei's approval did kill the "two Chinas" idea. That the president did not consider this "tactic" possible from a domestic standpoint comes through in his reaction to a suggestion floated by Secretary of State Rusk in late May. Rusk suggested telling the Nationalists that they would definitely lose their seat if they did not accept a "two Chinas" track at the United Nations. To the president this plan was a non-starter. Its rationale, in any case, was quickly undercut by Kennedy himself when he secretly, in early August, agreed to veto Peking's membership in the world body if necessary. The United States also consented to Nationalist requests to drop its pre-diplomatic contacts with Mongolia. In exchange for these actions, Taipei agreed not to veto its former province's membership in the United Nations.[37] Kennedy, according to McGeorge Bundy, who tried to talk him out of the veto guarantee, explained his move in terms of domestic pressures. Without sufficient time to bring the public around to accepting Peking in the United Nations, he felt he would be forced by political considerations to veto the mainland's membership. Given this situation, the president felt he might as well agree to this step before his hand was forced, and "bank some capital with Chiang."[38] Kennedy's perception of the domestic problems he might encounter if he acted differently was shared by others. Appearing on ABC's "Issues and Answers" at the end of July, Senator Fulbright lamented that because of the emotionalism engendered by the China question, the "President has no freedom of action."[39]

Kennedy, though, was not anxious to cast America's first veto in the face of world opinion. Judging its "moratorium" strategy no longer viable, the United States sought to delay the "Chirep" debate further by assigning the problem to an international study commission. When this procedure failed to garner much support from either side of the aisle, Stevenson moved to advocacy of the "important question" procedure Dulles had spoken of seven years earlier. Now firmly set in its opposition to Peking's membership, Washington increasingly noted that it had "not seen any evidence as yet that the Chinese Communists wish to live in comity with us." Given this line, it is not surprising that Kennedy brushed off an October call by the Chinese for stepped-up contacts.[40] A little more than a week later, on 19 October, in a statement many found "highly gratifying," the president announced that "the United States has always considered the Republic of China the only rightful government representing China and . . . therefore firmly opposes the entry of the Chinese Communists into the UN or any of its components."[41] In disgust, "TRB" commented in the *New Republic* that Kennedy "has just reaffirmed the old orthodox Dulles dogma. . . . His position is not any better, so far as we can see, than Eisenhower's before him."[42]

In his reading of opinion as being solidly opposed to Communist China's UN admission Kennedy was correct. A late-September Gallup poll found such an event opposed by a 65 to 18 percent margin in the general public.[43] Less rigorous survey efforts generally found comparable results.[44] Except for a few voices in the wilderness, most of the press also cleaved to this view (see table 4). Perhaps the best evidence of a public trend against moderating America's opposition to the People's Republic of China at the United Nations is found in Gallup's question inquiring whether America should go along with a majority vote on the "Chirep" issue. Between mid-February and late-September 1961 support for accepting "majority rule" on China's UN admission fell from 59 to 46 percent of the public, while opposition to this rose from 25 to 38 percent. This negative preference shift appears to have occurred independently of the executive's actions, as publicly Washington had yet to announce its tactics on this problem. While it is difficult to conclusively say that opinion led policy (since policy changed prior to the September poll), a close examination of events seems to strongly suggest this. With opinion actively trending against China in this "tactical" area, and other polls indicating very hostile feelings toward the People's Republic of China, the government appears to have allowed its actions at the United Nations to be influenced by the public.[45]

The president in 1962, despite America's UN win and an upswing in public confidence over the administration's handling of overall foreign policy, remained hesitant in adopting the China policy innovations suggested by his bureaucracy. Kennedy held steady to his view that any policy alterations would have to be preceded by signs of Chinese moderation. Only if this occurred could the public be expected to fully accept new policy initiatives. Aggression, as the outbreak of World War II had proved to the American people, was not to be rewarded. This moderation would likely follow a Sino-Soviet split, and as the strains in

TABLE 4

PRESS OPINION ON SEATING CHINA IN THE UN
IN KENNEDY's FIRST YEAR

(a) Opposed to PRC Admission

America
Birmingham News
Boise Statesman
Buffalo News
Burlington Free Press
Catholic Men
Charleston (S.C.) News
Chicago American
Chicago News
Chicago Sun-Times
Chicago Tribune
Cincinnati Enquirer
Cleveland Plain Dealer
Columbus (Ohio) Dispatch
Dallas News
Detroit Free Press
Ft. Worth Star-Telegram
Hearst Newspapers
Houston Chronicle
Houston Post
Human Events
Indianapolis Star
Life

Los Angeles Times
Manchester Union Leader
Memphis Commercial Appeal
Milwaukee Journal
Nashville Banner
National Review
Newark News
New Orleans Times-Picayune
New York News
New York Times
Oakland Tribune
Portland Oregonian
Richmond Times Dispatch
St. Louis Globe-Democrat
Salt Lake City Desert News
San Diego Union
Saturday Evening Post
Savannah Press
U.S. News and World Report
Wall Street Journal
Wichita Eagle
Wilmington News

(b) Advocates of PRC UN Admission, "Two China" Policy

Charlotte Observer
Commonwealth
Dayton News
Denver Post
Des Moines Register
Honolulu's Star-Bulletin
Louisville Courier-Journal

New Republic
New York Post
Providence Journal
St. Louis Post-Dispatch
San Francisco Chronicle
Worcester Telegram

Source: Special Report on American Opinion: "Public
Attitudes during 1961 on Seating Red China in
the UN," 21 September 1961, Foster Papers,
Box 33.

Note: List refers only to those with explicitly
defined editorial policy. List is meant to be
representative, not exhaustive.

the communist bloc became increasingly visible, little reason existed to prematurely abandon Washington's "splitting" policy. The United States, though, did increasingly make known its willingness to be flexible in dealing with a restrained China. This occurred since Washington did

> not know what inner battles may be going on now and may occur in the future within the Chinese Communist leadership: Internal and external difficulties must surely be breeding differences within that leadership. Evidence that the U.S. would be willing to play a part in moving our relationship away from one of implacable mutual hostility might strengthen the hand of any elements which may favor doing so, now or later.[46]

While China never showed Kennedy the moderation he was looking for, administration statements of flexibility did have the effect of undermining the most rigid assumptions upon which much of the public based their views. Over the short term this had little effect on opinion, though it made more rapid attitude change possible in later years.

Short-term opinion and policy toward the People's Republic of China, however, remained very negative. This occurred despite the increasing bureaucratic clamor for change. Some of this underlying bureaucratic pressure grew out of W. Averell Harriman's appointment as head of State's Far Eastern Bureau in the course of Kennedy's November 1961 "Thanksgiving Day Massacre." Harriman, upon taking up his post, set up a separate desk to deal with "Mainland Chinese Affairs." This seemed to bear out Ted Lewis's prediction in the Boston *Herald* that the "naming of Averell Harriman unquestionably is a blow to Chiang Kai-shek."[47] This was the case, as Harriman's move helped to end the organizational subjugation of Washington-Peking relations to Washington-Taipei contacts.[48] Relations with the mainland could now, at least in their formative stages, be considered separately from the impact they would have on Taiwan.

With many members of his bureaucracy advocating gestures of reconciliation, and yet interested in keeping it clear to the Chinese that no basic changes in policy would occur unless they first moderated, the president cautiously approached his initial 1962 policy decision on China. Reports of severe food shortages on the mainland raised the sensitive question of whether American grain should be sent to combat hunger among the Chinese. The Kennedy Administration, keeping its liberal credentials in order, hinted that wheat shipments to China might be allowed—a move opposed by much of the press as "feeding the mouth that's biting you" and splitting the public into a close 48 to 43 percent plurality favoring such an action.[49] Government documents warned that the Chinese would not accept an American gift, yet when Kennedy's hint of food shipments did come, he was clear to frame it in such terms.[50] This hint was strongly rejected by the Chinese on 29 May. The American position in this matter, Dick Wilson wrote, seemed to be "that if China does need U.S. grain she should ask, as it were, on bended knee and accept it as aid—with each sack or crate clearly labelled 'from Uncle Sam.' "[51] The United States, in other words, would only aid, not trade with, the Chinese communist enemy. Trade was an international privilege—to be accorded to states lacking in external aggressive characteristics. For this reason, Washington refused to allow the International Trading Corporation of Seattle to export 10.5 million tons of grain to China and North Korea in the course of a three-year contract.[52] Kennedy's actions did show an interest in eventually improving relations with the mainland, but they also showed a barely concealed refusal to deal with a regime that acted like Peking's.

Complicating Chinese perceptions of the grain maneuvers in Washington were events occurring in Taiwan. Since March the Nationalists had verbally and logistically been preparing to begin their long-promised "final counter-offensive." The Nationalists, viewing this as perhaps their last chance, conscripted extra men into their army and updated their battle plans. Taipei hoped to establish a beachhead on the mainland and then await a general uprising among the economically hard pressed mainland population. While most of Washington was skeptical over this plan's chances for success—memories of the Bay of Pigs fiasco had yet to fade—certain officials were cautious lest an important opportunity be lost. Among these was the CIA station chief in Taipei who flew back to Washington to argue that China's invasion scenario deserved large-scale covert U.S. support.[53]

The very minor positive signals emanating from Washington at this time (such as talk of food aid) were "credibly contradicted by [this] evidence from Taiwan of preparations for invasion, presumably with the support of Washington."[54] Peking's nerves had been especially frayed by the early 1962 visits of Harriman and former CIA Director Allen Dulles to Taiwan. Though they had come to Taipei to discourage invasion sentiments, Peking apparently did not read the visits in that manner since Nationalist "counter-attack" preparations continued. Similarly, the appointment of Admiral Alan G. Kirk as America's ambassador to Taiwan caused a rise in mainland concern. One of Kirk's first tasks was to convince the Nationalists that an invasion would be suicidal. The admiral was well suited for this, having been heavily involved in amphibious warfare during the Second World War. It was just this expertise, though, that caused temperatures to rise in Peking. By early June these fears had been translated into a half million PLA troops deployed in the coastal regions facing Formosa. This, in turn, raised fears in Washington that these forces would eventually assume an offensive posture. "As time goes on and the extraordinary Chinese Communist military buildup continues," reads the president's 19 June Intelligence Checklist, "our confidence in the assessment that this movement is primarily defensive in purpose is dwindling."[55]

Concurrent with these "Straits events," tensions were also increasing on China's other borders. The Sino-Indian frontier dispute was becoming more serious with each passing day. Given past U.S. involvement with Tibetan rebels, it would not have been implausible for China to have linked these threats together. The "Chinese Communists," wrote the vice president's special assistant in recognition of this possibility, expect their greatest foes, i.e., Nationalist China, India and the United States, to attempt to take advantage of some of China's internal difficulties as well as their quarrel with the Soviet Union. The Communists are convinced that the U.S. will support any overt action by India or Nationalist China because of the conviction that no major effort would succeed without U.S. support.[56]

Indeed, there is some evidence that Colonel Burris was correct in this determination. Vice Premier Ch'en Yi, in the course of his 29 May "wheat rejection," stated that "the Pentagon generals . . . may support Chiang Kai-shek in starting a 'counter-offensive on the mainland.' . . . Or they may be planning to raise trouble on the western border of China by utilizing the China-India border dispute."[57]

At about this same moment, the fragile, year-old Laotian truce was also in the process of breaking down, leading to an increase in U.S. forces along China's periphery in Thailand and in the Gulf of Siam. Adding to Peking's concerns was further trouble along its northwestern border with Russia. There was apparently a large-scale Soviet attempt at subversion in Sinkiang Province at this juncture which escalated into an armed border clash.[58] Chinese fears thus may have been escalated by a belief that it now faced two major colluding adversaries in the world. Harrison E. Salisbury, writing in the *New York Times Magazine* two years earlier, highlighted the fact that China's fears were not completely irrational, suggesting then that "the time is not far distant when America and Russia might settle their differences in order to meet the common threat of China."[59]

Fear of war in the Straits area began to dissipate only when each side made its intentions clear at the 23 June Warsaw meeting. Four days later, Kennedy publicly reiterated America's non-aggressive posture at a news conference. In response to a questioner, the president "emphasized the defensive nature of our arrangement" with Taipei.[60] The lack of any major American build-up in the region, such as had accompanied the 1958 crisis, seems to have convinced Peking of the veracity of the president's words.[61] Washington's secural of Chiang's agreement to adopt a more peaceful overall military posture following this crisis also renewed talk in the press of the "reality" of two Chinas. Another assumption of the American right was being newly assaulted. It should be noted, though, that Chiang's acquiescence may have had a price—increased U.S. support for covert activities directed at the "other" China.[62]

The administration's handling of this third Straits crisis was well received. Before it could take too many bows, though, the long-simmering conflict between China and India broke into the open. Skirmishes along the disputed border regions began on 21 July, with large-scale fighting starting on 20 October. This outbreak of war boosted administration advocates of a continuing tough policy by serving to silence many of those officials who had been arguing that China's caustic rhetoric was belied by her more cautious actions. Though deserving of its share of guilt in the incident, India was not perceived in this way and received extensive

American aid. This aid, the president told a willing public, was "for the purpose of defeating Chinese Communist subversion" on the subcontinent.[63]

These events served to exacerbate Washington's already strong suspicions about China's commitment to peace. As early as 1 February 1961 Kennedy had publicly expressed fear over China's future military strength.[64] This official concern, already evident in the late 1950s, continued to grow as Peking's efforts to become a nuclear power moved ominously closer to success. The press, leaning this way for some time, definitely adopted this government-held view following the Cuban missile crisis as Soviet behavior seemed to moderate but Chinese actions and rhetoric did not. By late 1962, Oscar Gass, writing in *Commentary*, could present the issue in its starkest terms. Gass predicted that

as the 20th Century moves toward the 21st, the long-range missiles will probably come into range of Chinese production. Then, if not by stupidity or mischance sooner, the United States will have with China a great nuclear war unless far-reaching accommodations have been worked out. . . . And we cannot be confident that these changes will occur.[65]

These concerns seem to have affected the public as well. In an almost complete reversal from 1961, a March 1963 poll found that a 47 to 34 percent plurality of the American public considered China to be a greater threat to world peace than the Soviet Union.[66] Opinion had precluded any real changes in policy early in Kennedy's term and, having spurred on a tougher government stance, was now, in turn, being affected by it. Kennedy summed up the fears now afflicting the public when he told the nation in August 1963 that a China in the future which would have "700 million people, a Stalinist internal regime, nuclear powers, and a great determination of war as a means of bringing about its ultimate success, would be potentially a more dangerous foe than any we [have] faced since the end of the Second World War."[67] While such a view argued for American resolve, public acceptance that in the not-too-distant future American territory could be within range of Chinese nuclear weapons seemed to deny the legitimacy (and even sanity) of the conservative assumption that total isolation of Communist China was the best policy to follow for all times. Again, even with opinion and policy both trending in a negative direction, the march of events—and Washington's aboveboard interest in contacts with a moderate, if still communist, China—seemed to be undercutting the assumptions on which the public's negative attitudes were built.

In spite of these weakening assumptions, policy continued to be guided by the harsh rationale prominent since Kennedy's first year. An added impetus to this was the post missile crisis thaw in Soviet-American relations. American pressure had helped split the Sino-Soviet alliance, ending the need for "scolding" pressure on Peking, but it was now apparently the Russians, and not the Chinese, who were moving closer to the United States. Lest this tentative movement be derailed, several bureaucratically promoted China "trial balloons" were shot down.[68] With Russian and American relations warming, however, Chinese fears of encirclement were heightened. This led to an even more strident rhetorical posture that, with Washington's help, only served to heighten the public's negative impression of China. Peking's open verbal attacks on the Limited Test Ban treaty and its rejection of calls for disarmament talks were, perhaps, the final straws in causing the United States to view China as the predominant threat in the world. By mid-1963 Washington was also becoming greatly occupied with problems in Vietnam. These difficulties were increasingly laid on China's doorstep in public announcements. The press, too, saw China's policies as designed to increase tensions in the world—tensions the "misanthropic and hopeless Chinese Communist leaders" hoped would lead to a new world war.[69] Mao, pictured as a man calling for "worldwide racial war," was described as showing "a degree of hatred and desperation which can only be described as psychotic."[70] Perceptions such as these, ultimately traceable to both real (and imagined) fears in Washington and the White House's increasing need to build support for America's Southeast Asian policy, led the public to view the mainland in a very negative light.

The widening gulf between China and the Soviet Union was, as implied, presented to the American people in terms relatively favorable to the "moderate" men in the Kremlin. The struggle for dominance in the communist world, if won by Peking, was argued to augur poorly for world peace. "We would," John Kennedy told a December 1962 television audience, "be far worse off— the world would be—if the Chinese dominated the Communist movement, because they believe in war as a means of bringing about the Communist world."[71] (To this the *Washington Post* responded that Kennedy has now "put the administration on record by noting the Sino-Soviet rivalry and stating our preferences for the 'Khrushchev view.' ").[72] An example of this Chinese "belief system," it was argued, was the conflict in Vietnam; Washington would have to meet this expansionist Communist Chinese challenge with renewed resolve. Reflective of this American "mind-set" was an August 1963 decision to withhold a $4.3 million loan to Pakistan for improvements to Dacca airport as a protest against the scheduled initiation of flights from there to Peking. This move was reaffirmed in early January 1964 at the same time the United States was trying to undercut the international impact of France's recognition of the People's Republic.[73]

America's hostility toward Peking was, in some ways, balanced by Washington's continued statement of its conditions for Chinese entrance into the family of nations. On 14 November 1963, for example, Kennedy told what would be his last news conference that "when the Red Chinese indicate a desire to live at peace with the United States, with other countries surrounding it, then quite obviously the United States would reappraise its policies. We are not wedded to a policy of hostility to Red China."[74] A number of Kennedy confidants have suggested that new initiatives toward China were planned by the president for his second term, when any political damage arising from them could presumably be minimized.[75] While the logic of events may have precluded these future actions, clearly State's Far Eastern Bureau was hopefully looking forward to this occurrence. In their own way, these mid-level officials continued to lobby for policy changes and took some minor actions—such as telling a group of San Francisco businessmen that they could meet with People's Republic of China officials in Hong Kong—when appropriate. The Far Eastern Bureau's allies in this project included the *New York Times* (under more liberal editorial control since 1961) and Edwin P. Neiland, president of the U.S. Chamber of Commerce, both of whom advocated the opening of trade relations with the mainland.[76]

Roger Hilsman's 13 December 1963 San Francisco speech, calling for eventual reconciliation with Peking (perhaps on a two-Chinas basis), reflected this bureaucratic fermentation. Hilsman, then assistant secretary of state for Far Eastern Affairs, made explicit what had long been implicit in U.S. policy—that there was "no reason to believe that there is a present likelihood that the Communist regime will be overthrown."[77] The press response to this speech was generally enthusiastic; of twenty-one editorials focusing on the subject, State found that fifteen praised the speech (with three attacking it from the left and three from the right). Drew Pearson hailed Hilsman's words as "an amazing step on the thousand mile journey toward peace." Perceptively, though, the *Washington Post* saw little, other than rhetoric, new in the address and its statement that American policy was one of "strength and firmness and readiness to negotiate."[78] This had been U.S. policy since at least 1961 and represented only an evolutionary advancement over the policy Dulles followed in his last years. Writing to Adlai Stevenson on 19 December to explain his speech, Hilsman acknowledged that there had been "no new departure" in policy. His speech was made in order to clarify to the American people, and our allies and adversaries abroad, Washington's stance toward China—and of the possibilities for its change. The Kennedy Administration's policy was laid bare as Hilsman discussed another "cause" of the speech:

There was a need to clarify the reasons for the apparent divergence between U.S. treatment of Moscow and U.S. treatment of Peiping. As the Soviets have begun to behave more responsibly, the U.S. has become more responsive to Soviet initiatives; but with Peiping continuing to hew to a bellicose Stalinist line, we have been unresponsive to the Chinese. This apparent divergence stems from a consistent policy of firmness and flexibility, as applied to regimes whose behavior currently differs.[79]

While there was some expectation that Hilsman's speech would be followed up by new initiatives toward China, this did not turn out to be the case. His explanation to Stevenson makes clear that, failing a sudden outbreak of moderation in Peking, little could be expected in this direction. Indeed, it was reported that Hilsman's pronouncement was "followed by strenuous efforts to reassure America's 'old line' allies in Taipei, Saigon, Bangkok and elsewhere that there is no change in Washington's policy toward China."[80] In addition to strategic factors, personal and political reasons also played a role in the lack of movement on China policy that came to characterize 1964. Lyndon Johnson, moving to consolidate his power, faced a rising electoral challenge from the right. He was, given this, in no (political) position to undertake conciliatory gestures involving the mainland. LBJ wanted his own presidency and the best way to guarantee this was to "play from strength, not from weakness; domestic policy was strength, foreign policy was weakness."[81] A low profile in international affairs was called for.

This profile was especially necessary given the rising difficulties in Vietnam. When China was mentioned, it was in terms Rusk had been promulgating since mid-1963. China was an aggressive and expansionist communist state. It was necessary to stand up to China if we ever hoped to moderate its behavior. Firmness had to precede flexibility; otherwise China would learn the wrong lesson from its "appeasement."[82] The harsh rhetoric of the Democrats over the last few years (initially set off by the public outcry against Peking's UN membership bid in 1961), as well as China's own actions, led to a popular view of China even more negative than that which had existed in the late 1950s. An American Institute of Public Opinion (AIPO, the Gallup organization) poll released in February 1964, for example, discovered that support for China's admission to the United Nations had fallen to levels of a decade earlier.[83] Similarly, a June Harris poll found Peking's membership in the world body opposed by a seven-to-one margin.[84] A May Gallup query further showed that 56 percent of the public now agreed that the People's Republic of China was the chief danger to lasting world peace, up 9 percent from the previous March.[85] Opinion was so negative toward China that even when the admission question was phrased so as to posit presidential support a May-June Survey Research Center (SRC) poll reported that China's entrance into the United Nations was still opposed by a 53 to 31 percent gap among those aware of the mainland's communist type of government.[86] Some in Washington, however, perceived in these SRC results the hint of a public "willingness to follow some Presidential suggestions concerning China."[87] The fact that even 31 percent would be amenable to People's Republic of China UN admission (and a 54 to 31 percent majority to People's Republic of China recognition if recommended by the president) seemed to substantiate the feeling that old assumptions about China were evolving, masked for the time being by a surface hostility responsive to current government promptings.

These changing assumptions did not preclude a jaundiced view of China. Indeed, such an opinion situation largely reflected the administration's view: We could deal with a moderate China in the future, but for now we had to redouble our efforts against the current "misanthropic" regime. With the mainland conceded to be a threat to world peace there was, not surprisingly, an acceleration of the trend viewing Peking as an enemy of both the United States and Russia. The war in Vietnam was underwritten by China not only in opposition to the United States but also in defiance of Moscow's more conciliatory policies. Vietnam, administration sources argued, was an area where Peking sought to vindicate its "views" in the worldwide ideological struggle, thus embarrassing the

Russians.[88] By 1964 Sino-Soviet polemics, as filtered through Washington and the American press, seemed so vitriolic that more Americans expected the Chinese to use their weapons against their northern neighbor than against the United States.[89] This trend toward seeing China as America's and Russia's number one enemy would accelerate in the years of peak involvement in Vietnam (see figure 1)—a war largely fought to contain the spread of Chinese communism. *News-week*, in a late-1965 cover story, captured this feeling when it reported that "In recent years, as U.S. relations with Russia have eased, Communist China has increasingly come to occupy the international devil figure in the minds of millions of Americans."[90]

An important contributing factor to this "devil" image was China's 16 October 1964 detonation of its long-feared atomic bomb. Secretary Rusk, seeking to defuse any possible panic, had announced that a blast was imminent less than three weeks earlier.[91] This advance knowledge allowed Washington to react to the explosion with an outward calm that belied its inner sense of concern. "No matter what the truth is about Red China's comparative nuclear strength, this event is awesome," a State Department official let slip a few days prior to the explosion.[92] China, it was feared, would now become more assertive in world affairs. Even worse, Gass's prophecy seemed to be one giant step closer to fulfillment. This was certainly the fear in Washington as a 15 September meeting of Rusk, McNamara, McCone, McGeorge Bundy, and the president determined to approach the Russians over the growing Chinese nuclear potential. "We believe," Bundy summarized,

that there are many possibilities for joint action with the Soviet Government if that Government is interested. Such possibilities include a warning to the Chinese against tests, a possible undertaking to give up underground testing and to hold the Chinese accountable if they test in any way, and even a possible agreement to cooperate in preventive military action. We therefore agreed that it would be most desirable for the Secretary of State to explore this matter very privately with Ambassador Dobrynin as soon as possible.[93]

Any discussions with the Russians, though, were cut short as Khrushchev's fall from power was announced on the same day as the Lop Nor test. This October day, the *Christian Century* commented, was "a momentous one ... in world history."[94] The U.S. government continued to downplay the dangers arising from these international events, though Johnson did acknowledge, on a campaign swing through Ohio, that "in the last twenty-four hours the world has changed."[95]

Opinion polls quickly reflected public concern over this latest "nuclear" turn of events. Gallup, in a survey conducted on the heels of the People's Republic of China blast, found that opinion had, in a sense, flip-flopped and was now the most favorably disposed (though still heavily opposed) to China's being in the United Nations since Gallup's American Institute of Public Opinion began asking

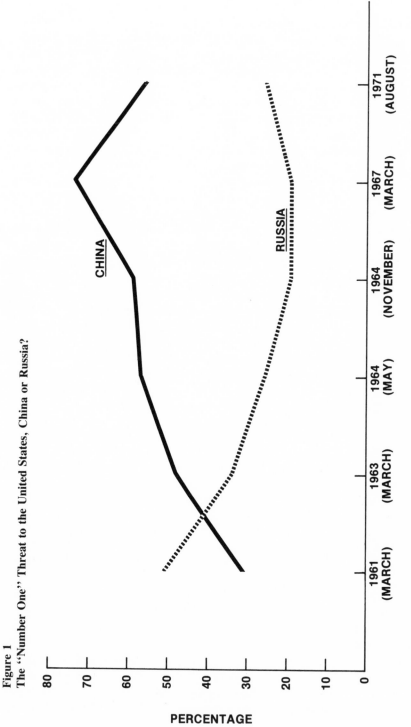

Figure 1
The "Number One" Threat to the United States, China or Russia?

CHINA

RUSSIA

PERCENTAGE

80 70 60 50 40 30 20 10 0

1961
(MARCH)

1963
(MARCH)

1964
(MAY)

1964
(NOVEMBER)

1967
(MARCH)

1971
(AUGUST)

Sources: *Opinion Index*, No. 76 (October 1971); Gallup polls, various years.

this question in 1954.[96] The Harris organization discovered that this was no fluke; a survey released at the end of November showed that those favoring People's Republic of China admission had risen 15 percent since June, while those opposed to such a move had fallen 17 percent.[97] Concern with Chinese intentions also came through in polls which now found three-to-one margins believing China would "turn out to be a greater threat to the U.S." than was the Soviet Union.[98] These polls reflect the fact that for "all the relative calm that greeted China's first step toward becoming a nuclear power, the American people could not entirely escape a new sense of foreboding."[99] This new sense of concern, State's opinion analysts noted, served to set into motion a "growing feeling" that there would have to be greater Sino-American contacts.[100] Though the majority still held China in disregard, it was increasingly accepted that reality demanded a heightened willingness to negotiate with Peking.

In spite of these post-bomb opinion bounces, American policy did not moderate. Given the logic behind U.S. actions in the Far East, this was not at all surprising. Washington contemptuously rejected China's call for a disarmament conference as a "sucker proposal" and went on to add, "We've seen very little [real] interest on the part of Peking in disarmament."[101] Two months after the detonation, in a further show of resolve, Washington stationed the first of seven planned ballistic missile subs off the Chinese coast.[102] However, the "China Cloud," as noted, had had an important impact on the American people. Many began to call for a more equal mixture of "firmness and flexibility" in U.S. policy. State's review of attitudes on China in 1964 confirmed that

the concept of "more open windows" between the peoples of Communist China and the peoples of the Western nations, to which President Kennedy gave expression in 1960, appears to be less repugnant at this writing than at any previous time. More and more frequently the argument is heard (in the words of *Commonweal*) that "the need is to hold open the doors to China just as we have to Russia."[103]

The tougher tone adopted by the administration following the Chinese explosion, in large part, was traceable to Secretary of State Rusk. Rusk, relatively flexible on past China concerns, remained convinced of the logic that only if American resolve was self-evident in Asia could China be induced to eventually moderate its world policies.[104] The secretary was, furthermore, "very doubtful" that allowing China into the United Nations would alter Peking's behavior. It seemed to him, rather, that a non-conciliatory approach was more likely to achieve this result. The United Nations was, after all "not a reform school. It was an organization of these states prepared to commit themselves to the principles of the world charter. Peiping has consistently announced to the world a militant doctrine of another sort." Continuing on in this 11 November 1964 television interview, Rusk stated that if China's leaders were not prepared to live in peace, then "I think we should not encourage them by rewarding them for a policy which is so contrary to the prospects of peace." Asked if this meant the United States and the People's Republic of China were on a collision course, Rusk answered that

this turns entirely on Peiping's decision on the crucial question, about whether they are prepared to leave their neighbors alone. We've made it very clear that we are not going to pull away and leave Southeast Asia to be overrun by these people from the north. . . . We feel that they must come to a decision to leave these people alone in South Asia. Now, if they don't, then there is trouble ahead.[105]

Rusk continued to pound on this containment theme; little more than a month later he again stated that it was necessary to stand up to Chinese expansionism as a way of forcing Peking to modify its policies. Conciliation or appeasement were out as the Chinese had "appetites and ambitions that grow upon feeding."[106]

Despite such rhetoric, the balance of opinion in the public remained roughly unchanged throughout 1965. The American people still viewed China in a very negative light, but their attitudes remained roughly stable following the mainland's explosion. The change in opinion following 16 October seems to have opened up some "running room" for those in the State Department favoring the more "opened windows" approach. Their latitude was also increased, paradoxically, by events in Indochina. Top-level officials, throughout 1965, were preoccupied with Vietnam, leaving the middle-tier analysts relatively unhampered in their China policy planning. A high State Department official of this period has recalled that

China—except as a possible intervenor in Vietnam—was largely ignored by high-level decision makers. For officials with Far East responsibilities, Indochina crises—Laos, the Tonkin Gulf episode of August 1964, and planning for Vietnam . . . consumed most waking hours.[107]

With some support from Capitol Hill, State's Far Eastern Bureau—the locus of this mid-level planning—urged the president to "give consideration to the initiative of limited but direct contacts with Red China through cultural exchange activities with emphasis on scholars, and journalists."[108] This move was given the distracted president's verbal approval on 24 August 1965. It would be Johnson's first move toward a more flexible posture vis-à-vis China. The public seemed willing to accept such a gesture as it might help reduce the probability of People's Republic of China intervention in Vietnam. The war, apparently to Johnson's mind, showed America's resolve in Asia; minor initiatives would not undercut this stance. Various problems, bureaucratic cross-currents, and lack of upper-level attention, however, held up official issuance of this policy statement until December. Interestingly, this move occurred even after some aggressive Chinese posturing in the Indian subcontinent. This minor 29 December relaxation in America's policy was widely applauded in the press. Public acceptance of this gesture had been foreshadowed two weeks earlier by the favorable reaction to the U.S. announcement that Washington would validate the passport of an American physician who had been invited to the mainland in order to demonstrate a new operating technique. In a statement released two days after this 12 December announcement, though, the State Department publicly implied that the mainland was the party responsible for holding up scientific exchanges. This statement led the Chinese to quickly cancel the doctor's trip, charging that America was playing politics with science.[109]

The applause that accompanied the 29 December announcement was very vigorous. This may have reflected the public's hope that such initiatives could head off a major Southeast Asian conflict with China. Concern in Washington over a PLA intervention in Vietnam had grown in the last quarter of 1965. Though officials were circumspect in speaking of this possibility, fear of war with China still "hovered over Washington like a cloud."[110] War concerns were heightened by intelligence reports showing that 50,000 mainland troops had infiltrated into the north since September 1965.[111] Though this data was not publicly played up, fear of a Sino-American confrontation was never far from the front pages of this nation's newspapers. Lin Piao's September "Long Live the Victory of the People's War" manifesto helped to further heighten public worries as some saw in this a Chinese *Mein Kampf*.[112] Declarations such as this were seized on by some members of the press as proving that "a clear element of irrationality, of craziness, of paranoia, exists in Communist China's view of the world." With this the case, negotiations to prevent a war could, Stewart Alsop reasoned in the 15 January 1966 *Saturday Evening Post*, only fail.[113] A Senate report issued two days after the *Post*'s cover date agreed that an Asian land battle with China was a very live possibility. Raising temperatures even more was a month-long discussion in a mainland-controlled Hong Kong newspaper on the imminence of a Sino-American war.[114] "Reluctantly and apprehensively," concluded Seymour Topping in the 30 January *New York Times*, "Communist China and the United States are drifting toward a military confrontation over Vietnam."[115]

A great deal of this official concern was passed on to the general public through televised hearings on Vietnam conducted by the Senate Foreign Relations Committee. In the course of these discussions it became clear that "certain China experts in our Government [believe] that the Chinese leaders expect to be at war with the United States within a year and ... some of our officials also expect war with China."[116] The public agreed with this assessment as a March 1966 Gallup poll found a 46 to 27 percent plurality of persons expecting "Communist China ... to send a great many troops to fight in Vietnam." If this occurred, the public, like Rusk, felt (by a 73 to 8 percent margin) that America should not "feed" the expansionist appetite of China—American troops should stay in Asia and continue fighting.[117]

In an attempt to ward off a People's Republic of China intervention, the Johnson Administration took a few more hesitant steps toward Peking in mid-February. Washington announced that it would allow Chinese journalists into the United States with no strings attached and, more quietly, moved to dissuade

Seoul and Taipei from entering into a formal alliance. Johnson, as always attuned to opinion, was aware of the changes in the public's views since 1964 and believed that mainland-directed initiatives would find favor with the American people. The United States also publicly suggested that medical teams from each nation might wish to exchange visits; to facilitate this, travel restrictions were eased once more. Senator Fulbright further announced in February that beginning 8 March his Foreign Relations Committee would initiate hearings on America's China policy. At these widely publicized hearings, which Johnson encouraged once he was convinced they would not be used as a forum to attack his Vietnam policy, America's rigid stance vis-à-vis China was called into question by several Asian experts.[118]

Interestingly, starting in March and for a short time thereafter, policy toward China began once more to take on a life of its own. With public interest (and fear) rising, this policy area again started to be closely attended to. Prior to this interlude, as the *Wall Street Journal* noted, Vietnam was still gripping "policy-makers' attention, limiting other initiatives. Rusk and McNamara generate no serious new ideas except for Vietnam; they lack the time and energy. Aides say it is hard to snare Johnson's attention for anything but the war."[119] A key figure in increasing the attention paid to China at this juncture was Bill Moyers, once described as "the number-2 man in the United States government."[120] Moyers, Johnson's principal assistant in 1966, encouraged both Gallup and Harris to conduct opinion polls on the China question in the hopes of buttressing his bureaucratic argument for a new approach to the People's Republic of China.[121] Persuaded by such opinion soundings, Johnson did lighten up further on America's harsh stance toward the People's Republic of China. Not all policy-makers, though, were pleased with this forward movement. This led, as *Newsweek* reported, to "intense internal disagreements" in Johnson's inner circle.[122] Reflective of these disagreements was the contradictory character of American actions in March. On the eighth of that month, Secretary of Defense McNamara publicly warned of China's growing nuclear threat. Two weeks later, after initially raising no objections, the United States sought to derail the sale of a European steel mill to China. On 13 March, though, in a significant statement, Vice President Humphrey announced that America's policy toward the People's Republic of China was one of both containing Chinese expansionist tendencies *and* seeking to establish better relations with the mainland regime.[123]

The hesitant U.S. moves toward China during this period were increasingly encouraged by the favorable public response they seemed to garner. A late March Gallup poll, for instance, found that opposition to People's Republic of China representation at the United Nations had fallen twelve percentage points since December.[124] At about this time, Americans were also found to favor China's admission to the United Nations by a two-to-one margin if this action would aid in reducing tensions in the Far East.[125] A June Harris survey similarly reported wide public support for negotiating with the Chinese, easing our travel ban, and remaining in the United Nations should China gain admission. The latter finding was not surprising given that Harris found a majority of those with opinions on the subject favored a "two-Chinas" solution to the United States–United Nations recognition problem.[126] Survey evidence suggestive of a public willingness to follow official moves toward a rapprochement with the mainland also appeared at this time with the publication of A. T. Steele's pioneering book on American public opinion regarding China.[127] Emboldened by evidence that opinion was open to increased government initiatives, President Johnson made a 12 July 1966 nationwide television speech advocating "reconciliation" with the mainland on terms of "cooperation, not hostility." While cautious in its overall tone, the president's speech did call for a "free flow of ideas and people and goods" between the two nations.[128] Judging the public ready, Johnson also initially accepted the advice of several State Department officials to move toward a two-China UN policy. This plan, pushed on the president when Secretary Rusk was out of town, was abandoned when the secretary returned and convinced Johnson that the time was not ripe to "reward" a still aggressive China.[129]

Before greater movement could be attempted in 1966, however, the specter of the Vietnam War began to again haunt America's decision-makers. As in the past, this left little time for other policy thoughts. The immediate impetus for dealing with China—fear of war—also receded as the year continued. By spring, Washington had apparently reached an implicit, if not explicit, understanding with Peking on the limits of war China would tolerate without actively intervening.[130] Of equal importance was the rising feeling that perhaps there was little real reason to be concerned about a China racked by internal conflicts. Max Frankel, writing in November 1966, noted this rapid change in public and official perceptions:

In just a year the upheavals inside China have changed its reputation from that of a formidable challenger of the United States throughout Asia and of the Soviet Union inside the Communist world—to that of a hobbled giant riddled by dissent and incapable of sustained growth and self assertion.[131]

This feeling did not appreciably alter over the next two years as China was still seen as "scared to death of the United States."[132] Concern over China's future course of action, though, remained high on the rhetorical list in Washington. After all, Peking retained its "special quality of militancy" and

within the next decade or two, there will be a billion Chinese on the mainland, armed with nuclear weapons.... Now, we believe [is the time] that the free nations of Asia must brace themselves, get themselves set, with secure, progressive, stable institutions of their own, with cooperation among the free nations of Asia stretching from Korea and Japan right around the subcontinent, if there is to be peace in Asia over the next ten or twenty years.[133]

The need to maintain domestic support for the Vietnam War put an additional brake on the extent of policy change toward China following mid-1966. Pointing the finger of guilt at China, Washington eventually took to accusing the Chinese of running "a unified Asian Communist movement directed from Peking."[134] Moving relations forward too fast would risk undercutting this already flimsy rationale for the Vietnam War. Equally important in slowing the evolution of United States–People's Republic of China ties was China's unyielding isolation in the first two years of its Cultural Revolution. This turbulent period of People's Republic of China history led to a deterioration of relations with, and public opinion about, China throughout the entire world. Reflective of this was China's loss of support among nations in its annual bid for UN membership.[135] A further indication of Peking's lack of attention to the sensitivities of other countries during the 1967-1968 height of the Cultural Revolution was its breaking off of the Warsaw talks with the United States, using the terse explanation that "there was nothing to talk about."[136] Robert Sutter has aptly described this chaotic period of Chinese history and its effect on world opinion:

The 1966-1969 Cultural Revolution brought normal PRC foreign policy functioning to a halt. Senior Chinese diplomats were recalled to China and junior officers remaining overseas were required to proselytize in the name of Mao Tse-tung. Rigidly ideological conduct in foreign affairs was the order of the day, leading to a severe downturn in Chinese relations with a large number of previously friendly states. This resulted in increasing PRC diplomatic isolation, to a point where China's inner circle of friends was limited to Albania, Pakistan, and a handful of African states.[137]

The xenophobic stance of the Chinese during the Cultural Revolution severely harmed their already poor image within the United States. Television specials covering the developments on the mainland appeared with biased titles such as "Roots of Madness."[138] One late-1967 survey found that China ranked lowest in American esteem among the twenty-eight nations measured in that poll.[139] A March 1967 survey by the Gallup organization similarly discovered that China was now seen as the main threat to world peace by 71 percent of the population (versus 20 percent for the Soviet Union).[140] Two years later Harris found equivalent results and concluded that "a majority of the public now believes that over the long pull the Russians might emerge as an ally working for peace in the world, while China was viewed as the predominant and growing threat." Harris also discovered that among those expressing a preference (39 percent), twelve times as many Americans wanted to see the Russians "win" the Sino-Soviet dispute as the Chinese. Harris further found that a plurality of Americans now favored a policy of continued non-recognition of China, reversing the previously favorable trend extending back to at least 1966.[141]

Curiously, though, not all poll data from this era ran in the direction Harris found. Support for America's defense treaty with Taiwan, probably suffering from the growing disenchantment with Asian wars, fell ten percentage points while opposition to the treaty rose from 6 to 19 percent in the same three-year period.[142] Similarly, Gallup found that between 1966 and 1969 those in the public favoring the seating of Peking in the United Nations, and in going along with a majority vote to do so, rose in a continuation of the trend begun in 1964.[143] The public, while still opposed to warmer relations with our expansionistic enemy, had increasingly come to accept that Peking, not Taipei, represented the bulk of the Chinese people.

The acceptance of this assumption was largely in line with U.S. policy. In the final years of the Johnson Administration a "containment yes, isolation no" stance became primary in Washington.[144] In mid-1967, reflecting this trend, Congress's Joint Economic Committee "strongly urged" a re-evaluation of U.S. trade policies toward China.[145] At this time, President Johnson may also have used Rumanian diplomatic channels to signal to China Washington's interest in better United States–People's Republic of China relations.[146] Signaling its intentions more publicly, the administration had offered in April 1967 to allow pharmaceuticals to be shipped to China, an offer firmly rebuffed by Peking. Early the following year, in a continuation of Washington's evolving stance, it was reported that America was once more pressing Chiang to reduce or remove his forces from Quemoy and Matsu.[147] These small moves continued with a May 1968 offer to Chinese newsmen by Leonard Marks, the U.S. Information Agency director, to cover the upcoming U.S. elections in person. A review of America's China policy later that month by Under Secretary Nicholas deB. Katzenbach also publicly laid out America's hopes for better relations with the mainland (while still blaming the lack of contacts on Peking).[148] Quietly, in the spring, RCA, in a significant gesture, was given approval to attempt to conclude some corporate business with the mainland involving telecommunications links.[149] The *Christian Century*, no friend of administration policy in Asia, nonetheless saw this period as one in which

Pres. Johnson, Vice-Pres. Humphrey, Under Secretary of State Nicholas Katzenbach, William Bundy and others in the administration and Congress, as well as a host of academic and other specialists, [have] called for steps . . . leading to reconciliation. All the major presidential candidates, including Mr. Nixon [have also] advocated liberalization of U.S. China policy.[150]

These efforts finally bore fruit when China agreed, three weeks after the November elections, to resume the Warsaw discussions early in 1969.

This upsurge in activity in Johnson's final year may have helped account for the positive changes in opinion toward China that Gallup found in his January 1969 UN questions. While it was difficult to publicly pass on the positive tenor of Johnson's policy in 1967, due to Rusk's explicit reiteration of an anti-Communist Chinese rationale for the Vietnam War and McNamara's (half-hearted) anti-Chinese justification for the anti-ballistic missiles (ABM) system,[151] this was less the case in 1968 when further escalation in Southeast Asia seems to have been ruled out. It is possible, though, that the movement of opinion in these years occurred autonomously of any government clues. The Vietnam War

was such an absorbing event that it may have precluded any real public attention
to the changes occurring in Washington's China policy. America was, after all,
still fighting to prevent the expansion of Communist Chinese influence in the
world.

Evidence for this proposition is presented in table 5. A breakdown of opinion
on Gallup's UN admissions question by age shows that much of the opinion
change in Johnson's final years was traceable to a shift in the views of the young.
While caution must be exercised in dealing with opinion sub-groups given the
small number of persons involved, this seems to be a trend that remained in
place through Nixon's first two years in office. The young, if this age breakdown
is to be given credence, may have been either disillusioned with Johnson's overall

TABLE 5

SHOULD CHINA BE IN THE UN?   AN AGE BREAKDOWN
(% in favor/ % opposed)

| Poll | Age | | |
Date	21-30	31-50	51+
7-54	7/76	7/80	6/80
5-55	14/62	9/67	8/70
8-55	25/66	18/71	12/75
12-56	22/62	15/69	12/73
2-57	17/66	15/67	9/75
8-58	22/60	22/60	15/69
2-61	25/58	17/61	12/69
2-64	19/64	16/69	10/75
11-64	38/45	22/61	13/65
12-65	26/68	26/63	17/69
3-66	26/61	28/55	22/53
9-66	28/58	29/54	21/56
1-69	45/46	33/56	27/56
9-70	55/36	33/51	28/54
5-71	48/34	45/41	42/36

Source: Gallup Polls, various years. Age breakdowns
         provided by Roper Archives (Storrs,
         Connecticut), Gallup Opinion Indexes, and
         author from computer tapes supplied by Tom
         Smith of the National Opinion Research Center.

Asian policy or simply more attentive to Washington's conciliatory actions toward China.[152] Either explanation could account for this disparity between age
categories, though one posits autonomous opinion movements on the part of the
young and the other suggests a more reactive model. The older age groups,
while showing some positive movement from 1966 on, apparently were focused
more on the Vietnam War–induced need to contain China than on Washington's
simultaneous interest in ending its isolation. Not until the Nixon years would
the opinions of elder citizens begin a similarly dramatic shift.

In any case, both the general public and its government were trending in a
positive direction, as regards China policy, by the end of Johnson's term. The
1960s represent an era where opinion played a powerful role in the formation
of policy. The public's hostility toward the mainland put a cap on any changes
Kennedy hoped to make in his first year in office and also seems to have started
the young president down a more negative road in United States–People's Republic of China relations. Johnson, perhaps the quintessential politician-presi-
dent, was always closely tuned in to the public's wishes.[153] Only after opinion
changed did he feel comfortable in moving policy forward. The actions of both
Democratic leaders highlight the interactive nature of opinion and policy. When
opinion changed, as in 1961 or the 1964-1966 period, it allowed for policy
alterations to safely take place. These alterations, in turn, helped encourage later
opinion changes. When Richard Nixon took office he would harness and accelerate the positive late 1960s preference changes, clearly moving in advance of
a still somewhat sluggish public. His rapprochement efforts, though, might not
have reached fruition if changes in opinion had not begun prior to his election.

NOTES

1. A 2 March 1960 Gallup poll (no. 624-KA) found the "overwhelming majority
of those interviewed (on America's most important problem) named issues dealing with
foreign policy." A July 1 Special Gallup Survey of Republican and Democratic County
Chairmen found that the vast majority of them expected the main campaign issue in the
1960 election to be one of foreign policy. Stephen Hess in "Does Foreign Policy Really
Matter?" *Wilson Quarterly* 6 (Winter 1980):96-111, argues that this expectation was not
fulfilled.

2. Robert A. Divine, *Foreign Policy and U.S. Presidential Elections: 1952-1960*
(New York: New Viewpoints, 1974), pp. 258-265; Richard M. Nixon, *RN: The Memoirs
of Richard Nixon* (New York: Grosset and Dunlap, 1978), pp. 219-220.

3. *Time*, 24 October 1960, p. 25.

4. *Monthly Survey* 223 (3 October 1960), Foster Papers, Box 13; "China Telegram"
19 April 1960, Foster Papers, Box 31; *Christian Century* 77 (2 November 1960):1269.
Despite his veto pledge, Nixon reportedly told a question-and-answer period at San
Francisco University that "in the long run" the People's Republic of China could qualify
for United States–United Nations recognition. See "China Telegram," 14 April 1960,
Foster Papers, Box 31.

5. Chester Bowles, "The 'China Problem' Reconsidered," *Foreign Affairs* 38 (April

1960):476-487; David Halberstam, *The Best and the Brightest* (New York: Fawcett Crest, 1972), pp.18-28.

6. John K. Fairbank, *Communist China and Taiwan in the United States Foreign Policy* (Paper delivered at the University of Connecticut, Storrs, Connecticut, 21 November 1960), p. 5.

7. *Wall Street Journal*, 14 March 1961. This article names Stevenson, Rusk, and NATO Ambassador Thomas Finletter as the chief advocates of a new China policy in Kennedy's Administration; *Far Eastern Economic Review* 30 (29 December 1960):655.

8. Adlai E. Stevenson, "Putting First Things First: A Democratic View," *Foreign Affairs* 38 (January 1960):202-203.

9. *Monthly Survey* 236 (3 January 1961), Foster Papers, Box 13 (emphasis in original).

10. James C. Thomson, Jr., "On the Making of U.S. China Policy, 1961-9: A Study in Bureaucratic Politics," *China Quarterly* 50 (April-June 1972):226. Franz Schurmann, *The Logic of World Power: An Inquiry into the Origins, Currents, and Contradictions of World Politics* (New York: Pantheon Books, 1974); Richard J. Walton, *Cold War and Counterrevolution: The Foreign Policy of John F. Kennedy* (New York: The Viking Press, 1972). A White House memo of 27 March 1961 entitled "The Sino-Soviet Border Dispute and the Berlin Situation," DDRS, 1978, 67C, noted that

in addition to all the basic reasons for the United States continuing its policy of no concessions to the Russians on Berlin, the Sino-Soviet dispute offers one other: a completely firm U.S. position would in the long run be more rather than less likely to increase Sino-Soviet differences on this issue.

11. *Public Papers, 1961* (2 June), p. 436.

12. "China Telegram," 12 July 1960, Foster Papers, Box 32.

13. *Christian Century* 77 (6 July 1960):795.

14. *Monthly Survey* 232 (2 September 1960), Foster Papers, Box 13.

15. J. Chester Cheng, ed., *The Politics of the Chinese Red Army: A Translation of the Bulletin of Activities of the People's Liberation Army* (Stanford, Calif.: Hoover Institute, 1966), p. 486. This 25 April 1961 PLA bulletin also states that "the smell of gun powder is more evident in Kennedy's Administration than in Eisenhower's, for it is more reactionary, treacherous, elusive and deceitful." It should be noted that the perception of China as a rising world threat was likely encouraged by the new administration's statements concerning the Far East. In contrast to its Republican predecessor, the new Democratic regime in Washington had to be careful to balance any signs of "softness" toward China with a display of its firm understanding of the menacing threat posed by the mainland.

16. Thomson, "On the Making," p. 223; William Gleysteen in a 6 July 1982 interview in Washington also stated that the Consulate in Hong Kong sent a report pointing to the need for a policy change around this time.

17. Gallup poll, no. 641-K (24 March 1961); "Gallup Poll Begins 3-Part Series on Red China" (March 1961), Foster Papers, Box 33. The public favored this move by a 53 to 32 margin. By a 52 to 37 percent majority, the survey population approved of sending U.S. "surplus foods" to China to combat "a severe food famine." This poll also found 47 to 38 percent plurality approval for "the United States and Communist China ... work[ing] out a business arrangement to buy and sell goods to each other."

18. Warren I. Cohen, *The American Secretaries of State and Their Diplomacy: Dean Rusk* (Totowa, N.J.: Cooper Square Publishers, 1980), p. 164.

19. *Business Week*, 25 March 1961, pp. 105-106.

20. "China Telegram," 14 March 1961, Foster Papers, Box 32; *Monthly Survey* 259 (2 April 1961), Foster Papers, Box 13.

21. *Wall Street Journal*, 27 March 1961. Among conciliatory moves toward the People's Republic of China mentioned by some historians was the administration's early efforts to get Taipei to remove its remnant troops (estimated at 4,000 with 6,000 dependents) from Northern Burma. This move, though, reflected more a fear of the collapse of United States–Burmese relations than an effort to improve United States–People's Republic of China relations, as riots broke out in Burma blaming the troop's existence on the American government. Fears of People's Republic of China direct intervention into Burma to "solve" this problem were also high. See "China Telegram," 28 February 1961, Foster Papers, Box 32.

22. *Newsweek*, 10 July 1961, p. 22.

23. Roger Hilsman, *To Move a Nation: The Politics of Foreign Policy in the Administration of John F. Kennedy* (Garden City, N.Y.: Doubleday Co., 1967), p. 306; Chester Bowles, *Promises to Keep: My Years in Public Life* (Evanston, Ill.: Harper and Row, 1971), p. 398, fn 2.

24. *Far Eastern Economic Review* 33 (20 July 1961):103.

25. *Christian Century* 77 (19 October 1960):1203-1204.

26. Arthur M. Schlesinger, Jr., *A Thousand Days: John F. Kennedy in the White House* (Boston: Houghton, Mifflin, 1965), p. 483. Adding to Kennedy's concern may have been a private statement Eisenhower reportedly made to the president-elect. According to Warren I. Cohen, "American Perceptions of China," in *Dragon and Eagle: U.S.-China Relations: Past and Future*, ed. Michel Oksenberg and Robert B. Oxnan (New York: Basic Books, 1978), p. 79, Eisenhower told Kennedy that he would return to public life to lobby against Washington's approval of the People's Republic of China's admission to the United Nations if Kennedy advocated such a course.

27. *Wall Street Journal*, 14 March 1961.

28. *Business Week*, 16 December 1961, p. 103.

29. Quoted in "China Telegram," 26 September 1961, Foster Papers, Box 32. It is interesting to note, in this vein, that unconfirmed press reports at the time had Kennedy telling British Prime Minister Harold Macmillan in April that it would take him at least twelve months to prepare the American public for accepting China's UN admission. To act sooner would be to risk potential political damage. See *Congressional Quarterly Weekly* 19 (28 April 1961):721.

30. That Kennedy was opposed to People's Republic of China admission for the time being in private, as well as in public, comes through in a letter he sent to Henry Luce in mid-1961. This can be deduced from Luce's reply of 9 June 1961, which is contained in the Adlai E. Stevenson Papers, Princeton University, Princeton, New Jersey, Box 829 (hereafter Stevenson Papers).

31. *Monthly Survey* 242 (3 July 1961), Foster Papers, Box 13 (emphasis in original).

32. "Current Public Concerns about U.S. Foreign Policy," 4 May 1961, Foster Papers, Box 1 (emphasis in original).

33. "Current Public Attitudes toward President Kennedy's Handling of Foreign Affairs," 2 November 1961, Foster Papers, Box 1.

34. This analysis, then, is compatible with Michael Leigh's notion that yesterday's manipulation of opinion could prove to be a constraint on today's policy actions.

35. Stevenson Papers, Box 829 (undated, 1961).

36. *Monthly Survey* 242 (3 July 1961), Foster Papers, Box 13.

37. Cohen, *Dean Rusk*, pp. 166-167; Hilsman, p. 307, argues that congressional pressure on Kennedy's foreign aid bill by "anti-Mongolian" legislators also affected his decision to drop this move. See also Thomson, "On the Making," p. 226.

38. Cohen, *Dean Rusk*, p. 167.

39. "China Telegram," 1 August 1961, Foster Papers, Box 32.

40. *Public Papers, 1961* (11 October), p. 658.

41. *Monthly Survey* 246 (2 November 1961), Foster Papers, Box 13; "China Telegram," 24 October 1961, Foster Papers, Box 32.

42. *New Republic*, 30 October 1961, p. 2.

43. Gallup poll, no. 650-K (26 October 1961).

44. Negative opinion toward China's UN admission was found in a number of surveys taken by congressmen. See *Special Report on American Opinion*, "October 1961 Concerns about U.S. Foreign Policy" (20 October 1961), Foster Papers, Box 1. An article by Senator Goldwater entitled "What to Do about Red China" in *This Week* magazine brought in 115,000 letters to that journal in five days, with a "ratio of 20-1 against Red China in the UN." See "China Telegram," 10 October 1961, Foster Papers, Box 32. Congressional opposition was shown by a resolution, passed without dissent in both houses, opposing recognition of China or its admission to the United Nations. Running contrary to this trend was a survey by the Council of Foreign Relations of 650 members of its local committees in twenty-nine cities. This poll found 46 percent of members "definitely opposed" to People's Republic of China membership in the United Nations, and another 4 percent "unfavorably inclined." However, 45 percent reported themselves "favorably inclined" toward this proposition. Perhaps accounting for this even opinion split among these attentive citizens was the question they responded to which asked if they favored Chinese representation "on the basis that it [i.e., the United States] could not stem the tide in this direction, and rigid opposition would prove disadvantageous in the long run" to America's world position. See *Monthly Survey* 242 (3 July 1961), Foster Papers, Box 13.

45. Gallup polls, no. 641-K (24 March 1961) and no. 650-K (26 October 1961). It should be noted that, despite the trend, these polls showed a public still in favor of going along with the majority at the United Nations. This instance helps to highlight the value of looking at the *entire* opinion picture before drawing any substantive conclusion.

46. Memo from W. Averell Harriman to the secretary, "United States Policy on Shipments of Medicines and Food Grains to Communist China," 13 April 1962, DDRS, 1980, 396C.

47. Quoted in "China Telegram," 5 December 1961, Foster Papers, Box 32.

48. Thomson, "On the Making," pp. 226-229.

49. *Monthly Survey* 251 (3 April 1962), Foster Papers, Box 13. Gallup poll (27 June 1962), no. 659-T. Kennedy's hints on the grain shipment question can be found in *Public Papers, 1962*, on 14 March (p. 230); 23 May (p. 431); and 14 June (pp. 487-488). This issue first publicly surfaced on 25 January 1961 (*Public Papers, 1961*, p. 15) at a news conference when Kennedy was asked if he favored sending food aid to China through international bodies (a suggestion raised by Senator Humphrey). Kennedy gave a noncommittal answer to this question. The *Christian Century*, in 1961, consistently advocated

a plan such as Humphrey's (see, for example, *Christian Century* 78, 8 March, pp. 293-294). This journal pointed out that a "Food for Peace" organization (headed by George McGovern) already existed within the State Department and could undertake such a humanitarian food distribution.

50. Roger Hilsman to Dean Rusk, "Proposed U.S. Food Offer to Communist China," 26 May 1962, DDRS, 1977, 397B.

51. *Far Eastern Economic Review* 35 (29 March 1962):699.

52. The official reason given for the rejection was a "lack of documentary evidence that the request had come from the Governments concerned and that they had foreign exchange to pay for it." Avery F. Peterson, deputy assistant secretary of state for Far Eastern economic affairs, later told the House of Representatives' Foreign Affairs Committee that such sales might be a good idea in the future since they would use Chinese funds for food and not bullets. See, ibid. 42 (17 October 1963):143.

53. Hungdah Chiu, "China, the United States and the Question of Taiwan," in *China and the Taiwan Issue*, ed. Hungdah Chiu (New York: Praeger Publishing, 1973), p. 173; Hilsman, pp. 310-314. The *Far Eastern Economic Review* 37 (19 July 1962):115, reported that a March bid for invasion support by Chiang was turned down, "though in terms considered too gentle by some officials in the State Department."

54. Allen S. Whiting, *The Chinese Calculus of Deterrence: India and Indochina* (Ann Arbor: University of Michigan Press, 1975), p. 65.

55. "The President's Intelligence Checklist," 19 June 1962, DDRS, 1975, 5G.

56. Memo to the vice president from the special assistant to the vice president (Colonel Howard L. Burris) [1962] "Deteriorating Conditions inside China," DDRS, 1979, 99C.

57. Whiting, *Chinese Calculus*, p. 63.

58. Ibid., p. 32; *Time*, 13 September 1963, p. 39.

59. Harrison E. Salisbury, "Haunting Enigma of Red China," *New York Times Magazine*, 12 June 1960, p. 75.

60. *Public Papers, 1962* (27 June), p. 511.

61. Taking no chances, however, elements of the Seventh Fleet did begin to sail toward the Straits before tensions completely subsided. See *Wall Street Journal*, 25 June 1962.

62. Cohen, *Dean Rusk*, p. 281.

63. *Public Papers, 1962* (20 November), p. 832. India, in the course of this crisis, went so far as to request American airstrikes on Chinese forces if the PLA advanced beyond the disputed territory. See Whiting, *Chinese Calculus*, pp. 149, 167.

64. *Public Papers, 1961* (1 February), p. 36.

65. Oscar Gass, "China and the United States," *Commentary* 34 (November 1962):397.

66. Gallup poll, no. 669-K (24 March 1963).

67. *Public Papers, 1963* (1 August), p. 616.

68. Thomson, "On the Making," pp. 228, 233; Bryce Nelson, "Ex-Administration Officials Discuss U.S. Policy in Asia," *Science* 154 (25 November 1966):990.

69. George F. Kennan, "Can We Deal with Moscow?" *Saturday Evening Post*, 5 October 1963, p. 40. In the course of the polemics denouncing the Test-Ban treaty, China charged that the Soviet Union had "reneged" on an atomic aid agreement. This revelation, according to State's analysts, "had [a] considerable impact on opinion" to the detriment of the People's Republic of China and the benefit of the USSR. See "Public Concerns about U.S. Foreign Policy since Signature of Test-Ban Treaty," 23 August 1963, Foster Papers, Box 1.

70. *Christian Century* 80 (11 September 1963):1091. For an argument charging that the press consistently misinformed the American public on this issue (and others) see Felix Greene, *A Curtain of Ignorance: How the American Public Has Been Misinformed about China* (Garden City, N.Y.: Doubleday, 1964).

71. *Public Papers, 1962* (17 December 1962), p. 900.

72. Quoted in *Monthly Survey* 260 (2 January 1963).

73. *Time*, 31 January 1964, pp. 25-26; 21 February 1964, p. 37. See also *NYT*, 2, 26, 29, and 30 January, 11 February 1964; Cohen, *Dean Rusk*, p. 187; Outgoing Telegram no. 812, Rusk to American Embassy, Taipei, 28 February 1964, DDRS, 1976, 179F.

74. *Public Papers, 1963* (14 November), pp. 845-846.

75. See, for example, Bowles, pp. 391-403; Theodore H. White, *In Search Of History: A Personal Adventure* (New York: Warner Books, 1978), pp. 499-500.

76. *Far Eastern Economic Review* 42 (17 October 1963): 144; *NYT*, 1 October 1963; Herbert L. Matthews, *A World in Revolution: A Newspaperman's Memoir* (New York: Charles Scribner's Sons, 1971) p. 372.

77. Roger Hilsman, "United States Policy toward Communist China," *DSB* 50 (16 January 1964):11-17.

78. Thomson, "On the Making," p. 231; *American Opinion Survey*, "U.S. Policy on China," 27 December 1963, Foster Papers, Box 33.

79. Letter from Hilsman to Stevenson, 19 December 1963, Stevenson Papers, Box 860.

80. *Far Eastern Economic Review* 43 (2 January 1964):11.

81. David Halberstam, *The Best and the Brightest* (New York: Fawcett Crest, 1972), p. 488.

82. Cohen, *Dean Rusk*, pp. 187, 284-285; Townsend Hoopes, *The Limits of Intervention*, rev. ed. (New York: David McKay, 1973), pp. 92-116.

83. Gallup poll, no. 684-K (14 February 1964).

84. Harris release, *Washington Post* (30 November 1964). This June poll also presented some evidence that the idea of negotiating with the People's Republic of China had lost support since the late 1950s.

85. *Special Report on American Opinion*, "U.S. China Policy, 1964" (14 December 1964), Foster Papers, Box 33.

86. Council on Foreign Relations, *The American Public's View of U.S. Policy toward China*, A Report Prepared by the Survey Research Center, University of Michigan (New York: Council on Foreign Relations, 1964).

87. James C. Thomson, Jr., "U.S. Opinion regarding Communist China," NSC Memo to Mr. Bundy, Mr. Komer, 21 August 1964, DDRS, 1978, 55C.

88. *Pentagon Papers* 3, *Public Statements*, pp. 714-715.

89. Harris release, *Washington Post*, 30 November 1964.

90. *Newsweek*, 29 November 1965, p. 44.

91. *NYT*, 30 September 1964; *Wall Street Journal*, 30 September 1964.

92. *U.S. News and World Report*, 12 October 1964, p. 38; Foster Rhea Dulles, *American Policy toward Communist China* (New York: Thomas Y. Crowell Co., 1972), pp. 223-224.

93. McGeorge Bundy, "Memorandum for the Record," 15 September 1964, DDRS, 1978, 119B. McCone left the meeting prior to its conclusion, the president joined after it had begun.

94. *Christian Century* 81 (28 October 1964):1323.

95. *Public Papers, 1964* (16 October), p. 1366. Johnson made a televised speech on 18 October to calm any fears that might have arisen. Washington became even more concerned once intelligence sources indicated that the bomb was of a more advanced design than first believed. See William L. Ryan and Sam Summerlin, *The China Cloud: America's Tragic Blunder and China's Rise to Nuclear Power* (Boston: Little, Brown and Co., 1968). Not above making political capital from this explosion, Humphrey told a Madison, Wisconsin, campaign meeting that China's having the bomb was dangerous, but it would be "unbelievably dangerous" for Red China to have atomic weapons and to have Senator Goldwater's "finger on the nuclear trigger." See Memo from James L. Greenfield to the Secretary, "Political Statements on Foreign Policy, October 24-30" (30 October 1964), Foster Papers, Box 1.

96. Gallup poll, no. 701-K (27 November 1964).

97. Harris release, *Washington Post*, 30 November 1964.

98. A poll conducted for Free and Cantril found 54 to 19 percent approval for this statement. See Lloyd A. Free and Hadley Cantril, *The Political Beliefs of Americans: A Study of Public Opinion* (New Brunswick, N.J.: Rutgers University Press, 1967), p. 200. Gallup's question on the world's most dangerous nation now showed China chosen over Russia by a 59 to 20 percent margin, up from 56 to 27 in May. See *Special Report on American Opinion*, "U.S. China Policy 1964" (14 December 1964), Foster Papers, Box 33.

99. Foster Rhea Dulles, pp. 223-224.

100. *American Opinion Survey*, "Nuclear China: Next Step for U.S." (28 October 1964), Foster Papers, Box 1.

101. *NYT*, 24 October 1964.

102. *Newsweek*, 22 February 1953, pp. 13-14. This move, however, may have also reflected the need to free surface ships for duty off the Vietnamese coast.

103. *Special Report on American Opinion*, "U.S. China Policy 1964" (14 December 1964), Foster Papers, Box 33.

104. Cohen, *Dean Rusk*, p. 283. In June 1965 Rusk, reflecting this view, told a cabinet meeting that

we have tried in the past three or four years to see if we cannot do a better job in meeting these wars of liberation. If we can find an answer to that question and make it quite clear to Peking, as well as Moscow, that this course of aggression has nothing in it for them and that prudence requires them to move towards peaceful co-existence, then it may well be that the poor human race can look ahead for a considerable period without the threat of a major war on the horizon. But it is going to take a lot of effort.

See "Minutes of the Meeting of the President's Cabinet, in the Cabinet Room, The White House," 15 June in *The Presidential Documents Series, President Lyndon B. Johnson: Minutes of President Johnson (1963-69)*, reel 1 (microfilm), University Publications of America, Frederick, Maryland.

105. Dean Rusk, 11 November interview with Marvin Kalb on "CBS Reports: The United States and Two Chinas," in *DSB* 51 (30 November 1964):772; *Far Eastern Economic Review* 46 (10 December 1964):527.

106. *DSB* 52 (11 January 1965):38.

107. Thomson, "On the Making," pp. 233-234.

108. A House subcommittee had earlier recommended this move. See ibid.

109. *Far Eastern Economic Review* 47 (7 January 1966):14. During 1965, Arthur

Goldberg, America's UN representative, in another move championed by State's advocates of better United States–People's Republic of China relations, stated that the United States was willing to meet Chinese representatives at the bargaining table of a nuclear disarmament conference. See Roger Kahn, "I'm Not Discouraged Either, Got It?" *Saturday Evening Post*, 29 January 1966, p. 88.

110. Richard Strout (TRB), "Taking in a New Idea," *New Republic*, 19 March 1966, p. 2.

111. Whiting, *Chinese Calculus*, pp. 186-190.

112. Foster Rhea Dulles, pp. 224-225; *DSB* 53 (11 October 1965):581-582; and 53 (8 November):944-947. Officials did not easily abandon the imagery of World War II. On 11 March 1966, for example, Tom Wicker, writing in the *Times*, could report that some in Washington were painting China as "relatively expansionist . . . and dedicated to spreading Communist and Chinese power throughout the world, advocacy toward threatening nuclear strength, and needing to be stopped now—in Vietnam—as the world should have stopped Hitler on the Rhine."

113. Stewart Alsop, "The Mind of Mao," *Saturday Evening Post*, 15 January 1966, p. 14.

114. Whiting, *Chinese Calculus*, pp. 186-190.

115. *NYT*, 30 January 1966.

116. Ibid., 7 March 1966. James Reston in his 13 February "Washington" column in the *Times* notes,

It was the decision of the National Broadcasting Company to televise the Fulbright (Vietnam) hearings that gave them so much influence. Open hearings without TV cameras do not influence the White House to the same extent, do not bring Senators to the caucus room with the same interest, and do not have the same impact on the general public.

117. Gallup Opinion Index, no. 10 (March 1966).

118. See *U.S. Policy with Respect to Mainland China*, Hearings before the Committee on Foreign Relations, United States Senate, 87th Cong., 2d sess., Washington, D.C. 1966. The Council on Foreign Relations 1966 Yearbook (Stebbins, *The United States, 1966*, p. 267) described this period as one in which there was

a gradual but highly significant modification of American attitudes on the whole China question. Not only was every aspect of China policy being discussed in the United States with a freedom that would have been unthinkable a few years earlier. Even the substance of China policy appeared to be undergoing subtle modifications as Washington, without relaxing its opposition to Chinese expansion, sought cautiously . . . [to encourage] new forms of Sino-American contact.

119. *Wall Street Journal*, 4 March 1966.

120. Nicholas Lemann, "How to Get a Job in the New Administration," *Washington Monthly* 8 (January 1977):8. One aide to Moyers sent him poll results showing a fair amount of public acceptance of China and added the comment that this "material might be helpful to your cause." See Hayes Redmon to Bill Moyers, 11 July 1966, White House Central Files, EX C050-2, Lyndon Baines Johnson Library, Austin, Texas. This memo focused on the results revealed in a 27 June 1966 Harris release. It pointed out that a majority of the public (with views) favored diplomatic recognition of the mainland (57 to 43 percent) and "two Chinas" in the United Nations (55 to 45 percent). This memo also quoted results showing that the public favored nuclear arms negotiations with China (74 to 26 percent), allowing Americans to travel to the mainland (68 to 32 percent), and staying in the United Nations should China win admission (92 to 8 percent). Redmon

did not note data less favorable to China (e.g., its admission to the United Nations was still opposed by a 63 to 37 percent margin in the general public).

121. Thomson, "On the Making," p. 239. Thomson also reports that the White House conducted its own opinion polls at this time, though none of this reported material appears to be filed at the Johnson Library (letter to the author from David C. Humphrey, Archivist, The Lyndon Baines Johnson Library, 18 May 1982, Austin, Texas). The Gallup and Harris releases are contained in the White House Office Files of Fred Panzer, Box 179, "China," at the Johnson Library.

122. *Newsweek*, 21 March 1966, p. 25.

123. Other non-executive events to occur at this time included Senator Javits's call for a new China policy (21 March 1966, *NYT*). The House, too, took moves in this direction as the House Foreign Affairs Subcommittee on the Far East and the Pacific, on 19 May, issued a report recommending an increase in contacts with the People's Republic of China.

124. Gallup poll, no. 726-K (22 April 1966).

125. Ibid.; 56 percent would favor admission, 28 percent would oppose it.

126. Harris release, 27 June 1966, in the *Philadelphia Inquirer*. A 24 February 1969 Harris release in the *Long Island Press* showed that this view continued to have support. From a 55 to 45 percent base reported in 1966 (actual breakdown, 37 to 31 percent), opinion held roughly steady—with a slightly different question—in 1969 at 52 percent in favor, 48 opposed (actual, 41 to 38 percent). A 1971 poll found this situation favored by 73 percent (actual, 55 to 20 percent). See 31 May 1971 Harris release in *Washington Post*.

127. Many of State's conclusions were based on the SRC survey of May-June 1964. The Steele book grew out of a suggestion to the Council of Foreign Relations by Dean Rusk in 1962. See James C. Thomson, Jr., "Dragon under Glass," *Atlantic Monthly*, October 1967, p. 35.

128. *Public Papers, 1966* (12 July), pp. 721-722. This speech was perhaps the high point in the trend forward in relations during 1966. Congress, for instance, passed a bill prohibiting U.S. food aid for China under the Food for Peace program and on 18 October (ibid., p. 1222) Johnson reiterated his formula for better relations with the mainland but dropped the notion of trade, saying, "We shall keep alive the hope for a freer flow of ideas and people between mainland China and the United States."

129. Interview with William Gleysteen, 6 July 1982, Washington, D.C. Mr. Gleysteen noted that Nicholas deB. Katzenbach played an important role in this effort. As early as 26 March 1966 the *New York Times* was reporting that a "two-China" policy was being considered in the White House.

130. Stebbins, *The United States, 1966*, p. 53; Schurmann, p. 513.

131. *NYT*, 3 November 1966.

132. Ibid., 22 October 1967. The quote is from a British official the *Times* interviewed.

133. Dean Rusk, 12 October 1967 news conference, in *DSB* 57 (30 November 1967):563; and Rusk in *DSB* 57 (6 November 1967):596.

134. Dixon Donnelley to the secretary, "American Press Reaction to the Secretary's Press Conference of October 12" (25 October 1967), Foster Papers, Box 44. This is cited as a perception of some of Rusk's Vietnam critics. This memo goes into detail over the "Yellow Peril" perception that several news organizations picked up from the secretary's speech. It should be noted, in reference to Rusk's "unified" imagery, that some government documents were reporting that "Hanoi still has considerable freedom of

action vis-à-vis both Peking and Moscow." See Special NIE 13-66 (4 August 1966), "Current Chinese Communist Intentions in the Vietnam Situation," DDRS, 1976, 223E. David Halberstam reports (pp. 649-650) that in 1966 Vice President Humphrey was sent on a tour of Asia with instructions from Johnson that his final report "brand China as *the* aggressor throughout Asia."

135. The vote totals for the years 1965-1969 were as follows (two-thirds required for admission):

	For Admission	Against Admission (U.S. Position)	Abstentions
1965	47	47	23
1966	46	57	18
1967	45	58	17
1968	44	58	23
1969	48	56	21

136. Robert G. Sutter, *China-Watch: Toward Sino-American Reconciliation* (Baltimore: Johns Hopkins University Press, 1978), p. 62.

137. Robert G. Sutter, *Chinese Foreign Policy after the Cultural Revolution, 1966-1977* (Boulder, Colo.: Westview Press, 1978), p. 6.

138. *Time*, 27 January 1967, p. 57. The review of this film notes that a voice-over (written by Theodore White) comments, as Mao appears on the screen, that "his aging mind still lusts for permanent strife; the theme he preaches to old and young alike is hate."

139. Gallup poll, Special Survey (7 February 1968).

140. *Gallup Opinion Index*, no. 76 (October 1971).

141. Harris release in the 5 May 1969 *Boston Globe*, 8 May 1969 *Miami Herald*, 24 February 1969 *Long Island Press*. The questions used, however, vary slightly. Evidently the poll Harris lists in the *Long Island Press* as having been conducted in 1969 was conducted in 1968. On this see Harris release, 11 September 1978, when the 1968 date was listed.

142. Harris release in *Long Island Press*, 24 February 1969.

143. Gallup poll, no. 774-K (20 February 1969).

144. Internal documents also reflect an understanding of this policy. See American Consul General (Hong Kong), "Communist China-U.S. Policy Assessment," 17 February 1967, DDRS, 1979, 69B; "Visit of Vice President Yen Chiu Kan of the ROC," May 9-10, 1967 (3 May), DDRS, 1979, 71A.

145. *Far Eastern Economic Review* 57 (13 July 1967):88.

146. Ibid. 59 (11 January 1968):61.

147. *Christian Century* 86 (29 January 1969):166. In March 1968 Johnson also halted pilotless reconnaissance flights over South China. See *Nation* 210 (2 February 1970):232. Nixon resumed these flights in October 1969, and ended them again in January 1970. High-altitude manned flights apparently continued.

148. Nicholas deB. Katzenbach, "A Realistic View of Communist China," *DSB* 58 (10 June 1968):737-740.

149. *Far Eastern Economic Review* 63 (16 January 1969):117.

150. Hwa Yu writing in *Christian Century* 86 (20 January 1969):166. Similarly, Dick Wilson, writing in the *Far Eastern Economic Review* 59 (11 January 1968):59, noted

that "the U.S. Government has done more in the past year or two to get closer to China than the Chinese have done on their side to bridge this gulf."

151. In many ways, the anti-Chinese rationale for an ABM system announced on 18 September 1967 was an outgrowth more of bureaucratic politics than strategic need. See Robert S. McNamara, "The Dynamics of Nuclear Strategy," *DSB* 57 (9 October 1967):443-451; Morton Halperin, "The Decision to Deploy the ABM Bureaucratic and Domestic Politics in the Johnson Administration," *World Politics* 25 (October 1972):62-95; John Newhouse, *Cold Dawn: The Story of SALT* (New York: Holt, Rinehart and Winston, 1973), pp. 84-89.

152. If the young were more responsive to the government's China policy, this might be explained as an extension of Gamson and Modigliani's (p. 189) "mainstream" model of opinion change. Their central hypothesis is, "The greater the attachment to the mainstream of society, the greater the degree of conformity of one's foreign policy opinions to official policy." Modifying this hypothesis slightly, it can be suggested that the greater the *felt need to form an attachment* to the mainstream, the closer would an individual's policy views parallel those dominant in the government. It may be this felt need to join "adult society"—of which the national government is perhaps the most visible and authoritative symbol for foreign policy questions—which leads to a youthful individual's views in this area paralleling those dominant in government in a time of turbulence. See William A. Gamson and Andre Modigliani "Knowledge and Foreign Policy Options: Some Models for Consideration," *Public Opinion Quarterly* 30 (Summer 1966). There is evidence that, despite outward appearances, the foreign policy views of the young were most in line with executive policy in the Vietnam War years. See William L. Lunch and Peter W. Sperlich, "American Public Opinion and the War in Vietnam," *Western Political Quarterly* 32 (March 1979): 21-44; John E. Mueller, *War, Presidents and Public Opinion* (New York: Wiley, 1973), p. 137. Another possible reason for more youthful attention to events concerning China has been pointed to by Ole R. Holsti and James N. Rosenau, "Does Where You Stand Depend on When You Were Born? The Impact of Generation on Post-Vietnam Foreign Policy Beliefs," *Public Opinion Quarterly* 44 (Spring 1980):8. They note that young adulthood "encompasses for many the beginning of eligibility for military service.... Consciousness of and interest in foreign affairs may be enhanced when the prospect of personal involvement hinges upon the outcome of foreign policy undertakings."

153. At the time when Johnson was considering far-reaching China policy changes in 1966 he had Robert Kintner prepare a few words for him to deliver on the importance of polls at a 15 July cabinet meeting. Johnson was to tell the other members of his government that he "takes a lot of interest in national polls. My reason is that these polls are becoming more and more a part of our national life—they are influencing public opinion a great deal; elected officials are very interested in them as is the public." See Robert E. Kintner, "Conference Memorandum for the President," 7 July 1966, *The Presidential Documents Series, President Lyndon B. Johnson*, Reel 2 (microfilm).

7

From Nixon to Normalization: Policy and Public Preferences, 1969–1979 ⎯⎯⎯⎯

The beginning of 1969 saw several important developments occur that, within the next three years, would have an enormous impact on the rhetoric and substance of American governmental policy regarding China. Chief among the developments were the election of Richard Nixon and the gathering momentum behind the more pragmatic members of the Chinese leadership, resulting from Soviet military actions in Europe and Asia. Just as a decade earlier some had seen the harbinger of a new China policy in Nixon's defeat, some now expressed the belief that his victory might open the way to an era of improved Sino-American relations. James Thomson, writing in the February 1969 *Atlantic Monthly*, expressed this viewpoint when he suggested that a

Republican President, and pre-eminently *this* Republican President, brings to the China problem some very special assets.... Who, for instance, can pin the label of "softness on Communism" on Richard M. Nixon when he makes overtures to Peking? If little else is clear about the new President, his anti-Communist credentials are impeccable. The ironic fact is that *any* Republican would have greater domestic room for maneuver on China policy than a Democrat, and that Mr. Nixon will have more room than most Republicans.[1]

The president-elect quickly displayed an interest in improved relations with the People's Republic of China by concurring with the Johnson Administration's decision to respond favorably to Peking's 26 November 1968 call for a resumption of the suspended Warsaw talks. The Chinese call for a resumption of these talks, as well as their continued withdrawal of PLA troops from North Vietnam (begun in March 1968), signalled Peking's interest in re-entering world diplomacy.[2] Any impetus on the American side for greater Sino-American contacts, though, would have to come from the new president. This proved to be true as Congress remained wary of the political costs of advocating better relations with the People's Republic of China prior to a shift in public attitudes. A December 1968 poll by Congressman Don Edwards of all his colleagues in the House, for example, found that 76 percent of those responding expected to be politically damaged if they publicly spoke in favor of gestures designed to improve relations with Peking.[3] Still, the cautious words from leaders in both capitals led the *Far Eastern Economic Review*'s New Year's editorial to speculate that the coming months brought with them "the promise that old, hardened attitudes will be rethought."[4]

Once in office, Nixon's interest in moving closer to China quickly manifested itself. An early Nixon memo sent to National Security Adviser Henry Kissinger, for instance, urged that improved relations with the mainland become a high priority for Washington.[5] The newly elected president, though, was still treading cautiously in public. At his first press conference, which "dismayed" advocates of rapprochement, Nixon stated that "until some changes occur on [the Chinese] side ... I see no immediate prospect of any change in our policy."[6] Again it seemed firmness might triumph over flexibility in America's Asian policy. Despite this initial "hawkish" exterior, Nixon's memo had set off a review of China policy in the upper reaches of government. Not privy to such information, the Chinese leadership remained divided in early 1969 over the wisdom of contacts with the United States. With advocates of isolation once more gaining the upper hand, the People's Republic of China cancelled the upcoming 20 February resumption of the ambassadorial talks by using the pretext of an alleged American role in "enticing" a Chinese chargé d'affaires in the Netherlands to defect.

Undaunted, Washington continued to press its China initiative. A 21 February news briefing was informed by Kissinger that "the President has always indicated that he favors a policy of maximum contact" with mainland China. More quietly, diplomatic messages of reconciliation were sent in March through the offices of France and through Rumanian and Pakistani channels in July and August.[7] Significant movement was also occurring in the press at this time. In a departure from past editorial policy, the 6 June 1969 *Time* magazine suggested that the United States seek to establish better relations with the mainland:

Any overtures toward China at this point may turn out to be a mistake because they may be based on a misreading of Chinese psychology and the country's political mechanisms. But on balance the risks involved seem relatively slight and the case for a change in U.S. policy is powerful.[8]

As 1969 continued, the Nixon Administration began to become more public in its gestures toward the mainland. Moves such as the enunciation of the Nixon Doctrine and the 7 November removal of the Seventh Fleet's permanent patrol in the Taiwan Straits showed America's willingness to disengage from China's periphery. Rhetorically, Washington increasingly stressed that it would be quite flexible toward Peking. The United States would "take the initiative to reestablish more normal relations with Communist China and shall remain responsive to any indications of less hostile attitudes from their side."[9] Washington also began to play down the military threat posed by the mainland—noting, with occasional lapses, that the ABM system was as much "targeted" at the Soviet Union as at China.[10] Public pronouncements on the course and purpose of the Vietnam War began to similarly alter as administration sources began to stress that China was "playing only a minimal role ... in Vietnam compared with the Soviet Union."[11] As Kissinger has written, "We needed no additional enemies."[12] At the United Nations, while holding steady in its opposition to Peking's seating, the 1969 speech by American General Assembly Representative Irving Whalley did appear to be cast in a somewhat less vitriolic tone than had been true in previous years.[13]

By year-end several further steps designed to bridge America's differences with China had taken place. On 21 July, for example, trade and travel restrictions involving the People's Republic of China were eased. "The actual change," according to Kissinger, "was unimportant but the symbolism was vast."[14] These restrictions were further lightened on 19 December, eight days after China had agreed to American importunings to resurrect the suspended ambassadorial talks. A further signal of Washington's peaceful intent toward the mainland occurred on 15 December 1969 when it was announced that all nuclear weapons would be removed from Okinawa within fifteen days. The administration was not shy about promoting its views among the public; it even went so far as to issue a discussion package for high school and college students on American relations with China, concluding with President Nixon's words that "whenever the leaders of Communist China choose to abandon their self-imposed isolation, we are ready to talk with them in [a] frank and serious spirit."[15]

These initiatives did not go unnoticed by Congress and the press. Several senators, taking their cue from the White House, began to call for better relations with China. The Senate, in a move reflective of this change, approved an administration-backed resolution which stated that "when the United States recognizes a foreign government and exchanges diplomatic representatives with it, this does not of itself imply that the United States approves the form, ideology or policy of that foreign government."[16] At about the same time, CBS television—in a move consonant with much media opinion—presented a documentary entitled "Triangle of Conflict," which seemed to argue for the necessity of a fundamental change in America's China policy. The Committee of One Million, clearly on the defensive, could only argue that having already gone the "extra mile" to heal long-standing wounds with China, Washington should go no further, as "any further initiative on our part would be counter-productive—and humiliating."[17]

Washington, though, continued to press its initiative forward. This occurred despite any clear movement (since early 1969) of opinion within the public itself.

The 8 January 1970 public pronouncement that the Warsaw talks would resume twelve days later brought further evidence of the changing nature of American policy. At his regular noontime briefing on the eighth, State Department spokesman Robert J. McCloskey told reporters that the ambassadorial talks would resume at the "Chinese Communist Embassy." Within a few hours, however, on

precise White House orders, McCloskey amended his remarks. The talks, he declared, would start "at the embassy of the People's Republic of China." Never before had any American spokesman referred to the Peking regime, founded in 1949, by its official name. Three times, McCloskey repeated "the People's Republic of China," just to make sure the signal bounced clearly across the Pacific.[18]

Though policy was rapidly altering, officials continued to caution that "we don't expect any major breakthrough and that we are realistic about the possibility of success."[19]

In its annual review of international relations for 1970, the Foreign Policy Association characterized American policy toward China as moving "away from strict containment and isolation of China, but far short of full coexistence and reconciliation."[20] This seemed to be the view of many top officials as a "one China, but not now" policy gained increasing credence in Washington. As one government memo put it in 1971, "Peking has often stressed its ability to wait for its desired outcomes. We should put its patience to the test."[21] The White House, though, seemed to be moving at a more rapid pace than its bureaucracy.[22] Even when Peking suspended the Warsaw talks as a protest against America's May 1970 Cambodian incursion, Nixon and Kissinger continued to press for closer ties with China. To this end, Washington quietly passed word through its UN representatives that it could support a "two-Chinas" solution at the world body if that option were to arise.[23] Presidential press secretary Ron Ziegler hinted at this in late October 1970 when he told a group of reporters that what the United States opposed happening at the United Nations was Taipei's expulsion, not Peking's admission.[24] Increasingly worried over abandonment, Taipei tried various methods to draw the United States more tightly to its cause. Among these methods was the expansion of airfields on Taiwan at its own ($30 million) expense in the hope of having the United States permanently station B-52 bombers on the island.[25] Not taking the bait, though, the administration continued to press for more "open windows" with Peking.

The winter of 1970-1971 saw a further easing of trade and travel restrictions concerning China, as well as the limited exchange of astronomical data between the two nations. The *Far Eastern Economic Review* described the United States' attitude toward China as "waiting for the phone to ring" and concluded that "the administration really seems concerned to start the long haul towards normalization of relations with China."[26] In order to make its "number" a little clearer, on 15 March 1971 the United States completely lifted travel restrictions to China—this despite the fact that Peking had granted visas to only three out of the more than one thousand Americans State had given permission to travel to China in the previous eighteen months. The lifting of the travel ban was seen as a small but significant gesture toward the mainland. The *New Bedford* (Massachusetts) *Standard-Times* reflected this cautiously hopeful belief when it wrote that

this straw is nothing to build a house of, nor to build hopes on, but it represents a change of some kind in an area in which there has been no change at all for a long time and that whets the interest of all who would like to see a better world than we now have.[27]

This interest was further "whetted" by the surprise April 1971 Chinese invitation to the U.S. table-tennis team to visit the People's Republic. Greeting the Americans upon their arrival, Chou En-lai remarked, "A new page has been turned. A new chapter has been opened in the relations between our two peoples. Your visit to China has opened the door to friendly contacts between the peoples of the two countries."[28] This event, encouraged as it was by the White House, was followed by vast changes in popular opinion—with a *majority* of Americans apparently coming to favor the recognition of the People's Republic of China for the first time.[29] The public, for the first time since the Gallup question began being asked in 1954, was also shown to now favor the People's Republic of China's entry into the United Nations.[30] Harris, finding similar results, labelled this "reversal [as] one of the most dramatic shifts in American attitudes in recent times."[31] Of thirty-three newspapers reviewed by the State Department, the vast majority concurred with these changed public attitudes, declaring in favor of seating Peking in the United Nations—though without Taiwan's expulsion. (See table 6.) "Virtually overnight," trumpeted the 15 April *Washington Post*, "it [i.e., China] has changed its popular image in the United States from stormy to sunny . . . suddenly it seems a bit ungracious to say Communist China."[32] This change, of course, was not an "overnight" phenomenon, having long been prepared for by Washington. Nixon, for example, rightly claimed in a 1972 interview that "I started a new policy in motion in February of 1969."[33] In any case, it appears that by the end of the table-tennis team's journey to China the majority of Americans had come to agree with Secretary of State Rogers's reply to Chou that "we hope it [i.e., our contact] will become a new chapter and that there will be several pages to follow."[34] Three days after this comment, a bipartisan presidential panel chaired by Henry Cabot Lodge issued a report that recommended American support for Peking's UN membership bid. "Surely this proposal," remarked the *Cleveland Plain Dealer*, "marks the burial of the remains of America's once automatic thumbs-down reflex against Red China."[35]

The United States followed up these April events with initiatives designed to further show concern for China's feelings. To this end Washington pressured American oil companies, which were considering drilling off China's coast, to take note of Peking's concerns and claims. The press was aglow with the sig-

TABLE 6

PRESS OPINION ON THE "CHIREP" QUESTION
IN MID-1971

Seat Peking, do not expel Taipei	Oppose Peking in UN
Atlanta Journal-Constitution	Boston Herald Traveler
Baltimore Sun	Chicago Tribune
Christian Science Monitor	Cincinnati Enquirer
Cleveland Plain Dealer	Dallas News
Denver Post	Richmond Times-Dispatch
Hearst Newspapers	St. Louis Post-Democrat
Houston Post	
Kansas City Star	
Los Angeles Times	
Louisville Courier-Journal	
Milwaukee Journal	
New Orleans Times-Picayune	
New York Post	
New York Times	
Newark News	
Norfolk Pilot	
Philadelphia Inquirer	
Providence Journal	
St. Louis Post-Dispatch	
Salt Lake City Tribune	
Scripps-Howard Newspapers	
Wall Street Journal	
Washington Star	

Seat Peking, no mention of Taipei

Miami Herald

Source: U.S. Opinion Survey 2 (May 1971), Foster
Papers, Box 13.

Note: List refers only to those with explicitly
defined editorial policy. List is meant to
be representative, not exhaustive.

nificance of such actions and generally reported them in a favorable light. Even old-time Nationalist journals began to show a new side. *Life*, for instance, devoted its 30 April edition largely to a favorable review of the mainland. In this issue Edgar Snow also reported on a December 1970 conversation he had had with Mao in which the chairman offered to meet with Nixon "either as a tourist or as President."[36] That the president wanted to go to China was in little doubt. Hugh Sidey reported that Nixon was "thirsting" to get to the mainland, though Sidey added that the chances of this occurring "are remote, of course."[37]

Within months of Sidey's words, and following an initially secret trip to Peking by Kissinger, a July 1971 announcement was made that Nixon would be visiting the People's Republic in February of the following year. The *Washington Post* commented, "If Mr. Nixon had revealed he was going to the moon he could not have flabbergasted his audience more.... It is very nearly mind blowing."[38] Such a statement, however, shows a neglect of the very real prior moves the president had made toward China and the way opinion reacted to these actions. As Philip A. Kuhn has written, "There are strong indications that the President's trip to China could not have taken place unless the White House had come to the conclusion that the public was ready for it."[39] Mindful of Eisenhower's U-2 debacle, Nixon now also suspended all intelligence-gathering flights over the mainland—though he was apparently unable to prevent the Nationalists from increasing their frequency of guerilla raids on the People's Republic of China.[40] Shortly after the trip's announcement, the Nixon Administration made official its implicit "China" policy. Speaking on 2 August, Rogers stated that the United States would vote in favor of seating the People's Republic at the United Nations and against the expulsion of Taiwan. The reaction to this announcement, according to State's opinion analysts, was "almost entirely favorable," with even some previously recalcitrant journals coming around to accept the administration's view.[41]

Acting in line with U.S. policy, UN delegate George Bush introduced two resolutions in the world body whose net effect would have been to allow the international organization to house both Chinas. The president reiterated that this was America's official policy when he told a September gathering of journalists,

We favor the admission and will vote for the admission of the People's Republic to the United Nations and that will mean, of course, obtaining a Security Council seat.... We will vote against the expulsion of the Republic of China and will work as effectively as we can to accomplish that goal.[42]

By this point, American policy seemed quite just to the press and public and little controversy arose over it. As Joseph Kraft, writing in the *Los Angeles Times* put it, "There is almost no public resistance to the not very gentle letting down of Chiang Kai-shek."[43]

Bush, though, did continue to work to retain Taiwan's seat. To act otherwise would not have been the politic thing to do. The *Far Eastern Economic Review*, in less than favorable language, described the American effort in the following terms:

Initially, the U.S. had given the impression it was sponsoring the retention of Taiwan only as a gesture intended to save Taiwan's face. But soon it became evident that the Americans really meant to go all out in defense of Taiwan, adopting the worst tactics of horse trading—even to the extent of flying in representatives of certain poverty-stricken countries, who would otherwise have been unable to attend.[44]

This maneuvering, however, was unsuccessful. (Bush, in his 1980 presidential campaign, would come to blame this loss on the evaporation of several votes he thought were safely in his pocket, including one from the delegate he came to call the "No man from Oman.") Not the least reason for Taipei's defeat was that Bush's efforts had been undercut by the continuing rapprochement between Washington and Peking. Indeed, on the day of Taiwan's expulsion Kissinger was in Peking—having extended his talks with Chinese leaders through the representation debate.[45] In a brief flurry, the Senate showed its distaste for the dancing in the aisles that accompanied the expulsion vote by refusing to allocate $141 million for the United Nations, a move opposed by most newspapers and a good portion of the general public.[46] Once having expressed its displeasure, though, the Senate moved on to other matters and the funds were eventually restored.

Despite the rapid change in U.S. policy, it would be incorrect to conclude that the years of public distrust of China had melted completely away. A majority of persons (56 percent) in August 1971 still saw China as the world's most dangerous nation.[47] *Reader's Digest*, continuing its decades old hostility to the People's Republic of China, published an article suggesting that Communist China, in dealing with the United States, was merely changing its tactics in seeking to fulfill its worldwide revolutionary goals. If we deal with them, argued this widely read publication, we must be prepared to be double-crossed.[48] Residual distrust of the Chinese was also evident in the plurality of persons who, on the eve of Nixon's visit to the mainland, agreed with the statement, "President Nixon can get fooled and trapped by the Communists in China."[49] Nixon's trip, preceded by further trade concessions, led to the issuance of the February 1972 "Shanghai Communiqué" which was to serve as the basis for Chinese-American relations throughout most of the 1970s. In this communiqué the United States pledged to "ultimately" remove its forces from Taiwan and acknowledge that "all Chinese on either side of the Taiwan Strait maintain there is but one China and that Taiwan is a part of China."[50]

Though a few editorial qualms arose over Taipei's treatment (the *Philadelphia Inquirer* headlined its article on the Shanghai Communiqué "They Got Taiwan, We Got Eggroll"), Nixon's actions appear to have been well received by the majority of the press and public. This trip may even have led to an increase in the "favorability" with which Americans viewed China. Gallup, for instance, found that of the 98 percent of those who had heard of Nixon's trip to China— the highest awareness score for any event in the history of the Gallup poll— many more persons chose favorable, rather than unfavorable, adjectives to describe the Chinese people.[51] Furthermore, as table 7 shows, there had been a large increase in those wishing China well. Also interesting in this respect is an April 1972 Minnesota poll which asked residents of that state if "President Nixon's trip to China had changed your impression of the Chinese people or not? and if so, how?" Thirty-one percent of those interviewed reported their impressions of the mainland had changed, with 29 percent now responding that they were "more favorably inclined" toward China than before the Nixon visit.[52] Seeking to bask in its reflected glow, the president kept Air Force One parked on the tarmac in Anchorage, Alaska, for nine hours on the return leg of his journey so as to arrive home in triumphant fashion during television's prime viewing hours.[53]

Contacts with the mainland continued to mount throughout 1972 and 1973. The United States placed Chinese trade on the same level as that of the Soviet Union and ended the ban on American commercial ships and planes traveling to China. By May 1973 liaison offices had been established by each nation in the other country's capital. The press and public also seemed to be adopting an increasingly favorable attitude toward the mainland. Thomas Massey, writing of these years, has noted that

during this state of foreign reportage . . . no country had a more successful propaganda run than the China of Chairman Mao. When Richard Nixon opened the door to respectability in 1972, the TV crews that accompanied him sent back pictures of what was soon to become the conventional view of China. . . . A frugal, honest and unified nation, with its ever-smiling face set to the future and its sense of common purpose firm. A nation, in short, that was everything we thought pioneer America had been.[54]

The *New York Times* was a leading proponent of such a view, with one critic stating that a "romance exists between the *New York Times* and Mao's China."[55] Such views had an impact on the public, as by 1973 more persons felt favorable toward China than had the opposite perception (see table 7).

In retrospect, though, the establishment of liaison offices appears to have been the high point of Sino-American relations in the first half of the 1970s. Internal policy disputes in China, Nixon's Watergate problems, and the increasingly shaky position of America's Asian allies all played a role in the stagnation that set in. Perhaps the major obstacle to relations' moving forward was Washington's unwillingness to accede to China's "three conditions" for normalizing relations. These conditions involved (1) the breaking of diplomatic ties with Taipei, (2) the abrogation of the Mutual Defense Treaty, and (3) the withdrawal of all U.S. forces from the island. Taiwan, clearly worried that the United States would eventually accede to these demands, asked for and got no less than fifty-two

TABLE 7

"FAVORABILITY" RATINGS OF PRC AND TAIWAN

	China		Taiwan	
	Favorable %	Unfavorable %	Favorable %	Unfavorable %
1954	12	67		
1967	5	91		
1972	23	71	53	38
1973	49	43		
1974	42	52		
1975	28	58	48	39
1976	20	73	55	34
1977	26	52	56	18

Source: Michael Y. M. Kau, Pierre M. Perolle, Susan H. Marsh, and Jeffrey Berman, "Public Opinion and U.S. China Policy," in Hungdah Chiu, ed., Normalizing Relations with the People's Republic of China: Problems, Analysis and Documents (Occasional Papers/Reprints Series in Contemporary Asian Studies, no. 2 1978, School of Law, University of Maryland); Gallup Polls, 7 February 1968 Special Survey; 19 June 1973, no. 868-K; 25 November 1976, no. 959-K; Current Opinion 2 (May 1974): 52. All polls are Gallup except the 1974 poll which is from NORC. Not all questions are identical, though the question wording varies very slightly from poll to poll.

"reassurances," in the three years following Nixon's trip, that they would not be cast adrift.[56] The inability of the United States to meet the mainland's demands helped to lead to a decline in Sino-American trade and cultural relations following their initial enthusiastic expansion (see figure 2). The stagnation in relations was also evident in the still small number of congressional visitors to the mainland.[57] A March 1974 NORC poll, and a 1975 Gallup survey, showed a continuing fall in People's Republic of China "favorability" among the American public (see table 7). This did not mean, though, that the public had turned against recognizing the People's Republic; new "assumptions" now existed. Gallup found mainland Chinese recognition still supported in the public by a 61 to 23 percent margin. This survey, however, also disclosed that by a 70 to 14 percent gap the public wanted to continue ties with Taiwan and, when asked directly, disapproved by a seven-to-one majority of the idea of "derecognizing" Taiwan as the explicit price for fuller relations with the mainland.[58]

Jimmy Carter, upon taking office in 1977, was somewhat of an unknown quantity on the China question. Given Ford's continued cutting of ties with Taipei, the Nationalists took solace in Carter's campaign pledge not to "sacrifice or abandon Taiwan."[59] This pledge, though, did not draw much domestic attention as the China issue "received no serious consideration in the presidential campaign of 1976."[60] After Nixon's actions, it no longer seemed possible to make China an area of partisan contention. Carter, though, was to disappoint the Nationalists. He was clearly interested in cutting the Gordian knot and finding a way to recognize Peking as the government of all China. A Presidential Review Memorandum (PRM-24) early in the new president's term codified this goal as government policy.[61] On 31 March 1977, Secretary of State Cyrus Vance announced he would be journeying to the mainland. This announcement, and the later public revelation of PRM-24, led to speculation—not discouraged by the administration—that full diplomatic relations with the mainland were close at hand. The 7 July *Boston Globe*, for instance, reported that Carter was determined to find a "formula" that would allow him to establish relations with the People's Republic of China.[62] Vance's trip was to be part of an overall administration plan involving both the Russians and the Chinese. Carter hoped to establish full *de jure* contacts with the mainland and, at roughly the same time, wrap up a SALT treaty with the Soviets, thus "enhancing leverage in both directions."[63]

The United States, however, would be unable in Carter's first year to secure the middle ground between the two communist giants. Peking, for its part, was being adamant in its demand for satisfaction of "the three conditions." Preliminary soundings on Capitol Hill showed little enthusiasm for any such move which might jeopardize the well-being of Taiwan.[64] Nor did the public appear ready to break ties with Taipei. Thus, on 17 August, it was reported that the decision to recognize Peking as the government of all China was being delayed. It was believed, however, that this act was now only a matter of time—the time required to convince the public and Congress of the necessity of breaking diplomatic relations with the Nationalists and to win better conditions from Peking.

Figure 2
Sino-American Trade, 1971-1978

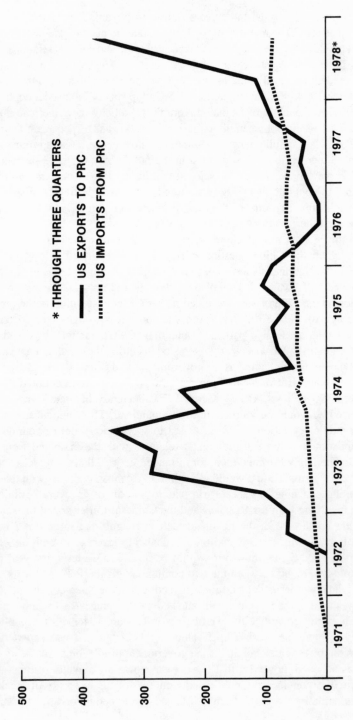

* THROUGH THREE QUARTERS
— US EXPORTS TO PRC
····· US IMPORTS FROM PRC

Source: Congressional Quarterly, *China: U.S. Policy since 1945* (Washington, D.C.: Congressional Quarterly, 1980), p. 66.

"The main obstacle to full normalization," an administration spokesman granted, "is the question of Taiwan, an issue of genuine concern to the American people."[65]

Support for the defense treaty with Taiwan, as such, continued to be strong among the American people throughout these years. Polls of the general public found the treaty's continuation favored by majorities of never less than three-to-one.[66] This may have reflected both a sense that America should keep its word to a steadfast ally, and a latent fear that the mainland might once again turn hostile toward the United States, necessitating an in-place framework for containment. A study by Yankelovich, Skelly, and White provides some evidence for this latter interpretation. A spring 1977 poll they conducted found that 58 percent of the public still saw "the emergence of Communist China as a major world power as a development unfavorable to U.S. interests."[67] A July-August poll of top political and media figures found an even stronger expression of support for Taipei, with three-quarters of the respondents favoring the defense treaty's continuation.[68] Congress, too, expressed its support of America's defense pact with Taiwan; on 25 July 1978, the Senate (by a 94–0 roll call vote) demanded to be consulted prior to any changes in the treaty.

It should be noted, though, that support for the treaty may not have been as great as it first appears. This may be due to the fact that only slightly over half of the general public and foreign policy "elite" believed that Taiwan was an area of "vital interest" for the United States.[69] When the notion of defending Taiwan was concretized into possible actions, a 1975 survey found only 8 percent of persons surveyed willing to send troops to defend the Nationalists. Another 27 percent favored sending supplies, while fully 54 percent felt America should "refuse to get involved" militarily in this situation. An earlier 1971 study, by Gallup for the Potomac Associates group, had found 11 percent willing to send troops and 30 percent willing to send supplies.[70] An April 1977 Potomac Associates poll and a ballot of Foreign Policy Association members that same month found roughly similar results.[71] Finally, a 1978 poll conducted by AIPO for the Chicago Council on Foreign Relations found continued reluctance for getting militarily involved in the Far East, though 20 percent of the public now seemed willing to back our commitment with troops. A "leadership sample" conducted in late 1978 and early 1979 found results of about the same magnitude, though this "attentive" group appeared somewhat more willing than the general public to get involved in a deteriorating military situation concerning Taiwan.[72]

One could, however, confidently report that, at least on a non-specific level, our defense pact with Taiwan was widely supported.[73] Similarly, support for the continued recognition of Taiwan as an independent entity remained quite strong throughout the 1970s. When polls linked the recognition of Peking with the derecognition of Taiwan, the previous support for establishing diplomatic relations with the mainland quickly evaporated. This was true in polls run by Gallup, Harris, the Potomac Associates, and the Foreign Policy Association. The withdrawal of Taiwan's recognition as the explicit price for improved relations with the mainland was opposed by a better than five-to-one margin in 1977 and a three-to-one majority in 1978.[74] If public opinion were to be followed to the letter, America's "two-Chinas" impasse in the Far East seemed destined to remain.

This, however, was not to be the case. Talks in Peking had begun in earnest over the normalization process in July 1978. In addition to its previous backers in the administration, Zbigniew Brzezinski, Carter's national security adviser, also began to push for recognition of the mainland as he became convinced of the "balance of power" rationale for such a move.[75] By October, though the discussions remained secret, Taiwan had come to realize that normalization of relations with Peking "could well be one of the next items on President Jimmy Carter's foreign policy agenda after the United States mid-term Congressional elections next month." While also not privy to the existence of these talks, the *Far Eastern Economic Review* continued,

The signs have been coming thick and fast. On the civilian front, the U.S. recently discontinued its aid participation in the Joint Commission on Rural Reconstruction, an agricultural project begun 30 years ago. Not long ago, Washington closed two of the three Taiwan offices of the U.S. International Communications Agency (formerly USIS), and the director of one of them was promptly whisked off for a new assignment in Peking. In addition to the continuing troop withdrawal, the U.S. indicated earlier this year that foreign military sales credits to Taiwan, declining from US $80 million in 1975 to a proposed US $10 million next year, will cease altogether by 1980.[76]

Perhaps the strongest sign that the days of diplomatic ties with Taipei were numbered involved Nationalist Ambassador Jimmy Shen. American officials reportedly informed Shen that he would be the last Republic of China ambassador in Washington. If he retired and Nationalist China attempted to appoint a successor the "State Department and White House would drag their feet indefinitely over accepting" the new appointee. Despite these signs, though, the majority of commentators expected the Chinese impasse to continue for a while longer, given the shape of American opinion. A hindrance to change was also felt to exist due to Taiwan's warm acceptance in Congress. In a poll of the upper chamber, the American Conservative Union had found, for instance, 64 senators opposed to, or leaning against, cutting America's defense and diplomatic ties with Taipei in exchange for recognizing Peking.[77]

In spite of this congressional sentiment, the White House was undeterred. On 15 December 1978, in a television address to the nation that one journalist called "dramatic and unexpected," President Carter announced the establishment of full diplomatic relations with Peking.[78] While Carter stressed that "normalization will not jeopardize the well-being of the people of Taiwan,"[79] his actions were clearly contrary to the wishes of the majority of Americans as expressed in various opinion polls taken prior to this declaration. It is unsurprising, then, that his speech brought a torrent of letters, cables, and phone calls to the White House, with 80 percent of these messages expressing disapproval (especially over the president's failure to gain People's Republic of China guarantees on Taiwan's future security).[80] The polls that followed Carter's statement also generally found that opinion was still against Taiwan's "derecognition" and the ending of the mutual defense pact as the quid pro quo for recognizing Peking. There is, though, suggestive evidence that Carter's actions did help to pull public opinion more in line with administration policy. This seemed to be Carter's expectation as after he finished his announcement he leaned over his dead microphone and said, "Massive applause throughout the nation."[81] (Upon hearing of this studio episode William F. Buckley commented, "No doubt Ribbentrop was ebullient too after concluding the pact with Molotov in 1939.")[82]

The first poll taken (on 16–17 December) following Carter's pronouncement found that 60 percent of the persons interviewed claimed to have heard of the president's Friday night announcement. This survey discovered virtually no change from an earlier 1977 study which had found a large plurality against the derecognition of Taiwan as the price for formal ties with the mainland.[83] As this poll does not, however, break down those who had heard of the president's announcement from those who had not, we are unable to directly say what effect Carter had on the opinion of the sampled group. A poll taken one week later also found a majority with reservations concerning the cancellation of the defense treaty with Taiwan. This poll, though, found nearly three-to-one support for the statement that America was "more right [than wrong] ... to have agreed to official diplomatic recognition of the PRC."[84]

A Gallup poll released one month after Carter's decision found similar results when it asked informed persons (86 percent) whether they, "all things considered," approved of the actions the United States had taken with regard to the China area. By a 57 to 23 percent margin people responded to this question affirmatively, though they also felt, by a 48 to 34 percent count, that the establishment of diplomatic relations with the People's Republic was not an "important enough reason to break off diplomatic relations with Taiwan." Perhaps the low level of information concerning the actual content of the president's actions accounted for this paradoxical attitude. Some evidence for this view arises from the fact that only 16 percent of the "informed group" correctly knew of the conditions of America's recognition of the People's Republic of China and the simultaneous derecognition of Taiwan.[85]

A CBS poll in late January 1979 also found concern over the plight of the people of Taiwan. However, only 11 percent of the persons sampled in this survey considered sending troops to aid allies such as the Nationalists an appropriate response to a military attack.[86] Finally, an early February poll found a slight plurality (44 to 40 percent) of those interviewed still opposed recognition of the mainland at the cost of the defense treaty with Taiwan.[87] Such opinion soundings reflected the ambivalence with which many Americans evaluated Carter's actions. The *Reader's Digest* offered forth a rare editorial that, though accepting the need to recognize the reality of the mainland's Communist regime, expressed concern over Taiwan's future plight.[88] The *Houston Post*, perhaps, best summed up these ambivalent feelings when it granted the inevitability of Peking's recognition yet lamented that "Americans can only feel a sadness over the end of our special relationship with Taiwan."[89]

This sadness manifested itself in Washington in more active terms. Many in America's capital agreed with the *Wall Street Journal*'s analysis that "the U.S. surrendered for a remarkably low price . . . [and] paid a high price in conceding the People's Republic's claim to Taiwan with so little assurance of Taiwan's security."[90] Congress generally showed concern, as well, over Carter's lack of prior consultation with it. "Even moderates in Congress who applauded the President's action are haunted by the way Mr. Carter went about it," commented Rod MacLeish on the 16 December CBS evening news.[91] This lack of consultation led some, such as Senator Goldwater, to charge the chief executive with "an outright abuse of presidential power" in cancelling the treaty. (A law suit was filed by Goldwater along these lines, though a federal appellate court later ruled in the president's favor.) Others, like House International Relations Committee Chairman Clement J. Zablocki, argued that there was little that could be done to reverse Carter's actions and that Congress had best concentrate its attention on legislating support for Taipei. Carter, having not properly prepared the public for his actions, was susceptible to such legislative counter-pressures. This was especially true given that his was the party of "weak" foreign policy. Having gotten too far ahead of opinion, some backtracking was now necessary lest an already hot issue turn into a future electoral liability. This backtracking eventually led to the April 1979 signing of the Taiwan Relations Act—a bill containing considerably stronger language guaranteeing Taipei against future threats than the president had initially hoped for.[92] This move, as might have been expected, was supported in the public by a 56 to 31 margin.[93] The Taiwan Relations Act, though, did not effectively alter Carter's actions. Congressional, public, and "elite" opinion notwithstanding, America's China policy had lastingly changed.

NOTES

1. James C. Thomson, Jr., "Nixon and China: Time to Talk," *Atlantic Monthly*, February 1969, p. 71.

2. Robert G. Sutter, *Chinese Foreign Policy after the Cultural Revolution, 1966-1977* (Boulder, Colo.: Westview Press, 1978), p. 12; Allen S. Whiting, *The Chinese Calculus of Deterrence: India and Indochina*, (Ann Arbor: University of Michigan Press, 1975) p. 170.

3. *Christian Century* 86 (31 December 1969):1676.

4. *Far Eastern Economic Review* 63 (2 January 1969): 3.

5. John Osborne, *The Third Year of the Nixon Watch* (New York: Liveright, 1972), pp. 65-66. Henry Kissinger, *White House Years* (Boston: Little, Brown, 1979), pp. 169-171, argues that this memo was not reflective of a yet-formulated policy and only sought to give the "impression" of movement in order to unnerve the Russians. Vernon A. Walters in his *Silent Missions* (Garden City, N.Y.: Doubleday and Co., 1978), pp. 523-

550, esp. p. 525, however, reports meeting with the president-elect in January 1969 and having Nixon tell him that he intended to move toward better relations with Peking.

6. *Public Papers, 1969* (27 January), p. 16.

7. Marvin Kalb and Bernard Kalb, *Kissinger* (Boston: Little, Brown, 1974), pp. 221-223.

8. *Time*, 6 June 1969, pp. 48-49.

9. William Rogers' statement of 21 April 1969 quoted in Foster Rhea Dulles, *American Policy toward Communist China* (New York: Thomas Y. Crowell Co., 1972), pp. 240-241. The removal of the permanent patrol meant that the two ships constantly assigned to that task would be removed. Ships of the U.S. Navy, however, would continue to sail through the Straits approximately fifteen times each month. See Kissinger, pp. 186-187.

10. Congressional Quarterly, *National Diplomacy, 1965-1970* (Washington, D.C.: Congressional Quarterly, 1970), p. 40. *New Republic*, 5 April 1969, p. 7.

11. *Public Papers, 1969* (25 July), p. 554.

12. Kissinger, pp. 167-168, notes that "one of the first and most important steps taken in the Nixon Administration was something we did *not* do. The Johnson Administration had used the specter of Asian Communism led by Peking as a principal justification for the Vietnam War. . . . By contrast, the Nixon Administration, from the beginning never cited, or even hinted at, an anti-Chinese motive for our Vietnam involvement; we did not agree with the analysis; we needed no additional enemies."

13. Speech reprinted in *DSB* 61 (1 December 1969): 476-479.

14. Kissinger, p. 179.

15. *Communist China* (Issues in United States Foreign Policy, no. 4, with a discussion guide), Department of State Publication 8499 (December 1969), pp. 31-32; Kalb and Kalb, pp. 225-229.

16. Congressional Quarterly, *China* (1980), p. 187.

17. Stanley D. Bacharach, *The Committee of One Million: China Lobby Politics, 1953-1971* (New York: Columbia University Press, 1976), pp. 263-265.

18. Kalb and Kalb, p. 229. Michel Oksenberg, "A Decade of Sino-American Relations," *Foreign Affairs* 62 (Fall 1982), p. 177, reports that the 20 January Warsaw meeting was productive in substantive terms.

19. "Secretary Rogers Interviewed for the Hearst Newspapers" (29 January 1970), *DSB* 62 (2 March 1970):221.

20. Foreign Policy Association, *Foreign Policy Priorities, 1970-1971* (New York: Foreign Policy Association, 1970), p. 40.

21. Richard Moorsteen and Morton Abramowitz, *Remaking China Policy* (Cambridge, Mass.: Harvard University Press, 1971), p. 9.

22. In this vein Oksenberg notes (p. 177), "Kissinger perceived foot-dragging at the State Department, while China specialists in the Foreign Service who privately supported changes in China policy hedged their memos, unaware of how rapidly the President was prepared to move."

23. *Television News Index and Abstracts*, 12 and 20 November 1970 (pp. 1796, 1849), Vanderbilt Television News Archive, Joint University Libraries, Nashville, Tennessee.

24. Kissinger, pp. 770-774.

25. James C. Thomson, Jr., "The Inscrutable Commitment," *Washington Monthly* 2 (February 1971):47. Thomson's article covers the November 1969 and May 1970 Senate

hearings on America's military and diplomatic relationship to the Republic of China; *Far Eastern Economic Review* 69 (6 August 1970):7.

26. *Far Eastern Economic Review* 70 (3 October 1970):37-38.

27. Excerpted in *Editorials on File, 1971* 2 (16-31 March 1971):373.

28. Quoted in Jacques Guillermaz, *The Chinese Communist Party in Power, 1949-1976* (Boulder, Colo.: Westview Press, 1976), p. 548.

29. Harris release in *Washington Post*, 31 May 1971.

30. Gallup poll, no. 830-K (14 May 1971). A mid-1970 telephone poll of 1980 households in six states by the Opinion Research Group of Princeton found, with a differently worded question, that People's Republic of China admission to the United Nations was opposed by a 42 to 40 percent margin in the general public. This roughly evenly split group was asked, "Do you favor or oppose the admission of Communist China to the United Nations?" Cited in Bacharach, p. 269.

31. 31 May 1971 Harris survey in *Washington Post*. Harris quote from *U.S. Opinion Summary*, no. 3 (July 1971), Foster Papers, Box 13.

32. *Washington Post*, 15 April 1971.

33. *Reader's Digest*, February 1972, p. 62.

34. Quoted in Guillermaz, p. 548.

35. Excerpted in *Editorials on File, 1971* 2 (16-30 April 1971):519.

36. Edgar Snow, "A Conversation with Mao Tse-Tung," *Life*, 30 April 1971, p. 47. This quote is Snow's paraphrase of Mao's words.

37. Hugh Sidey, "Thirsting to Get into China," in ibid., p. 4.

38. *Washington Post*, 17 July 1971.

39. Philip A. Kuhn, ed., writing in *"The China Trip: Now What?* (A discussion at the University of Chicago Center for Policy Study, 1972), p. 26.

40. Kalb and Kalb, p. 253; Thomson, "The Inscrutable Commitment," p. 47.

41. *U.S. Opinion Summary* 5 (August 1971), Foster Papers, Box 13.

42. *Public Papers, 1971* (16 September), p. 950. Rogers' 2 August announcement had stated that the General Assembly would determine whether Taipei or Peking deserved the Security Council seat allocated to China. However, by Nixon's news conference the United States, according to Kissinger (p. 774), had been "forced to retreat from this position and actually *recommended* that China's Security Council seat [sh]ould go to Peking, in the hope that the majority of nations would be attracted by the compromise."

43. *Los Angeles Times*, 16 August 1971.

44. *Far Eastern Economic Review* 74 (30 October 1971):5

45. Untitled telegram, American Taipei Embassy to State Department, 5 May 1971, DDRS, 1981, 9A. This telegram reports, for instance, that Chou told a visiting group of American scholars "that the Nixon trip was instrumental in gaining China's entry into the UN since many small nations swung to the Chinese position when it became known that Kissinger was in Peking."

46. *U.S. Opinion Survey* 7 (October 1971), Foster Papers, Box 13. Harris asked the following between October 26 and 31: "As you know just this week the United Nations voted to oust Nationalist China from the UN and to give its seat to Mainland (Communist) China. As a result of this action, do you think the U.S. should get out of the UN, cut back our support, continue with the UN as before, or increase our activity in the UN?" Eight percent of the public favored leaving the United Nations, 30 percent favored a "cut back," 33 percent recommended maintaining the status quo, 12 percent favored increasing

our "activity in the UN," and 7 percent were unsure of what to do. See *U.S. Opinion Summary* 8 (November 1971), Foster Papers, Box 13.

47. *Gallup Opinion Index*, no. 76 (October 1971).

48. Charles J. V. Murphy, "What Is behind Red China's Smile?" *Reader's Digest*, October 1971, pp. 69-73.

49. Harris survey release, 23 February 1972.

50. The Shanghai communiqué is reprinted in Hungdah Chiu, ed., *Normalizing Relations with the People's Republic of China: Problems, Analysis and Documents* (Occasional Papers/Reprints Series in Contemporary Asian Studies, no. 2, 1978 [14], School of Law, University of Maryland), pp. 145-153.

51. Gallup poll, no. 846-K (12 March 1972); *U.S. Opinion Survey* 12 (March 1972). State's analysts reported that while some commentators had qualms over the United States' actions, most editors supported it. See also James A. Michener, "China Diary," *Reader's Digest*, May 1972, p. 284.

52. Minnesota poll, April 1972. One percent responded that their feelings toward China had worsened and 1 percent were unsure how their impressions had changed.

53. Joel Swerdlow, "A Question of Impact," *The Wilson Quarterly* 5 (Winter 1981):92.

54. Thomas Massey, "China and India and Me," *The Washington Monthly* 10 (March 1978):44.

55. Unsigned review of Harrison Salisbury, *To Peking and Beyond*, in *The Washington Monthly* 5 (March 1973):64.

56. Terry L. Deibel, "A Guide to International Divorce," *Foreign Policy* 30 (Spring 1978):29.

57. According to the Congressional Quarterly's *China* (1980), p. 14, three members visited in 1972, eight in 1973, six in 1974, twenty-two in 1975, thirteen in 1976, ten in 1977, and sixty-five in 1978.

58. Poll cited in Michael Y. M. Kau, Pierre M. Perolle, Susan H. Marsh, and Jeffrey Berman, "Public Opinion and U.S. China Policy," in Chiu, ed., p. 95.

59. William R. Kintner and John F. Cooper, *A Matter of Two Chinas: The China-Taiwan Issue in United States Foreign Policy* (Philadelphia: Foreign Policy Research Institute, 1978), p. 81. For an in-depth review of Sino-American relations during Carter's term see Oksenberg, pp. 181-191.

60. O. Edmund Clubb, "Comment," in *Our China Prospects: Symposium on China-American Relations at the Autumn General Meeting of the American Philosophical Society*, 12 November 1977, ed. John K. Fairbank (Philadelphia: American Philosophical Society, 1977), p. 45.

61. *Washington Post*, 17 August 1977. This Evans and Novak report cites Michel Oksenberg, William Gleysteen, and Zbigniew Brzezinski as authors of PRM-24. The "spiritual fathers" of this policy were identified as A. Doak Barnett and John K. Fairbank.

62. *Boston Globe*, 7 July 1977. Taiwan reportedly became so involved in encouraging political opposition in the United States to normalization that Carter "added Taiwan to the secret interim list of hostile foreign intelligence services and targeted Taiwanese diplomats for surveillance and wiretaps." See *Chicago Sun-Times*, 1 June 1982.

63. Interview with William Gleysteen, 6 July 1982. In 1978, Middle East policy also became involved in China policy as Carter hoped to announce the signing of the Egyptian-Israeli treaty at the same time as announcing resumed relations with the mainland. He would then have been able to "present his austere budget on a high note and enter the

critical mid-way point of his Administration in a blaze of glory." See Dom Bonafede, "A Checkered Chinese Policy," *National Journal* 10 (30 December 1978):2078.

64. Gleysteen interview, 6 July 1982.

65. Warren Christopher (Deputy Secretary of State) speaking at Occidental College, 11 June 1977, reprinted in Appendix 6, p. 381, of *Normalization of Relations with the People's Republic of China: Practical Implications*, U.S. Congress, House, Hearings before the Subcommittee on International Relations, 95th Cong., 1st Sess., 20, 21, 28, and 29 September, 11 and 17 October 1977.

66. The Harris survey, in a 27 June 1966 release to the *Philadelphia Inquirer*, found continuance of the defense treaty favored by a 65 to 6 percent margin. A 1969 poll by Harris, released to the 4 February 1969 *Long Island Press*, found continuation of the treaty to be favored by a 55 to 19 percent margin. An 11 September 1978 Harris release found the treaty's continuation favored by a 64 to 19 percent gap; this compared with opinion that favored the treaty's continuance by a 65 to 6 percent margin in 1976 and by a 57 to 12 percent margin in 1977.

67. Daniel Yankelovich, "Cautious Internationalism: A Changing Mood toward U.S. Foreign Policy," *Public Opinion* 1 (March/April 1978):14.

68. This mail poll, conducted by Kau et al., in Chiu, ed., *Normalizing Relations*, pp. 97-99, may have a pro-Taiwan response bias in it. In any case, the defense treaty's continuation was favored by a 75 to 11 percent margin and this group opposed acceptance of the "three conditions" by a 93 to 5 percent margin. The academic community may have had a similar opinion profile. See Kintner and Cooper, p. 1.

69. John E. Reilly, ed., *American Public Opinion and U.S. Foreign Policy 1979* (Chicago: Chicago Council on Foreign Relations, 1979), p. 16. By a 53 to 26 percent margin the public felt the United States had a "vital interest" in the Taiwan region. The 366 members of the "elite" felt this way by a 55 to 43 percent margin. The general public was polled from 17 to 26 November 1978, the "elite" group from 20 November 1978 to 12 January 1979.

70. *Gallup Opinion Index*, July 1975, no. 121; Albert H. Cantril and Charles W. Roll, Jr., *Hopes and Fears of the American People* (New York: Universe Books, 1971), pp. 86, 89.

71. These polls, cited in Kau et al. in Chiu, ed., p. 96, found roughly similar results. FPA members, by a 43 to 40 percent plurality, backed military aid (i.e., troops and/or supplies) to Taiwan if it was attacked. The Potomac Associates found the public mildly opposed to this move by a 36 to 40 percent margin.

72. Reilly, p. 26.

73. This actually represents a quite logical stance. If America's commitments are clear to the world they won't be challenged and the United States, therefore, will not have to respond with force.

74. An August 1977 Gallup poll found the continuation of diplomatic relations with Taiwan favored by a 64 to 12 percent margin. The derecognition of Taiwan, as the price for recognizing the People's Republic of China, was opposed by a 65 to 8 percent spread. An April 1977 Potomac Associates poll found 61 to 22 percent support for continued ties to Taiwan and a 47 to 28 percent margin against derecognizing Taiwan in exchange for official relations with the mainland. An April 1977 ballot among FPA members found 68 to 19 percent support for continued diplomatic relations with Taiwan and a 53 to 33 percent majority against exchanging America's relations with Taiwan for relations with the mainland. Harris, in a 27 October 1977 release, reported the continuation of U.S.

recognition of Taiwan was favored by a 62 to 11 percent gap. An 11 September 1978 Harris release found, in response to a similar question, 66 to 19 percent support for diplomatic relations with Taiwan.

75. Gleysteen interview, 6 July 1982.

76. *Far Eastern Economic Review* 102 (27 October 1978): 17. By October only 600 U.S. troops remained on Taiwan.

77. Ibid., p. 20. The ACU also polled the House. Out of 270 responses, 264 were favorable (outright or "leaning") to Taiwan. In the Senate nine refused to answer, and twenty-three reported themselves undecided.

78. Terrence Smith in *New York Times*, 16 December 1978.

79. "Text of President's Statement on Ties with China," *NYT*, 16 December 1978.

80. Hungdah Chiu, "China, the United States and the Question of Taiwan," in *China and the Taiwan Issue*, ed. Hungdah Chiu (New York: Praeger Publishing, 1973), p. 196.

81. *Time*, 25 December 1978, p. 20.

82. *National Review*, 19 January 1979, p. 114.

83. CBS/*NYT* poll release, December 1978. This move was opposed by a 45 to 27 percent plurality. In the January 1977 poll it had been opposed by a 42 to 28 percent margin.

84. ABC/Harris survey release, 18 January 1979.

85. Gallup poll release, 14 January 1979.

86. CBS poll release, 23 January 1979.

87. NBC/Associated Press release, 6 February 1979. This poll also found that Russia was now seen by two-thirds of the population as the world's greatest threat to peace. Only 17 percent held a similar view of the People's Republic of China.

88. *Reader's Digest*, February 1979, pp. 136-138.

89. *Houston Post*, 20 December 1978, excerpted in *Editorials on File* 9 (16-31 December 1978):1527.

90. *Wall Street Journal*, 18 December 1978.

91. *CBS News Index* (Microfiche), 16 December 1978 (Evening News), p. ll; Bonafede, p. 2078. U.S. Ambassador Unger on Taiwan was only supposed to give Taipei one hour advance notice. He, however, disregarded these instructions and passed the word on to the Nationalists as soon as he got it—still only seven hours prior to Carter's announcement. See Chiu, "The Question of Taiwan," pp. 185, 205.

92. On the congressional aftermath of Carter's actions see Congressional Quarterly, *China* (1980), pp. 15-29; William J. Lanouette, "Congress Plays Its Card in Chinese Policy Game," *National Journal* 11 (3 March 1979):352-355.

93. NBC/Associated Press release, 6 February 1979.

8

Public Opinion and Foreign Policy: Some Substantive and Theoretical Conclusions _____

The relationship between opinion and policy in America's East Asian policy has been examined in broad stroke. The remarkable overall harmony that existed between the government's actions and the preferences of the public was not traceable to any one factor. Both opinion and policy, at varying times, have played a guiding role in the formation of America's China policy. Before elucidating the possible reasons for this finding, it is valuable to once more highlight those instances of significant opinion change on identically worded questions. Doing so will allow for a firmer base upon which to rest our concluding remarks.

OPINION AND POLICY

Military Aid to the Nationalist Chinese (NORC)

25 February 1948–25 March 1948

This short, one-month period finds, as table 8 shows, both opinion and policy moving in tandem. For a variety of strategic and political reasons, the president did not wish to completely cut off aid to the embattled Nationalists. This led the administration to seek economic aid for remnants of "free China." The granting of military aid to Chiang's forces was not, however, a high priority for the Truman White House. The need to protect the major provisions of the European Recovery Program—to which the House attached the China Aid Act— led the administration, though, to accept the inclusion of military aid in its overall package of economic help for the Nationalists. It is clear that the executive branch was, in this case, responding to congressional and not public pressure. Indeed, State's opinion analysts reported that what little public pressure existed was directed toward cutting aid off to Republican China. This conclusion was

TABLE 8

MILITARY AID TO THE NATIONALIST CHINESE

Question: "In China there is a serious civil war going
            on between the Chinese Communists and the
            Chinese Government. Do you think we should
            try to help the Chinese government by sending
            them military supplies, or should we stay out
            of it?"

Opinion Trend:	Send Supplies	No Supplies	Don't Know
25 February 1948	32%	60%	8%
25 March 1948	41	46	13

Significant Events:

1947 June 26   - Arms embargo on China lifted by US

     June 27   - Ammunition sold to Nationalists on
                 concessionary terms

     Oct 27   - US to provide foodstuffs to China

     Nov 10   - $300 million economic aid plan for
                 China announced by Administration;
                 will seek Congressional approval

     Dec 19   - Congress inserts $18 million in economic
                 aid for China into an unrelated bill

1948 Jan   - Fighting intensifies in north China

     Feb 18   - Truman submits $570 million economic
                 aid package for China to Congress

     Feb 20   - House begins hearings on aid bill;
                 Administration reveals sale of 10,000
                 tons of ammunition to Chiang at one
                 percent of cost

     Feb 25   - Czech coup; Russia presses Finland for
                 defense pact

     Mar 11   - Jan Masaryk, pro-west Czech Foreign
                 Minister, dies

     Apr 3   - Truman signs bill allocating China
                 $338 million in economic aid (later
                 reduced to $275) and $125 million in
                 military credits

unsurprising given that even the March poll found a plurality of persons opposed to pouring America's military supplies down the "rat hole" of Chiang's China.

Truman submitted his China aid package to Congress on 18 February. Hearings began on this bill two days later. These hearings brought forth a succession of witnesses in favor of extending military aid to the Nationalists. By early March it had become evident that Truman's bill would be changed to include a mix of arms and economic funding. It is likely that opinion was responding to this evolving policy on military aid, as well as to the crises in Europe (e.g., the Czech coup) which seemed to argue for the need to militarily back those resisting communism.[1]

22 April 1948–1 June 1949

This thirteen-month period presents an instance of both directional and majoritarian congruence as regards opinion and policy. The public once again turned against aiding Chiang's forces militarily, accepting administration arguments that the die in China was cast and the United States would be better off not wasting its scarce resources on a hopeless cause. At every turn the White House and State Department sought to divert interest away from aiding the Nationalists and to focus attention on the need to rebuild Europe as a bulwark against Russian expansionism. As table 9 makes clear, the public found this argument a plausible one.

Helping the Nationalists Attack the Mainland (NORC)

18 April 1951–10 September 1954

The majority approval of this measure (see table 10) is unsurprising given America's war-borne hostility toward Peking. While the United States briefly considered aiding Chiang's forces in a move against the mainland in January 1951 (as UN forces were being pushed to the brink of extinction), once the situation had stabilized in Korea this thought never again seriously arose. This was especially true following the end of hostilities in Korea as American officials from Eisenhower and Dulles downward worried over Chiang's ability to set off World War III. Rhetorically, the new Republican administration moved closer to this policy with its "unleashing" of Chiang, though its simultaneous "neutralization" of Nationalist forces showed where Washington's heart truly lay. Despite these rhetorical flourishes, opinion did trend more in line with government policy over these years, probably reflecting a slight lessening of the passions engendered by the Korean War.

U.S. Bombing of Mainland China during the Korean War (NORC)

(a) 27 August 1951–2 October 1951

(b) 2 October 1951–19 March 1952

These two separate instances of significant opinion change again show a public whose views were subordinated to war-time strategy. Throughout the Korean

TABLE 9

MILITARY AID TO THE NATIONALIST CHINESE

| Question: | "In China there is a serious civil war now going on between the Chinese Communists and the Chinese government. Do you approve or disapprove of our sending military supplies to help the Chinese government against the Communists?" |

Opinion Trend:	Approve	Disapprove	Don't Know
22 April 1948	55%	32%	13%
1 June 1949	40	48	12

Significant Events:

1948 Mar	31 -	Soviets begin obstructing traffic into West Berlin
Apr	3 -	Truman signs aid bill
June	20 -	Berlin blockade begins
Nov	1 -	PLA takes Mukden
Nov	2 -	Truman re-elected; Democrats win control of Congress
Dec	1 -	Mme. Chiang arrives in Washington to lobby for aid; receives polite but 'unresponsive' greeting
Dec	16 -	US announces it will not get involved in Chinese civil war or increase aid to a non-communist coalition government
1949 Jan	23 -	PLA takes Peking
Mar	10 -	50 Senators request action on $1.5 billion China aid bill. Administration refuses.
Apr	13 -	Congress extends 1948 aid bill ($56 million in economic aid remains to be spent from allocation)
Apr	20 -	PLA crosses Yangtze
May	12 -	Berlin blockade ends
May	25 -	Shanghai falls
Sept	28 -	Congress votes $75 million in military aid for the 'general area' of China. White House makes no move to use funds, which are later not employed to aid the Nationalists
1950 Jan	5 -	Truman announces US will stay out of Chinese civil war

TABLE 10

HELPING THE NATIONALISTS ATTACK THE MAINLAND

Question: "Would you approve or disapprove of the United
States giving the Chinese Nationalist
government on Formosa all the help it needs
to attack the Chinese Communists on the
mainland of China?"

Opinion Trend:	Approve	Disapprove	Don't Know
April 1951	58%	25%	17%
May 1951	56	28	16
Sept 1951	59	24	17
Mar 1952	56	28	16
Sept 1954	53	33	14

Significant Events:

1951 July 10	-	Korean truce talks begin
Nov 27	-	Provisional Agreement reached
1953 Feb	-	Chiang publicly 'unleashed,' privately 'neutralized'
July 27	-	Korean armistice signed
late	-	Tensions rise in Indochina
1954 March	-	Intervention in Indochina considered by Washington
April	-	Geneva conference begins; ends 21-22 July
Sept. 3	-	PRC shells offshore islands

hostilities, American forces allowed communist supply "sanctuaries" to exist in Manchuria. Washington did not respond to changes in opinion with changes in battlefield tactics. Perhaps the closest America came to bombing the mainland was its June 1952 attacks on the Yalu power stations, which occurred despite a downward trend in (the still-majority) opinion favoring attacks on the People's Republic of China (see table 11). In these war-time conditions, Washington did not let its tactics be dictated by opinion. Nor is it likely many in the public would have advocated such a suicidal responsiveness during the war.

Should Dulles Meet with Chou En-lai (NORC)

29 September 1955–26 January 1956

The question of whether John Foster Dulles should meet with Chinese Foreign Minister Chou En-lai presents a case of majoritarian non-congruence and directional harmony traceable to government actions. As table 12 shows, a clear majority of persons polled favored such a meeting. The Chinese, once the am-

TABLE 11

U.S. BOMBING OF MAINLAND CHINA DURING THE KOREAN WAR

Question:	"Do you think United States airplanes should or should not cross the Korean border now, and bomb Communist supply bases inside China?"		
Opinion Trend:	Should	Should Not	Don't Know
(a) 27 August 1951	54%	31%	15%
2 October 1951	60	23	17
(b) 2 October 1951	60	23	17
19 March 1952	54	31	15

Significant Events: (See also table 10)

1952 June 26   – U.S. ends three days of bombing of Yalu power plants which provide electricity to Manchuria as well as North Korea.

TABLE 12

SHOULD DULLES MEET WITH CHOU EN-LAI

Question: "Do you think it would be a good idea or a
             bad idea for Secretary Dulles to meet with
             the Chinese foreign minister in the near
             future, to try to reach an agreement on some
             of the problems in Asia?"

Opinion Trend:	Good Idea	Bad Idea	Don't Know
29 September 1955	82%	10%	8%
26 January 1956	74	18	8

Significant Events:

1955 Aug   1   - Ambassadorial talks begin; 11 imprisoned
               American airmen released by China

     Sept 10   - Repatriation agreement reached

1956 Jan   - Level of public acrimony over talks
               increases

     June 12   - U.S. publicly rejects 12 May Chinese
               offer for a Foreign Minister's meeting.
               Statement reiterates long-standing
               U.S. opposition on this point

bassadorial talks began, pressed for this event. The American public and press
were also ready for high-level talks to resolve tensions in the Far East. Dulles,
however, had no interest in engaging in discussions that would accord the People's Republic of China a greater degree of legitimacy than it already had. From
the moment of the ambassadorial talks' announcement, the secretary of state
made this clear to all who would listen. Opinion, though still heavily positive,
did respond to this government policy by becoming less enthusiastic over a
foreign ministers' conference. Undoubtedly affecting opinion was the increasingly acrimonious atmosphere at the Geneva talks, resulting from intransigent
American negotiating tactics and Chinese ''foot-dragging'' on the 10 September
1955 repatriation agreement.

Should Trade Be Allowed with the Chinese Communists (NORC)

July 1956–January 1957

American commerce with the People's Republic of China was neither en-couraged nor allowed until the 1970s. Opinion in the mid-fifties, though, seems to have become more accepting of the idea of eventually opening trade relations with the mainland (see table 13). This attitude change, which may have been encouraged by the actions of our allies, led to no change in government policy—though a subtle rhetorical shift may have been encouraged by this opinion alteration.

Should Communist China Be in the United Nations (Gallup)

7 July 1954–25 August 1958

With broad outlines, this roughly four-year period represents an instance of majoritarian and directional congruence. As policy moderated in Washington, a small but significant change in public attitudes occurred (see table 14). Allowing the People's Republic of China into the United Nations would grant it interna-tional legitimacy. Dulles's actions in setting up negotiations with the Chinese Communists was a step in this direction. Only after the administration responded positively to Chou En-lai's April 1955 initiative did some of the war-bred hostility toward the mainland begin to fade. The general thrust of American policy in these years, despite some occasional backing and filling, was in a slightly positive direction; the same could also be said of public opinion Toward China.

25 August 1958–4 February 1964

This borderline case of significant opinion change presents another situation of congruence. This congruence, though, appears traceable to opinion's influence on the policy process. This was especially true in the Kennedy years, as any change in America's "Chirep" policy was ruled out by an adamant public. Policy under Kennedy, after some initial hesitation, fell into line with the citi-zenry. Spurred on by Washington's words and deeds (in response to opinion's original harsh stance), popular attitudes drifted into an increasingly negative posture in this era (see table 15).

4 February 1964–17 May 1971

This longest of China-United Nations cases presents a dramatic instance of congruent opinion and policy change. Opinion altered first in response to the October 1964 Chinese nuclear blast. Policy, in response to this threat, initially hardened, but by late 1965 was consciously trending in a positive direction. The change in public attitudes that allowed for these moves was, in turn, reinforced and deepened by Washington's actions in 1966. Policy and opinion toward the mainland continued to moderate in Johnson's last year, though continuing Peo-ple's Republic of China intransigence and the White House's Vietnam problems

TABLE 13

SHOULD TRADE BE ALLOWED WITH THE CHINESE COMMUNISTS

Question: "Now a question about Communist China. Would
you approve or disapprove of Americans
carrying on trade with Communist China, if
this trade did not include war materials?"

Opinion Trend:	Approve	Disapprove	No Opinion
July 1956	40%	55%	5%
January 1957	47	46	7

Significant Events:

1956 Feb 1   - U.S. and Great Britain agree that Chinese
                "trade controls should continue and
                should be reviewed . . . periodically as
                to their scope, in the light of changing
                conditions . . ."

     May 16   - Britain informs U.S. of planned expansion
                of PRC trade

1957 Apr 4   - Commerce Secretary Weeks says U.S. will
                continue total trade ban

     Apr 20   - Under allied pressure, U.S. agrees to
                discuss modification in "China controls"
                that allies follow. Washington, however,
                reiterates its intention to maintain its
                own trade ban

     May   - U.S. and allies meet in Paris. They fail
                to reach agreement. England unilaterally
                eliminates "China Differential" on trade
                placing PRC commerce on same footing as
                other communist states. Allies follow
                England; U.S. announces it is "most
                disappointed" by allied actions

     June 5 - President, at news conference, indicates
                an interest in eventual trade relations
                with PRC

   June 11,28 - Dulles moves to counteract President's
                words

     July 9 - Weeks announces Administration will "not
                gamble with national security" by ending
                its total embargo

TABLE 14

SHOULD COMMUNIST CHINA BE IN THE U.N.

Question: "Do you think Communist China should or should
            not be admitted as a member of the United
            Nations?"

Opinion Trend:		Should	Should Not	Don't Know
7 July	1954	7%	78%	15%
15 May	1955	10	67	23
30 August	1955	17	71	12
June	1956	11	74	15
12 February	1957	13	70	17
29 January	1958	17	66	17
25 August	1958	20	63	17

Significant Events:

1954	June 5	- Bilateral talks on prisoners begin
	July 8	- U.S. announces it will veto PRC in U.N.
	Sept 3	- Shelling of offshore islands begins
1955	early	- Arms shipments to Taipei continue at rapid pace
	Jan 29	- Formosa Resolution signed
	Feb 9	- Defense pact ratified
	Apr 2	- U.S. says 76 detained Chinese technical students are now free to depart
	Apr 23	- Chou Bandung offer; positive U.S. response follows
	Aug 1	- Ambassadorial talks begin
1956	Jan	- Acrimony over Geneva talks rises
1957	May	- Matador missiles to Taiwan; Taipei riots
	Aug	- State to allow reporters to China
	Dec	- Three mothers of imprisoned Americans allowed to go to PRC
1958	Aug 23	- Shelling of coastal islands resumes

TABLE 15

SHOULD COMMUNIST CHINA BE IN THE U.N.

Question: See table 14

Opinion Trend:	Should	Should Not	Don't Know
25 August 1958	20%	63%	17%
15 February 1961	20	64	16
26 September 1961	18	65	17
4 February 1964	15	71	14

Significant Events:

1958 Aug 23	- Shelling of coastal islands resumes
1959	- Sino-Indian border dispute; Tibet revolt
1960 Nov	- Kennedy elected
1961 Aug	- Kennedy secretly pledges to veto PRC U.N. admission
Oct/Nov	- U.S. determines to follow 'important question' tactic
1962-1963	- Sino-Soviet split worsens
1964 mid	- Rusk reiterates secret veto pledge to Taipei

put off any tangible sign of real progress until late 1968, when an agreement was reached to resume the suspended Warsaw talks. Nixon, upon entering office, was the beneficiary of the public's changed (but still negative) view of China. He took America's relatively stagnant policy toward Peking and vigorously moved it forward, in the process permanently altering the American people's way of thinking about the Chinese Communists (see table 16).

TABLE 16

SHOULD COMMUNIST CHINA BE IN THE U.N.

Question: See table 14

Opinion Trend:		Should	Should Not	Don't Know
4 February	1964	15%	71%	14%
11 November	1964	20	57	23
24 February	1965	22	64	14
16 December	1965	22	67	11
29 March	1966	25	55	20
13 October	1966	25	56	19
28 January	1969	33	54	13
28 September	1970	35	49	16
17 May	1971	45	38	17

Significant Events:

1964 mid		- Rusk visits Chiang; reiterates veto pledge
	Oct 16	- Chinese A-bomb test
	Dec 26	- U.S. missile subs to patrol China coast
1965 Dec	29	- Travel restrictions eased
1966 Feb	14	- U.S. ready to accept PRC newsmen without reciprocity
	Feb	- Washington suggests U.S.-PRC medical teams exchange visits
	Mar 8	- China hearings begin; Vietnam hearings began 4 February
	Mar 9	- LBJ revealed to be planning further easing of travel restrictions
	Mar 13	- Humphrey frames U.S. policy in conciliatory terms
	Mar 20	- U.S. seeks to reassure China on Vietnam at Warsaw talks
	July 12	- Johnson calls for "cooperation, not hostility" with PRC
	Dec 7	- State appoints 10 man panel to "stimulate new ideas" on China policy

Table 16 *continued*

1967			- China justification for ABM, Vietnam prominent
	Apr	20	- Medical drugs offered to China
	Summer		- LBJ reportedly signals hope for better U.S.-PRC relations through Rumanian diplomatic channels
1968	May		- U.S. invites PRC newsmen to cover American election
	Aug	21	- Soviet invasion of Czechoslovakia
	Spring		- RCA commercial gesture to China
	Nov	26	- PRC proposes resumption of Warsaw talks, U.S. accepts
1969	Feb		- U.S. reviews China policy; seeks stepped up contacts despite PRC cancellation of talks
	Mar		- Sino-Soviet border clashes
	July	21	- Trade and travel restrictions eased
	July	25	- Nixon Doctrine
	Nov	7	- Permanent patrol of Straits ended
	Dec	15	- All nuclear weapons to be off Okinawa by year's end
1970	Jan	20	- Warsaw talks resume; broken off by Cambodian invasion
	Apr	29	- Trade restrictions eased; further eased on 28 July, 26 August
	Oct		- U.S. hints at new UN policy
1971	Mar	15	- Travel restrictions completely lifted
	Apr		- "Ping-pong" diplomacy
	July		- Nixon's February 1972 trip announced
	Aug	2	- New UN policy made official

Should the United States Follow the Majority at the United Nations (Gallup)

30 August 1955–15 February 1961

The large change in opinion over these years reflected a moderating government policy. Though this attitude reversal was traceable to Washington's actions and the passing of Korean War hatreds, it did give hope to advocates of a policy change (see table 17).

15 February 1961–4 February 1964

This instance of significant opinion change is one of directional congruence and apparent majoritarian non-congruence. The Kennedy Administration, in response to the trend in public attitudes (and the still overwhelmingly negative public "vote" on Gallup's UN admission item), privately agreed to veto the People's Republic of China's entrance into the United Nations. Publicly Kennedy determined to follow the "important question" tactic at the world body, thus also opposing the United Nation's majority will (see table 17). The United States was still following both of these obstructionist paths in 1964. The public's already negative trajectory was seemingly deepened by the increased U.S. public hectoring of the People's Republic of China in the years following 1961.

4 February 1964–28 January 1969

Opinion on following the majority at the United Nations again reversed itself in this period (see table 17). The catalytic event, as with the Gallup UN admission item, appears to have been the 16 October 1964 Lop Nor explosion. Public attitudes changed before America's policy, though Washington's later actions in the "proper" direction certainly added force to this trend. Only in the 1970-1971 period did Washington officially abandon the "important question" tactic (though it was employed in an attempt to prevent Taiwan's 1971 UN expulsion).

Should Communist China Be in the United Nations (Harris)

June 1964–November 1964

This wide swing in opinion presents further evidence of the importance of China's atomic bomb in shaping American attitudes (see table 18). As with other cases focusing on this time-span, policy first acted contrary to the movement in public opinion and only later fell in line with moderating popular attitudes.

Should America's Defense Alliance with the Nationalists Be Continued (Harris)

27 June 1966–24 February 1969

Opinion on continuing the defense treaty with Taiwan, as table 19 shows, fell throughout the late 1960s—though it was always heavily supported by the public.

TABLE 17

SHOULD THE U.S. FOLLOW THE MAJORITY AT THE U.N.

Question: "Suppose a majority of members of the United
Nations decide to admit Communist China to
the United Nations. Do you think the United
States should go along with the UN decision,
or not?"

Opinion Trend:			Should	Should Not	No Opinion
(a)	30 August	1955	31%	53%	16%
	15 February	1961	59	25	16
(b)	15 February	1961	59	25	16
	26 September	1961	46	38	16
	4 February	1964	42	44	14
(c)	4 February	1964	42	44	24
	24 February	1965	49	35	16
	16 December	1965	47	41	12
	28 January	1969	56	33	11

Significant Events: (See also tables 14, 15, 16)

1954 July 8   - U.S. will veto PRC membership, use
'important question' tactic if
necessary

1961 Aug   - Kennedy pledges to veto PRC at U.N.

Oct 19   - Kennedy publicly denounces PRC U.N.
membership

Oct/Nov   - U.S. pursues 'important question'
tactic

1963 Dec 19   - Hilsman speech

1964 mid   - Rusk reiterates secret veto pledge

1971 Sept/Oct   - U.S. drops 'important question' tactic
to keep PRC out, uses tactic in attempt
to keep ROC from being removed from
the U.N. U.S. supports PRC admission
to U.N., but opposes Taiwan's
expulsion.

TABLE 18

SHOULD COMMUNIST CHINA BE IN THE UNITED NATIONS

Question:	"As far as you are concerned, do you favor or oppose giving Red China a seat at the United Nations as a member?"		
Opinion Trend:	Favor	Oppose	Not Sure
June 1964	10%	73%	17%
November 1964	25	56	19
Significant Events:	See table 16		

Congruence, in this instance, thus existed within the majoritarian model, but the change model exhibited a divergence between opinion and policy.

While using government military aid figures for supplies sent to Taiwan seems an appropriate policy measure for this issue, it is important to be aware that revisions of these figures have been made in the past with disquieting regularity. Despite this lack of solidity, it appears that military aid to Taiwan did increase in these years as support for the treaty—probably reflecting the disillusionment with Asian wars—faded (see table 20). It is true that military assistance, as recorded in Washington, fell in the 1969 fiscal year. Secret negotiations, however, were begun in that year which led to the fiscal 1970 bulge in assistance. (This secret transfer only entered onto government books in 1975, despite its "deleted" 1970 disclosure at congressional hearings and its subsequent mention that year in the *New York Times*.) The increase in aid was probably pursued to reassure Taiwan, as Washington was making its first hesitant steps toward diplomatic ties with the mainland at this time. The exact extent of American aid in this period, though, may never be known. Not only did Taipei benefit from the upgrading of facilities on the island to cope with American support troops for Vietnam, but apparently the U.S. Military Assistance Group on Formosa was not adverse to appropriating used or slightly damaged equipment from Vietnam and having the Nationalists refurbish it (for pay) and then keep the arms.[2]

1976–11 September 1978

Whether America's defense treaty with Taiwan should remain in effect again became an issue in the mid- to late 1970s. This occurred due to Peking's demand that this pact be abrogated before full diplomatic ties were established. American

TABLE 19

SHOULD AMERICA'S DEFENSE ALLIANCE WITH THE
NATIONALISTS BE CONTINUED

Question: "Our country has a defense alliance with
             Chiang Kai-shek and Nationalist China
             (Formosa). Should we continue or end
             this defense alliance?"

Opinion Trend:		Continue	End	Not Sure
27 June	1966	65%	6%	39%
24 February 1969		55	19	26

Significant Events:

1967 Jan 10   - State Department says Chiang cannot
                move on mainland without U.S. approval,
                which is not forthcoming

1969 Summer   - Negotiations on weapons transfer to
                Taiwan begin in secret, completed
                in fall

     Nov 7   - Permanent patrol of Straits ended

1970 Jan 9   - U.S. to send 'excess' squadron of
                F-104 Starfighter jets to Taiwan

     Jan 28   - Senate deletes funds added by House
                for Taiwan to buy a squadron of F-4D
                fighters. Administration neutral
                overall, Pentagon in favor

     Jan 31   - U.S. to supply 34 F-100 Super Sabre
                fighter-bombers to Taiwan

     Mar 20   - It is revealed that U.S. secretly
                agreed to supply $157 million in
                arms aid to the ROC

TABLE 20

MILITARY AID TO THE REPUBLIC OF CHINA, 1966-1977

Fiscal Year	Aid (in millions of dollars)
1966	100.1
1967	111.2
1968	161.5
1969	122.6
1970	263.1
1971	127.5
1972	141.4
1973	146.2
1974	95.7
1975	82.7
1976	81.1*
1977	35.5

Source: United States Agency for International
          Development, Statistics and Reports
          Division.

*Transitional Quarter 13.4.

policy was clearly moving in this direction between 1976 and 1978, and opinion seemed to be responding to these gestures. Military aid for Taiwan fell precipitously in these years (see table 20), though Taipei's purchase of U.S. arms— it saw the "handwriting on the wall" and stocked up accordingly—continued at a high level (see figure 3). Even the arms sales the United States allowed, though, showed America's disengaging intentions. Washington, for example, repeatedly denied Taiwan's request for an advanced jet fighter. The White House also refused to approve Taiwanese co-production of a GE jet engine on the grounds that it had some limited military use. In addition to these and other steps, America's military presence on the island had dwindled to about 500 troops by October 1978, as opposed to a Vietnam War high of 10,000 seven years earlier.[3]

These signals proved to be apt indicators, as on 15 December 1978 Carter ended America's defense treaty with the Republic of China. In a directional sense, as table 21 makes clear, opinion followed Washington's "detaching" gestures. Carter, however, acted too hastily in voiding the treaty, as a large majority of Americans continued to favor its existence. The "cost" of this premature action for Carter would be his acceptance of stronger language than

Figure 3
U.S. Military Equipment Deliveries to Taiwan

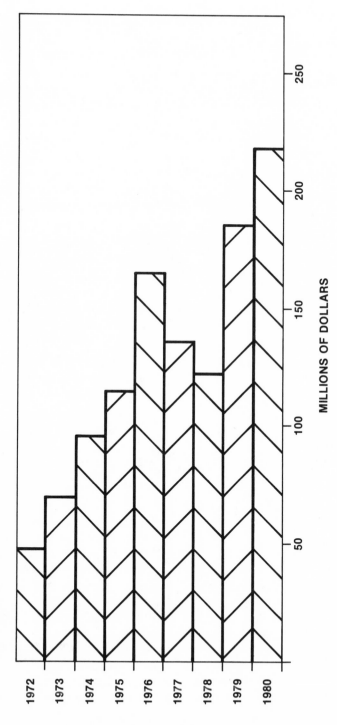

MILLIONS OF DOLLARS

Source: *Chicago Tribune*, 15 April 1982. Reprinted with permission.

TABLE 21

SHOULD AMERICA'S DEFENSE ALLIANCE WITH
THE NATIONALISTS CONTINUE

Question: "Should we continue or should we end our
defense alliance with the Nationalist
Chinese government on Taiwan?"

Opinion Trend:	Continue	End	Not Sure
1976	65%	6%	29%
1977	57	12	31
11 September 1978	64	19	17

Significant Events:

1976	- U.S. terminates $1 million program at MIT designed to teach engineers from Taiwan inertial guidance (i.e., missile) expertise
June 24	- U.S. to withdraw military advisers from Quemoy and Matsu
Aug	- U.S. reportedly turns down request for 60 F-4 jets
1977 Mar 10	- Administration announces it is "in the process of phasing out" military aid to Taiwan
June 30	- SEATO dissolved
1978	- U.S. blocks licensing agreement on GE jets
	- Administration announces it will seek only $10 million in military credits for Taiwan next year; credits to cease by 1980
June 30	- Taipei jet request turned down
July 4-6	- As a substitute for American jets, Washington suggests Taipei buy 50-60 Israeli Kfir jets. Suggestion rejected by Nationalists
Nov 3	- Secretary of State Vance says U.S. would not oppose allies selling military equipment to Peking
Dec 15	- Defense pact abrogated

desired in the 1979 Taiwan Relations Act regarding America's commitment to the defensive well-being of Formosa.

CONCLUSION

The influence of the American people on foreign policy has often been dismissed. If the findings presented here are correct, though, this "wave of the hand" response may be misdirected for America's East Asian policy. Individual government actions involving China have occasionally moved in opposition to opinion, but *overall* there has been a remarkable degree of harmony between policy and public preferences. This harmony has arisen through the adjustment of opinion and policy to one another. Each of these factors, at different times, has led the other. This varying relationship in the China policy area has largely turned on the political party in control of the White House.

The examination of modern-day United States–Chinese relations must begin, at the latest, with the Truman years. American policy in the late 1950s was one of slow disengagement from China's decades-old civil war. Despite some congressional and bureaucratic misgivings, which served to slow the pace of the White House's preferred policy, Truman and Acheson were able to "control" public attitudes as the Nationalists retreated into collapse. The president, however, did accommodate public opinion through his delay of United States–United Nations recognition of the People's Republic. In these years, a hesitant public influenced the speed and manner with which Washington pursued its chosen course, but popular attitudes did not affect this policy's substance. Affecting the speed of policy prosecution, however, can ultimately have substantive implications since at least two actors are involved in every international situation. An opportunity delayed may become an opportunity lost. If the United States had been able to move more rapidly in cutting its ties with Chiang, the later decades of People's Republic of China–United States hostility might have been avoided.

Truman and Acheson, in this period, sought to prevent the formation of a strong Sino-Soviet alliance. The executive branch followed a dual path in attempting to accomplish this goal. In disengaging from China's civil war, the United States hoped to make clear its non-threatening intentions to China's new regime. Rhetorically, though, Washington continued to hammer on the subservience of the CCP to Moscow. This public line was followed in the expectation that it would heighten nationalistic sentiment among Peking's new leaders and thereby encourage them to adopt an independent international posture. Even though these "scolding" statements provided ammunition for Truman's critics, the president encountered few problems in holding to his policy course. In the absence of any major galvanizing historical event, Washington's Democrats were able to continue advancing policy ahead of opinion.

In addition to showing the president's ability to lead opinion, the Truman years are also of interest in displaying how the organizational outlines of the government's foreign policy machinery can affect the input various actors have into the policy process. Congress, a body with many voices and little initiative, was able to influence policy in only minor ways despite the hesitancy many legislators felt over abandoning the Nationalists. Within the executive branch, the structural characteristics of foreign policy formation also exerted themselves. Those traditionally charged with the planning of international actions played the greatest role in influencing the president's policy course. Others outside these channels were, at best, reduced to ineffectual scheming behind the chief executive's back. In all instances, though, the final policy choice did devolve to an opinion-conscious president.

Truman resisted the pressure from his China critics even after the 25 June start of the Korean War. Only when Chinese "volunteers" crossed the Yalu in late 1950 did the administration begin to set aside its accepting policy toward Peking's Communists. The PLA intervention in Korea, however, served to focus public attention on America's East Asian policies in a manner unflattering to the in-power Democrats. By December 1951 the public had developed a strong "tendency to agree . . . that U.S. policy 'failed' in dealing with China and that it is still confused at present."[4] Public attitudes turned very hostile toward China in the course of the Korean conflict, so much so that polls repeatedly found a majority of citizens in favor of taking military action directly against the mainland. The wide support for such moves, though, represented more a willingness to accept these attacks than an insistence on their occurrence. Government documents showed a recognition of this, displaying an understanding that in times of crisis or war the public generally defers to the judgment of its leaders on tactical matters.

The negative opinion alteration during the Korean War was encouraged by the administration as a way of bolstering the public's flagging enthusiasm for the conflict. Even though this preference shift was encouraged by the Democrats, it redounded to their detriment. Eisenhower, in many ways, rode into office on the discontent engendered by Truman's Asian policies. Once in office, Eisenhower was able to harness and shape popular views toward China. As policy slowly moderated in the 1950s, so also did opinion. A key factor in this preference movement was Dulles's decision, over initial bureaucratic and public hesitancy, to accept Chou's Bandung offer of ambassadorial-level talks. Despite their ability to lead opinion, though, Eisenhower and Dulles were also affected by its overall contours. Public attitudes on China often influenced the manner in which policy was pursued in these years. The administration, in acting in this way, displayed an understanding that to not attend to opinion's overall shape was to chance later political problems. Along these lines, Dulles acted in 1957 and 1958 to moderate the shift in public attitudes he had begun, lest the White House be forced to ease its pressure on Peking prior to inducing a Sino-Soviet split.

This attention to overall opinion, though, did not rule out the government's occasionally acting contrary to popular wishes. Instances of the public's preferences being violated did surface from time to time. An example of this occurred in the mid-1950s when Dulles refused to meet with Chinese Foreign Minister

Chou En-lai. This refusal came in the face of seven-to-one public approval for such a conference. This incident thus serves to make clear that the citizenry's wishes can be violated on a minor facet of policy, if, overall, the government is acting in line with general preferences in a particular issue area.

While Eisenhower was largely in control of East Asian policy, the same could not be said for his successor. Kennedy, unlike his Republican predecessor, was often forced by political considerations to follow opinion's lead. This heightened concern with public preferences was a result of earlier historical events; it was, after all, Kennedy's party that had "lost" China. The public's influence on policy can be discerned most clearly in the young president's UN actions during his first year in office. Opinion in 1961 was already quite negative to the idea of allowing Peking into the United Nations. This preference trend accelerated as the year went on and Kennedy weighed his various "Chirep" policy options. Under the weight of opinion, Kennedy disregarded the advice of several of his top policy aides and decided to veto the People's Republic's admission to the world body should the need to do so arise. This secret pledge to Taipei was accompanied by a more open determination to prevent Peking's entrance into the United Nations through the use of the "important question" tactic.

Kennedy's actions in disregarding his bureaucracy's advice should give pause to those who disregard opinion in the policy formation process, choosing instead to exclusively focus on international or bureaucratic factors. On a salient and partisan issue, opinion must be added into the policy "equation" for a true understanding of the government's output to result. It should also be noted that Kennedy's negative actions involving China, initially set off by the public's mood, led to an even sharper downturn in popular attitudes toward the mainland. The relationship between opinion and policy in these years thus serves to highlight the generally interactive nature of the public preference–government action dyad.

Several of Kennedy's closest associates have argued that the president planned to alter America's China policy at a politically prudent moment in his second term. It is impossible to know whether this would have come to pass. What is clear, though, is that when Johnson acceded to the presidency he too was strongly influenced by the public in forming the United States' East Asian policy. Johnson felt comfortable in accepting the arguments of some members of his bureaucracy that initiatives toward the mainland were desirable only after an opinion change seemed to make a moderating course feasible.

The catalyst for changing public attitudes in the early Johnson years was the October 1964 Chinese detonation of a nuclear warhead. Together with the on-going Vietnam War, this incident helped to focus public attention on the People's Republic once more. Johnson clearly did not lead these event-induced preference shifts as he, at first, hardened policy in response to China's Lop Nor explosion. Within a relatively short period of time, though, this Texas Democrat began to act more in line with opinion's trend. The actions Johnson took in response to this attitude shift, again in line with the interactive nature of opinion and policy, served to encourage an even greater positive shift in popular preferences. Domestic and international problems, however, retarded the president's forward movement in the China policy area during his last years in office.

It remained for Richard Nixon to re-invigorate the rapprochement process. Nixon resumed the Eisenhower-Dulles pattern of moving in advance of opinion, relatively secure in the knowledge that his anti-Communist Republican credentials would cover his political flank. The new president, in his urge to re-adjust America's China policy, benefited from changes in attitudes that had occurred prior to his term. Nixon, however, recognized that a period of public preparation was still necessary if his new policies were to be accepted without a large public outcry. Only when opinion had altered would a lasting China policy change be possible. In restrospect, this preparatory process is one of the most striking features of Nixon's first-term Asian policy. Nixon was quite successful in this endeavor, bringing the American people around to the idea of accepting the People's Republic into the world community.

Gerald Ford, taking over in unique circumstances, was unable to make much headway in relations beyond what Nixon had already accomplished. Jimmy Carter, however, determined to put Washington back on the track of increased Sino-American contacts. Carter believed that the passage of time, and events of the previous decade, had effectively removed China from the sphere of political conflict.[5] In his opinion reading, however, Carter was only partially correct, as a lingering partisan flavor remained to America's China policy. The public, in addition to this, still remained opposed to breaking ties with Taipei. Without having properly prepared opinion, Carter was forced to backtrack some after his 15 December 1978 action. A Republican may have been able to lead opinion by the degree Carter attempted; for a Democratic President, though, such actions presented political problems.

Public opinion, as we've seen, greatly affected Washington's policies toward the People's Republic of China. This citizen influence stemmed largely from the adversarial nature of American politics. Since Korea, America's China policy has been both a highly visible and a partisan issue. In addition to this, popular attitudes involving East Asia have been relatively stable over the years, changing in a non-random manner.[6] These beliefs thus were a factor of which politicians had to take account. The *possibility* of electoral retribution, in other words, led officials to attend to the overall shape of China opinion. The theoretical objection that most citizens would not endure the "costs" of informing themselves on the distant China issue, thereby leaving decision-makers with a free hand in this international policy area, fails due to the competitiveness of electoral politics.[7] Opposition politicians, simply put, will bear the costs of informing the electorate on an issue if they feel some gain might result.[8] These partisan charges, if they take hold, might damage an incumbent's political future (and, by extension, his ability to currently govern). Elected officials live in an uncertain world. A prudent policy-maker will take few chances, lest such actions later burst into detrimental prominence. Diminishing this possibility requires an office-holder to attempt to shape opinion or, failing this, to fall in line with popular preferences. In politics, like economics, expectations rather than current realities often play a determining role in behavior.

The degree of political uncertainty an elected figure faces on an issue is a function of both historical circumstances and personal background. Republicans, with their foreign policy credentials secure on East Asian issues, had to worry less about being attacked for their moves in response to "structural demands" than did the Democrats. Having "lost" China once, the Democrats could move on mainland relations only if opinion first altered; to do otherwise would risk being charged with having completed their earlier "betrayal" of the Nationalists. Though able to move in advance of opinion, Republicans did not have enough latitude to completely ignore popular views. They could lead opinion but had to be cautious about getting too far ahead of these attitudes lest they also open themselves up to potential political damage. In all political eras, then, lasting China policy change has had to be accompanied by significant alterations in the public's outlook.

While it is clear that public opinion importantly influenced the United States' actions in East Asia, caution is called for in generalizing this finding to other foreign policy issues. The opinion-policy relationship found in the China policy area resulted from historical circumstances and may not indicate an invariant causal pattern. Along these lines, it should be recalled that prior to the Korean War, a Democratic administration was able to shape popular impressions of the People's Republic. Firmly establishing the extent of public influence over the gamut of international issues requires further research as several broad theoretical interpretations of our findings are possible. It may ultimately be discovered, for instance, that presidential leadership of foreign policy is the norm for most external issues, though this pattern can be disrupted by an event (such as the Korean War) that heightens the partisan saliency of a particular policy area. Even if this turned out to be the case, the findings in this study would still provide some backing for notions of democratic responsiveness, as it was found that, whether led or followed, opinion always impacted on policy.

The finding that domestic opinion influences external policy casts doubt on those theories of international behavior that completely ignore a state's internal political processes. While this type of theory, whether labelled "realist," statist" or "system," is helpful in clarifying the structural and geopolitical underpinnings of state policy preferences, it seriously undervalues the role the general public can play in the formation and conduct of a democratic nation's foreign policy. On important and partisan issues like China, at least, it appears that whether an official can act on personal policy preferences is often a function of opinion's profile. The view of the state as autonomous of public pressures is certainly insufficient to explain the course of America's China policy. This insufficiency may very well hold for other areas of international concern.[9]

The case study undertaken here has highlighted the importance of domestic opinion in the formation of America's China policy. Personal preferences of decision-makers, geopolitical concerns, and allied interests all played a role in molding U.S. foreign policy in East Asia. To focus solely on these factors, though, is to miss the essence of the real world situation. In the China area, without opinion's approval an overall line of external action could not long be pursued by Washington. While further research is called for, it is clear that America's "ritual deference" to opinion, at least as regards its East Asian policies, is more than show. Opinion, if our case study is any indicator, does affect the substance and conduct of American foreign policy.

NOTES

1. George F. Kennan, "The International Situation," *DSB*, pp. 399-400, has described in vivid fashion the effect of the Czech coup on U.S. public opinion. He also noted that the public was further jolted by the 11 March news of the death of that country's pro-West foreign minister, Jan Marasyk. In official circles, a war scare also occurred at this time. This scare grew out of General Lucius Clay's 5 March telegram from Berlin prophesizing a war with the Russians which would "come with dramatic suddenness."

2. *NYT*, 29 March; 5 April 1970.

3. "Propping Up a Fading Friendship," *Far Eastern Economic Review* 102 (27 October 1978):17.

4. "A Summary of U.S. Attitudes on China Policy, 1949-1951" (7 December 1951), Foster Papers, Box 33.

5. Gleysteen interview, 6 July 1982.

6. Perhaps the best known statement of a public whose views are volatile is to be found in Gabriel A. Almond, *The American People and Foreign Policy*, rev. ed. (New York: Frederick A. Praeger, 1960). An opposing view, more in line with what has been suggested here, is to be found in William R. Caspary, "The 'Mood Theory': A Study of Public Opinion and Foreign Policy," *American Political Science Review* (June 1970):536-547. See also Robert Y. Shapiro, "The Dynamics of Public Opinion and Public Policy" (Ph.D. dissertation, University of Chicago, 1982), pp. 11-42.

7. On "information costs" see Anthony Downs, *An Economic Theory of Democracy* (New York: Harper and Row, 1957), pp. 207-259.

8. No information is, of course, ever costless since it requires the expenditure of a scarce resource—time—to perceive and assimilate. See ibid., p. 209. While strictly speaking some "cost" remains to the perceiver in our scenario, this cost is, especially within the context of a political campaign, quite minimal.

9. It might be useful to digress for a moment and clarify what is meant by this autonomy idea. Typically, those who hold to this view believe that "except for instances of overwhelming societal opposition," state policy-makers are free to translate their own policy preferences into government actions (Eric A. Nordlinger, *On the Autonomy of the Democratic State* [Cambridge, Mass.: Harvard University Press, 1981], p. 202). While individual instances of what these theories might label "autonomous actions" may exist in the China policy area, overall this case study points strongly to the conclusion that autonomy theories seriously undervalue the role opinion can play in the formation and conduct of American foreign policy.

This under-valuation generally occurs for three reasons. First of all, many of the works in this vein are ahistorical in nature. By abstracting from history, autonomy theories lost much of the flavor of everyday real-world political events. This ahistorical bent thus leads into two further problems prominent in works along these lines. One of these difficulties involves the generally bureaucratic and technical view these works take of the policy process. Top policy-makers, however, do not work in a vacuum—attending only to data and never opinion. Even when such a course is followed by government bureaucrats, higher level officials add opinion into the decision-matrix before deciding on a course of action. Instances of this opinion-addition process occurred repeatedly in our China case.

The final problem with autonomy theories is that they seriously undervalue the role America's adversarial political system can play in enhancing the strength of the public's views. Sophisticated autonomy arguments often claim that few will oppose the government on a policy choice due to the fear that this opposition will be rewarded with state-imposed sanctions. These sanctions, though, would be unlikely to deter an opposition politician from acting should some political gain be viewed as resulting. This sanctions idea would seem to have greater validity for those issues that are non-partisan, not very salient to the general public, and affecting only a finite and well-organized opposition. This may account for the fact that some recent studies of U.S. foreign policy and international business have found that the government is the dominant actor in this arena. (See, for example, Stephen D. Krasner, *Defending the National Interest: Raw Materials Investments and U.S. Foreign Policy* [Princeton: Princeton University Press, 1978].) This thought also leads to the speculation that "corporatist-type" democracies, that is, states with very well organized interest intermediation groups, could be more subject to government manipulation than plural democratic polities.

Bibliographic Essay

The opinion-policy field is only now beginning to blossom. Those working in this area, however, owe a great intellectual debt to Gabriel A. Almond. His seminal *The American People and Foreign Policy*, rev. ed. (New York: Frederick A. Praeger, 1960) framed the field's major questions for later researchers. Recently, several scholars have again begun to move this area forward. Among the most important recent contributions to the literature in the opinion-policy field have been John E. Mueller, *War, Presidents and Public Opinion* (New York: Wiley, 1973); Robert Weissberg, *Public Opinion and Popular Government* (New York: Wiley, 1973); and Barry Hughes, *The Domestic Context of American Foreign Policy* (San Francisco: W. H. Freeman, 1978). Donald J. Devine's thoughtful *The Attentive Public: Polyarchical Democracy* (Chicago: Rand McNally and Co., 1970) is also quite valuable, though it must be read cautiously. All of these works can be read for both their substantive and methodological insights.

To study the interrelationship of opinion and policy, measures of both are necessary. An excellent start on tracing American preferences on any policy question can usually be made by using George Gallup's compilation of opinion soundings, *The Gallup Poll: Public Opinion, 1935-1970*, 3 vols. (New York: Random House, 1972). These three volumes, along with their successor books in the Gallup series, contain information on most of the major foreign policy questions of our era. *Public Opinion Quarterly* also regularly publishes useful summaries of opinion on important questions of the day. Works focusing exclusively on American opinion toward China are few in number. A. T. Steele's 1966 book, *The American People and China* (New York: McGraw-Hill, 1966), is useful, though inadequate even for the period it focuses upon. The most valuable opinion source on China—the Foster Papers at the National Archives—remains unpublished.

Clear policy measures are generally more difficult to find than unambiguous opinion yardsticks. To fully understand the last thirty years of Sino-American relations it is necessary to go beyond the previously published sources. The private papers of Wellington Koo (at Columbia University), and John Foster Dulles's and Adlai Stevenson's papers (both at Princeton University), are invaluable to this task. Also helpful in getting a handle on U.S. policy in Asia are the Declassified Documents Reference System (DDRS), and the *Foreign Relations of the United States* (*FRUS*) series. Among more readily accessible sources, the *Public Papers of the Presidents* (Washington, D.C.: U.S. Government Printing Office, 1965) and the *Department of State Bulletin* are most helpful.

Few works span the past thirty years of Sino-American relations in an adequate manner. Even rarer is the researcher who shows a sensitivity to American opinion while attempting this task. Of the researchers active in this field, I have found that Warren I. Cohen's works most closely approach this ideal. His historically based works are quite illuminating. Among the best of these efforts are "Acheson, His Advisers and China, 1949-1950" in the excellent *Uncertain Years: China-America Relations, 1947-1950*, edited by Dorothy Borg and Waldo Heinrichs (New York: Columbia University Press, 1980), and (more selectively) *The American Secretaries of State and Their Diplomacy: Dean Rusk* (Totowa, N.J.: Cooper Square Publishers, 1980).

In addition to Cohen's works, several quite excellent books exist on various aspects of America's China policy in the late 1940s and early 1950s. Included among these are Ross Y. Koen, *The China Lobby in American Politics* (New York: Macmillan Co., 1960); H. Bradford Westerfield, *Foreign Policy and Party Politics: Pearl Harbor to Korea* (New Haven: Yale University Press, 1955); Norman A. Graebner, *The New Isolationism: A Study in Politics and Foreign Policy since 1950* (New York: The Ronald Press, 1956); and Thomas H. Etzold, "The Far East in American Strategy, 1948-51," in a book edited by Etzold titled *Aspects of Sino-American Relations since 1784* (New York: New Viewpoints, 1978). On period military matters, few books approach the rigor of Allen S. Whiting, *China Crosses the Yalu: The Decision to Enter the Korean War* (New York: Macmillan Co., 1960). Melvin Gurtov, *The First Vietnam Crisis: Chinese Strategy and United States Involvement, 1953-1954* (New York: Columbia University Press, 1967), and J. H. Kalicki, *The Pattern of Sino-American Crises: Political and Military Interactions in the 1950s* (New York: Cambridge University Press, 1975), are also very useful.

Surprisingly, the course of Sino-American relations from the mid-1950s to the present remains largely unexplored. Among the volumes focusing on this era that I found most informative were Kenneth T. Young, *Negotiating with the Chinese Communists: The United States Experience, 1953-1967* (New York: McGraw-Hill, 1967); Michael A. Guhin, *John Foster Dulles: A Statesman and His Times* (New York: Columbia University Press, 1972); John Gittings, *The World and China, 1922-1972* (London: Eyre Methuen, 1974); Foster Rhea Dulles, *American Policy toward Communist China* (New York: Thomas Y. Crowell Co., 1972); Roger Hilsman, *To Move a Nation: The Politics of Foreign Policy in the Administration of John F. Kennedy* (Garden City, N.Y.: Doubleday Co., 1967); James C. Thomson, Jr., "On the Making of U.S. China Policy 1961-9: A Study in Bureaucratic Politics," in the April-June 1972 issue of the *China Quarterly*; and— from a more journalistic angle—David Halberstam, *The Best and the Brightest* (New York: Fawcett Crest, 1972). More recently, Marvin Kalb and Bernard Kalb, *Kissinger* (Boston: Little, Brown, 1974); Robert G. Sutter, *China Watch: Toward Sino-American Reconciliation* (Baltimore: Johns Hopkins University Press, 1978), and *Chinese Foreign Policy after the Cultural Revolution, 1966-1977* (Boulder, Colo.: Westview Press,, 1978); Ralph N. Clough, *Island China* (Cambridge, Mass: Harvard University Press, 1978); and Michel Oksenberg's Fall 1982 *Foreign Affairs* article, "A Decade of Sino-American Relations," have added greatly to the still sparse literature on our relations with Peking over the past decade.

The popular press also proved invaluable to the completion of this book. The *New*

York Times has been called the most thorough daily intelligence briefing available; I have found no reason to quarrel with this assessment. The *Washington Post*, *Wall Street Journal*, and other dailies were also invaluable in the information they provided. To work in the field of opinion and policy research, one must have a feel for the era being studied. This can best be accomplished by reading the popular press of the day. The media is a source not only of information, but also of opinions and the intangibles that make up the atmosphere of a period under review. Until recently a large segment of the press— television news—remained unrecorded. The *Vanderbilt Television News Index and Abstracts* has partially alleviated this still-serious problem.

No less valuable in doing opinion and policy research are periodicals. To read *Time*, *Life*, *U.S. News and World Report*, *Newsweek*, the *Atlantic Monthly*, *The New Republic*, *Christian Century*, the *Washington Monthly*, and other journals is to relive the intellectual and opinion battles that raged over the landscape of America's China policy in the past. Information gathered from non-American sources such as the *Economist* and the *Far Eastern Economic Review* also proved valuable in framing the American debate in world terms. Of academic journals, the *American Political Science Review* and *Public Opinion Quarterly* provided the best methodological insights, while the *China Quarterly* and *Diplomatic History* proved most valuable in substantive terms. None of these non-book sources should be overlooked when researching an opinion and policy question.

Index

About the Author

LEONARD A. KUSNITZ is a Foreign Service Officer in the United States Department of State.

DATE DUE

NOV 0 8 1999			